# Disability Benefits, Welfare Reform and Employment Policy

# Disability Benefits, Welfare Reform and Employment Policy

Edited by

Colin Lindsay
*University of Strathclyde, UK*

and

Donald Houston
*University of St Andrews, UK*

First published 2013 by
PALGRAVE MACMILLAN

Palgrave Macmillan in the UK is an imprint of Macmillan Publishers Limited, registered in England, company number 785998, of Houndmills, Basingstoke, Hampshire RG21 6XS.

Palgrave Macmillan in the US is a division of St Martin's Press LLC, 175 Fifth Avenue, New York, NY 10010.

Palgrave Macmillan is the global academic imprint of the above companies and has companies and representatives throughout the world.

Palgrave® and Macmillan® are registered trademarks in the United States, the United Kingdom, Europe and other countries.

ISBN 978–0–230–34994–0

This book is printed on paper suitable for recycling and made from fully managed and sustained forest sources. Logging, pulping and manufacturing processes are expected to conform to the environmental regulations of the country of origin.

A catalogue record for this book is available from the British Library.

A catalog record for this book is available from the Library of Congress.

Typeset by MPS Limited, Chennai, India.

# Contents

# List of Figures

# List of Tables

# Notes on Contributors

**Clare Bambra** is Professor of Public Health Policy and Director of the Wolfson Research Institute for Health and Wellbeing at Durham University. Clare studied political science and comparative public policy before moving into public health research. Her research is highly interdisciplinary, applying theories and methods from the social sciences to epidemiology and public health. Her research focuses on health inequalities and the social determinants of health. She has three main areas of interest: (1) labour markets and the relationships between work, worklessness, and health; (2) the influence of welfare state policies and political structures on international variations in public health and health inequalities; (3) tackling health inequalities by addressing the wider social determinants of health. She has published over 75 articles as well as a sole-authored book: *Work, Worklessness and the Political Economy of Health* (Oxford University Press, 2011).

**Helen Barnes** is an independent social policy researcher and consultant. She was previously Principal Research Fellow at the Institute for Employment Studies, where she led the evaluation of Employment and Support Allowance. As well as disability and ill-health issues, Helen's research interests include ageing and the labour market, mapping individual transitions and trajectories, and the experiences of minority ethnic groups in education and work.

**Christina Beatty** is Professor in the Centre for Regional Economic and Social Research (CRESR) at Sheffield Hallam University. A statistician by background, she has published widely on unemployment, the growth in incapacity benefit claimants, welfare reform, and the economic geography of Britain.

**Judith Brown** is a research associate in the Healthy Working Lives Group in the Institute of Health & Wellbeing at the University of Glasgow. Her work focuses on investigating the nature, dynamics, and needs of the workless population and the health-related benefit-claiming population in Glasgow, Scotland and the UK. This work resulted in the establishment of the Scottish Observatory for Work & Health (SOW&H, www.gla.ac.uk/sowh). She is the lead researcher of the SOW&H, which monitors and evaluates the interactions and determinants of work and health in Scotland.

**Martin Brussig** studied Sociology in Berlin and New York, and received his PhD from the Friedrich-Schiller-University Jena. Since 2003, he has been working at the Institute for Work, Skills and Training (IAQ) within the

University of Duisburg-Essen, where he is now leading the research unit 'Employment – Inclusion – Mobility'. His main fields of interest are labour market sociology and human resource strategies of firms. He has published widely about transitions into retirement and labour market policy reforms in Germany.

**Steve Fothergill** is a Professor in the Centre for Regional Economic and Social Research (CRESR) at Sheffield Hallam University. An economist by background, he has published widely on issues of employment, unemployment, and regional development. Since the 1990s, his research with Christina Beatty has pioneered much of the understanding of the scale, causes, and location of disability claims across the UK.

**Kayleigh Garthwaite** is a post-doctoral researcher at the Wolfson Research Institute, Department of Geography, Durham University. Her research interests focus on the relationship between health and disability, welfare-to-work policies, and self-identity, with a particular interest in reflexivity within the research process. She has published in the field of disability studies, sociology, youth studies, and public health. Previously a research assistant at Teesside University, she co-authored a report for the Joseph Rowntree Foundation entitled *The Low-Pay, No-Pay Cycle: Understanding Recurrent Poverty*. She is also a co-author of *Poverty and Insecurity: Life in 'Low-Pay, No-Pay' Britain*, to be published in 2013 by Policy Press.

**Anne Green** is a Professorial Fellow at the Institute for Employment Research at the University of Warwick. Her research interests span local labour market issues, urban and rural development, the impacts of labour migration, and geographical mobility more generally (including long-distance commuting), the geography of employment and worklessness, local skills strategies, ICT and employability, and the role of social networks and place attachment in understanding labour market behaviour. She has contributed to evaluations of welfare-to-work programmes and area-based initiatives and led the national evaluation of the City Strategy initiative.

**Daniel Horsfall** is a Research Fellow in the Department of Social Policy and Social Work at the University of York. His research interests are broad, ranging from global health issues such as the implications of medical tourism, to the political economy of welfare states. Among his publications are works that question whether the welfare state has been replaced by a competition state, explore the role played by the internet in informing prospective medical travellers, and outline how medical value travel impacts upon national health systems.

**Donald Houston** is Lecturer in Urban Studies at the University of St Andrews, Scotland. He has 15 years' experience of research on poverty and inequality in the UK, spanning benefits, unemployment, housing, and poor health.

He has been a visiting fellow at universities in Sweden and the United States. He has undertaken research funded by the UK Economic and Social Research Council to examine the rising numbers claiming disability benefits. He has conducted several projects commissioned by government, including the UK Department of Work on Pensions on aspects of welfare reform. He has published over 30 academic journal articles, books, and reports.

**Matthias Knuth**, sociologist, headed the research unit 'Employment – Inclusion – Mobility' at the Institute for Work, Skills and Training (IAQ) within the University of Duisburg-Essen, where he was appointed Associate Professor. He continues working as a member of the department. He is president of the German Association for Social Scientific Labour Market Research. His fields of research are mobility on the labour market, labour market policies, the international comparison of welfare state reforms, employment and retirement under conditions of demographic ageing, and the integration of ethnic minorities in the labour market. He was involved in several evaluations of the German labour market reforms.

**Colin Lindsay** is Senior Lecturer in Human Resource Management and an Associate Member of the Scottish Centre for Employment Research (SCER) at the University of Strathclyde. He has published extensively on labour market policies and welfare reform. With Donald Houston, he edited a Special Issue of *Policy Studies* (Vol. 31, No. 2, 2010) on 'Health, Employability and Challenges for UK Welfare Reform Agenda'.

**Neil Lunt** is Senior Lecturer at the Department of Social Policy and Social Work, University of York. His research interests include the organisation, management, and delivery of health and social services, research within policy and practice, and welfare policy. Between 1997 and 2006 he was based in New Zealand, teaching policy studies. He is co-author of *Employment Policies for Disabled People in Eighteen Countries: A Review* (1997) and co-editor of *New Welfare New Zealand* (2008).

**Ewan B. Macdonald** is an occupational physician and Professor at the Institute of Health and Wellbeing at the University of Glasgow. He is Head of the Healthy Working Lives Group, Public Health and Health Policy Section, University of Glasgow.

**John Macnicol** is Visiting Professor of Social Policy at the London School of Economics. Recent publications include *The Politics of Retirement in Britain 1878–1948* (second edition, 2002), *Age Discrimination: An Historical and Contemporary Analysis* (2006) (winner of the Social Policy Association's prize for 'Best New Publication, 2006–7'), 'Differential Treatment by Age: Age Discrimination or Age Affirmation?', in Robert B. Hudson (ed.) *Boomer Bust? Economic and Political Issues in the Greying Society* (2009), (as co-author) 'A Think Piece on Intergenerational Equity' (EHRC, 2009) and

'Intergenerational Equity: A View from History', in Cornelius Torp (ed.) *Challenges of Aging: Retirement, Pensions, and Intergenerational Justice* (2012). He is a Trustee of The Age and Employment Network (TAEN), a charity that researches the problems of older workers.

**Ian Shuttleworth** is a graduate of the University of Leicester and Trinity College Dublin, and has worked in Northern Ireland since 1990. He was appointed to a Lectureship in Human Geography in Queen's University Belfast in 1993 and since 2004 has been a Senior Lecturer. During his career he has conducted a wide range of research on topics ranging from education to segregation, and he has published over 35 journal articles and books. His current research interests include spatial mobility in the labour market, migration, residential segregation, and census analysis. He is currently Director of the NILS-RSU and is also a member of the Northern Ireland Census Advisory Group.

**Paul Sissons** is a Researcher at The Work Foundation where he is leading a programme of research on labour market polarisation. He was previously a Research Fellow at the Institute for Employment Studies working on a range of public policy evaluations. He has also worked at the University of Dundee on research into worklessness and housing market change. He holds a PhD from University College London where his thesis was a comparative study of the longer-term impacts of past regional deindustrialisation in the UK and the US. His research interests cover worklessness, health and employability, and skills and labour market disadvantage.

**Ivan Turok** is Deputy Executive Director at the Human Sciences Research Council in South Africa and Honorary Professor at Cape Town and Glasgow Universities. He has published widely on issues of spatial inequality, city economies, urban regeneration, unemployment, and local labour markets. Key publications include the *State of South African Cities Report* (2011), *The State of English Cities* (2006), *Changing Cities: Rethinking Urban Competitiveness, Cohesion and Governance* (2005), *Twin Track Cities* (2005), *The Jobs Gap in Britain's Cities* (1999) and *The Coherence of EU Regional Policy* (1997).

**Rickard Ulmestig** holds a PhD in Social Work and a Senior Lecturer in Social Work at University of Jönköping in Southern Sweden. His research focuses on social policy and labour market policy for marginalised groups. His publications in English include (with P.A. Köhler and Katarina Thorén) 'Activations Policies in Sweden: Something Old, Something New, Something Borrowed and Something Blue' in W. Eichhorst, O. Kaufmann and R. Konle-Seidl (eds) *Bringing the Jobless in to Work* (2009).

**Rik van Berkel** is associate professor at the Utrecht School of Governance, Utrecht University, the Netherlands. His research interests are situated on the interface of social policy, public administration, and public organisation studies, and include welfare state transformations, the introduction of new models for the provision of social services, and processes of change in public organisations responsible for the implementation of social policy and governance reforms. Recent publications include: R. van Berkel and P. van der Aa (2012) 'Activation Work: Policy Programme Administration or Professional Service Provision?', *Journal of Social Policy*, 41 (3), 493–510; and R. van Berkel, W. de Graaf, T. Sirovatka (eds) *The Governance of Active Welfare States in Europe* (2011).

**Jon Warren** is a sociologist who is currently Senior Research Associate in Public Health Policy, based at the Wolfson Research Institute, Department of Geography, Durham University. His research interests are centred on work, employment, the work/life interface, and the industrial history of the North East of England. He is involved with methodologically innovative research and is currently involved with projects using Qualitative Comparative Analysis (QCA) and Visual methods. He has published work in the fields of disability studies and the sociology of work. He was previously part of the School of Applied Social Science at Durham where he taught Sociology and Social Work. He undertook his doctoral studies on work/life relations in the call centre industry in the UK and India. Prior to coming to Durham he was a lecturer in Community and Youth Studies at Sunderland University and also a researcher for the Office for National Statistics.

**David Webster** is an Honorary Senior Research Fellow, Urban Studies, University of Glasgow, and a member of the editorial board of *Local Economy*. He was formerly Housing Strategy Manager with Glasgow City Council and has worked at the Board of Trade, London School of Economics, London Boroughs Association and Centre for Environmental Studies, and was an adviser to the House of Commons Environment, Social Security and Scottish Affairs Committees. He studied Economics at Queens' College, Cambridge and has an MBA and PhD from the University of Glasgow. His research is mainly on labour market and related issues, and on urban regeneration.

# 1
# Fit for Work? Representations and Explanations of the Disability Benefits 'Crisis' in the UK and Beyond

*Colin Lindsay and Donald Houston*

## Introduction

At the start of 2012, more than two and a half million people of working age were out of work and claiming disability benefits in the UK (see Box 1.1). Since 1979 the numbers on these benefits have more than trebled. Successive governments have argued that the large numbers of people spending long periods on disability benefits represents a social and economic crisis. Beyond the fiscal pressures placed on welfare budgets (which have become particularly acute in the context of recurring recession and public spending deficits), there is evidence that long periods spent on these benefits can further undermine individuals' health (Brown et al., 2009), increase the risk of poverty (Kemp and Davidson, 2010) and feed into 'risky behaviours' (Waddell et al., 2007). From an economic perspective, it is argued that high levels of working age inactivity represent a waste of human capital, as skills and labour are haemorrhaged from the productive economy (Beatty et al., 2010). Finally, population ageing and pressures on pension schemes mean that, in the long term, there will be a need to keep older people working, and working for longer, with the 'active management' of health conditions bound to be a key element of any policy solution (Loretto et al., 2007).

Given this context, it is unsurprising that policy makers have expressed a determination to reduce the numbers claiming disability benefits. Recent policy responses in the UK have focused on the reform of disability benefit regulations in order to establish a more 'active' disability benefits regime; restrict eligibility; extend means-testing; limit payment levels; and introduce active labour market programmes (Pathways to Work from 2003, and its successor, the Work Programme since 2011).

This book explores whether these policy responses (see Box 1.2) are fit for purpose by: presenting evidence on why benefit rolls have risen and why

1

## Box 1.1    What are disability benefits?

For the purposes of this book, we define 'disability benefits' as those monetary benefits granted under contributory and non-contributory state schemes and paid to people experiencing long-term sickness, disability or reduced work capacity as means of earnings replacement. This may include some early retirement schemes specific to disability or reduced work capacity (these operate in countries such as Denmark and Germany) and some broader social assistance schemes that have a specific disability component. Our focus is on the main state benefits, and not private disability insurance benefits. This definition is broadly similar to that used by recent cross-national studies (OECD, 2010).

## Box 1.2    Disability benefits and employability policy in the UK

The current benefits system for people with health problems arguably has its roots in the establishment of contributions-based Invalidity Benefit in 1971. For people with insufficient National Insurance contributions, support provided because of ill-health traditionally fell under the main general social assistance benefits (until recently Income Support, and before that its predecessors Supplementary Benefit and National Assistance). The first of a series of important reforms took place with the introduction of Incapacity Benefit to replace Invalidity Benefit in 1995. This reform was designed to tighten eligibility criteria via a more rigorous medical 'all work test' and stricter National Insurance contributions requirements. Further restrictions were applied with the introduction of the 'Personal Capability Assessment' and additional contributions requirements in 1999. Despite these changes, the numbers receiving disability benefits rose steadily during the 1980s and 1990s.

From 2008, new claimants have applied for Employment and Support Allowance, and all existing recipients – chiefly those on Incapacity Benefit – will be moved on to the new benefit by 2013. The new benefit divides claimants into a 'Work-Related Activity Group' considered capable of progressing towards employment and *mandated* to engage in activation programmes (previously participation was largely voluntary); and a 'Support Group', assessed as more sick or disabled, who are paid a higher rate of benefit and are excused from work-related activity. An even stricter medical 'Work Capability Assessment' has seen the majority of claims for disability benefits rejected, and most successful claimants directed towards work-related activity. The first large-scale activation programme directed specifically at Incapacity Benefit claimants was 'Pathways to Work', rolled out from 2003 to 2008. In 2011 Pathways to Work was replaced by a single 'Work Programme' providing activation for claimants of all working age benefits.

some people are more likely than others to become long-term claimants of disability benefits; critically assessing the content and outcomes of recent policy in the UK; and comparing experiences in the UK with those of other welfare states. A crucial conclusion is that, while the welfare system can in some instances hinder a return to work, the notion that insufficient work incentives and a lack of activation measures explain why so many people are on disability benefits is fatally flawed. Rather, labour market change and industrial restructuring, alongside individuals' employability and health-related problems, combine to explain why some people find themselves on disability benefits for long periods.

The comparative element of this book is important because high levels of disability claiming are not unique to the UK. Social democratic states such as Sweden (Hytti, 2006) and leading 'active' welfare states like the Netherlands (Koning and Van Vuuren, 2007) have faced similar problems, and even the liberal US welfare state, despite limited spending on benefits, saw a rapid growth in 'social security disability' in the 1990s and 2000s (Autor and Duggan, 2006). Meanwhile, other countries represented in this volume, such as Germany and New Zealand, have managed to avoid (Germany) or limit (New Zealand) the growth of large benefit rolls, but face substantial problems of working age sickness and disability (OECD, 2010).

If policy makers in the UK and beyond are to get to grips with the disability benefits crisis, then they first need to appreciate the nature of the problem; and then assess the evidence on what might work (and has previously worked) in terms of policy solutions. We set ourselves the same challenge in this book. We have gathered evidence from experts in a wide range of disciplines including economic geography, social policy, sociology, occupational medicine, and public health studies. We also present comparative perspectives from four welfare states beyond the UK.

The remainder of this chapter sets out one of the central issues for the book – that the disability benefits crisis in the UK and beyond can only be understood as the result of a combination of three key factors:

- **labour market processes** of job destruction, polarisation, and work intensification that have limited opportunities for work in post-industrial labour markets, particularly for those with poor health;
- **gaps in individuals' employability** and skills that mean they are left at the 'back of the queue' for those jobs that are available; and
- **health problems** that both explain why people claim disability benefits in the first place and limit their prospects of returning to work.

The UK evidence on these three interconnected issues is unpacked in Chapters 2 to 7, before we assess their relevance in other welfare states, and finally outline issues for policy. We first set the scene by providing more detail on how the disability benefits 'crisis' has been represented and misrepresented and on how the three themes of the book – labour market change, employability, and health – interact to leave many people claiming disability benefits for long periods.

## (Mis)Representations of the disability benefits crisis

According to the UK's General Household Survey, around 15% of the working age population have a limiting long-term illness or impairment, a proportion that has remained fairly constant since the 1970s. Approximately half are currently employed, down from almost two-thirds in 1980 (Berthoud, 2011). Disability benefits claimants rose from below 3% of the working age population in 1980 to 7.7% in 2010. Assuming that the overwhelming majority of claimants would report a limiting long-term illness, almost half of sick and disabled people in the UK are therefore in receipt of disability benefits. Of those claiming benefits, over 80% say their health means they can either do no work or substantially limits the amount or type of work they could do (Beatty et al., 2009).

In what respect – indeed if at all – this situation can be represented as a 'crisis' depends very much on one's point of view. From the government's perspective, the 'crisis' is the increase in the numbers claiming such benefits and the associated cost to the taxpayer over the last 30 years (DWP), 2010). From a social justice point of view, the 'crisis' is that the employment rate of the sick and disabled is significantly lower today than 30 years ago (Berthoud, 2011). From a social exclusion point of view, the 'crisis' is low income levels on benefits and the large numbers claiming concealing the true extent of involuntary worklessness (Beatty and Fothergill, 2012). From an economic point of view, the 'crisis' is cast as lost labour supply and increased pressure on pension schemes already stretched because of population ageing (OECD, 2010). On the other hand, the situation may not be seen as a 'crisis' at all, but merely a reflection of appropriate mechanisms of social protection for the sick and disabled who are unable to work in an increasingly competitive labour market.

The dominant rationales for policies to deal with the disability benefits crisis are arguably to reduce the cost to the state and to place more economic responsibility on citizens (DWP, 2010). Political and popular discourses typically revolve around disability benefits being: overly generous; too easily accessible for people who should be 'insufficiently' sick to qualify; excessively complex to administer; and too passive in that they do not place enough obligation on recipients to move off benefits (Freud, 2007; DWP, 2008, 2010; OECD, 2010). Thus, there is an assumption behind recent welfare reforms in the UK and beyond that the root cause of the high numbers claiming lies with the nature of the benefits system itself and its influence on the behaviour of individuals. These ideas are closely linked to the notion of 'dependency culture', which lies behind the emphasis on activation, coercion, and 'responsibilisation' within welfare reform

(Mead, 1986; Halvorsen, 1998; Peck, 2001). If the operation of the benefits system has led citizens to disengage from the labour market – so the reasoning goes – reforms to the system can 'correct' undesirable behaviour (Beck and Beck-Gernsheim, 2002). However, this behaviourist reading of the disability benefits problem appears to have run up against a more complex reality.

## What factors might explain the disability benefits crisis?

### A labour market problem?

The history and geography of disability benefits claiming in the UK indicate very clearly that job availability plays a pivotal role in determining the number of people on disability benefits. Disability benefits claimants in the UK are heavily concentrated in areas of industrial job losses (Beatty et al., 2007; Beatty and Fothergill, this volume). All periods of economic slowdown since the late nineteenth century have coincided with rises in disability insurance/benefit claiming (Macnicol, this volume). This was as true before the introduction of the Beveridge welfare state as it was after. Similarly, in many other states, claims of disability benefits have risen most strongly in the years following economic slowdowns (OECD, 2010).

Beatty et al. (2000, 2009) have made a convincing case that area-specific economic restructuring and 'job destruction' in traditional sectors during the 1980s and 1990s came to 'hide' unemployment among increasing numbers claiming disability benefits in disadvantaged labour markets, where there have been fewer opportunities available, and where those with health problems and other barriers have been pushed to the back of the jobs 'queue'. Such processes of job destruction have resulted in persistently high levels of worklessness and claiming of disability benefits in depressed urban labour markets (Webster, 2005), seaside towns (Beatty and Fothergill, 2004), former coalfield communities and industrial towns (Beatty and Fothergill, 2005) and some rural areas (Beatty and Fothergill, 1997).

There is a strong evidence base to support this theory. First, survey evidence suggests that there is little 'different' about the health or personal characteristics of people on benefits in 'high disability rate' labour markets – it's just that there are lots more of them (Brown et al., 2009). Second, spatial inequalities have remained remarkably consistent over time. The areas reporting the highest levels of benefit claiming barely changed from the early 1990s to the middle of the first decade of the 2000s (Beatty and Fothergill, 2005) and similar inequalities remain in place today (Beatty et al., 2010). These differences between areas seem resistant to changes to the benefits system (Lindsay and Houston, 2011), and to the introduction of active labour market strategies (Webster et al., 2010).

It would be simplistic, however, to suggest that job availability alone explains the patterns and trends in benefit claiming. In the UK, industrial redundancies largely affecting men in manual occupations explained a lot of the increased inflow onto disability benefits in the 1980s and early 1990s, which was dominated by men over 50 years of age in industrial districts. Since the mid-1990s, however, the inflow has come to be more varied with women and younger workers (aged 35–50) claiming in greater numbers. In parallel, poor health has replaced redundancy as the most common reason for job loss among disability claimants, and anxiety and depression have become more prevalent among claimants (Beatty et al., 2009). Despite these changes in the characteristics of claimants, the geography of claiming in the UK – including the inflow since major reform in 2008 – has remained heavily concentrated in areas of former industrial job losses that continue to be characterised by sluggish economic growth (Lindsay and Houston, 2011). This suggests that through time shortfalls in labour demand are transmitted onto those least able to compete for scarce jobs (Beatty et al., 2009).

Deindustrialisation has led to a reduction in the number of hazardous work environments in the labour market, which could be expected to reduce levels of disability among the working age population. Yet reported levels of disability have remained constant since the 1970s. An explanation may be that there has been an intensification of work and the emergence of new occupational hazards in the service sector relating more to mental than physical stress (Baumberg, 2012). Consistent with this is the fact that levels of depression and anxiety in the population have increased (although increased divorce and separation may also account for some of this rise) and that the proportion of disability benefits claimants recorded as having mental illness has also risen. Increased pressures for productivity have been noted in a range of workplaces in both public and private sectors (Loretto et al., 2010). Consequently, work intensification may be part of the explanation behind reduced employment rates among people with disabilities or poor health.

Furthermore, Davidson and Kemp's (2008) work on 'sickness benefits in a polarised labour market' pointed to the greater vulnerability faced by people with health problems working at the bottom end of the labour market. Individuals in weaker labour market positions may be less able to negotiate with employers for workplace adaptations, a change of work role or reduced hours; and those in casual or fixed-term positions may be more likely to be made redundant if they take time off for health problems. Many temporary and agency workers are also not entitled to statutory sick pay in the UK, while other casual staff can find themselves denied sick pay by employers – accordingly, disability benefits may 'act[s] as a functional equivalent of sick pay for people in poor health working in temporary jobs' (Kemp and Davidson, 2010, p. 213). In short, it seems that 'the inequality between those in "good" and "bad" jobs, in relation to both job security and other terms and conditions of employment, is reinforced while in sickness' (Davidson and Kemp, 2008, p. 229).

The first two chapters following this introduction closely connect with issues around how labour market inequalities shape the experiences of people on disability benefits. Christina Beatty and Steve Fothergill (Chapter 2) ask if the high level of disability claiming in some regions of the UK is best seen as 'an issue of health or jobs'. Some commentators have sought to caricature Beatty and Fothergill's previous work as focusing solely on 'hidden unemployment' as a cause of rising working age disability, but it is important to note that 'hidden sickness' has always been as important to their analysis (see, for example, Beatty et al., 2000, 2009). Beatty and Fothergill maintain such a balanced approach in these pages. Their recent research reported here, based on survey work with thousands of claimants, confirms health to be an important factor (most of their respondents left work because of health problems and reported substantial limitations as to the work that they could do), but again identifies spatial concentrations of disadvantage as the result of weak labour demand in regions that have experienced industrial restructuring. It's a problem of health *and* jobs.

John Macnicol (Chapter 3) provides an invaluable historical perspective, telling a recurring story of vulnerable people with health problems being shaken out of the labour market as a result of economic crisis or the 'redistribution of work' across regions and sectors. These first three chapters, along with the overwhelming weight of evidence from previous studies, show that labour market inequalities provide the crucial context for the worklessness experienced by many people with health problems and disabilities. As we have noted elsewhere:

> the weight and range of evidence is such that we can say that it is simply a fact that labour market changes, and especially the long-term impacts of area-specific industrial decline and job destruction, are essential to explaining the rise in, and continuing high levels of, [disability benefits] in some parts of the United Kingdom.
>
> (Lindsay and Houston, 2011, p. 710)

Of course, Beatty and Fothergill and Macnicol acknowledge that while labour markets and the uneven distribution of job opportunities frame the disadvantage encountered by many, individual factors, including gaps in employability and skills, explain why certain individuals rather than others are excluded.

### An employability problem?

We have noted above that labour market change has seen some regions and localities shed jobs that would otherwise be accessible for people who instead end up on disability benefits. So it would appear to be that spatially sensitive, and to some extent demand-oriented, economic policies will be required to address the labour market inequalities faced by people in these areas (see Chapters 12–13 for further discussion). However, the evidence suggests that the characteristics of individuals also matter, if only in explaining why some people rather than others are at greater risk of finding themselves 'towards the end of the jobs queue' (Beatty et al., 2009, p. 961) and consequently on benefits. Numerous survey exercises have been conducted with disability benefit claimants in the UK (Kemp and Davidson, 2010; Beatty et al., 2010; Green and Shuttleworth, 2010), so that we know that they are relatively more likely than most people of working age to report barriers to work including:

- low levels of occupational and basic skills (including gaps in literacy and numeracy);
- holding few or no qualifications;
- poor work records with long periods of unemployment or sickness absence;
- work experience concentrated in peripheral sectors characterised by low-paid and unstable job opportunities;
- fewer social networks linked to people in work;
- low household incomes and recurrent experiences of poverty;
- limited or no access to transport.

These problems are significant predictors of claiming benefits in the first place, and are associated with reduced chances of re-entering employment. Accordingly, if we want to help people claiming disability benefits to compete for jobs against people 'further towards the front of the jobs queue', then supply-side policies will be required to help improve their employability and skills.

There is little evidence, however, that disability claimants hold particularly negative attitudes towards work, as implied by the notion that the benefits system has produced a 'dependency culture'– for example, survey work by Beatty et al. (2010) found little evidence of prior knowledge of the benefits system or 'learned dependency', and in-depth qualitative interviews with claimants revealed strong latent desires to work being short-circuited by poor health and other obstacles to employment.

The chapters contained within the 'employability' strand of this book add to this evidence. Helen Barnes and Paul Sissons (Chapter 5) report the results of more than 3,000 interviews, during which disability claimants described a range of factors limiting their employability, with the weakness of work histories (often due to ill-health) emerging as a key barrier. Like the other authors of this book, Barnes and Sissons refuse to see employability and health as isolated issues, noting that illness and disability in themselves limit the employability of people on benefits. To this end they are sceptical about recent welfare reforms, which were meant to ensure that two groups – the permanently disabled and those who could work with support – were no longer 'conflated' within a single benefits regime (see Beatty et al., 2009 for discussion). Instead, Barnes and Sissons argue that multiple groups can still be identified among disability claimants, ranging from some who are engaged and near work-ready to others living with severe, limiting illness.

Anne Green and Ian Shuttleworth (Chapter 4) report on their survey research with more than 800 disability benefits claimants in Northern Ireland. As well as the sort of employability-related barriers uncovered by previous studies, they note how community divisions can reinforce a sense of spatial isolation for some disability claimants (a reminder that highly specific social and labour market contexts will shape perceptions at the local level). Green and Shuttleworth also find evidence of negative attitudes towards to work among a minority of respondents, but they understand this less as a symptom of a supposed 'dependency culture' than a reflection of the very real barriers faced by many who accurately identify their chances of re-employment as severely limited.

## A health problem?

One reason for ongoing interest in the high numbers of disability benefit claimants in the UK is that there has not been clear evidence of a corresponding rise in ill-health among the general population. Reviews of the General Household Survey and other national social surveys have found no consistent evidence that health trends predict changes in disability benefit rates (McVicar, 2008). Indeed, claimant disability rose during the 1980s and 1990s at the same time that life expectancy was increasing (Beatty et al., 2009). Furthermore, work by Beatty et al. (2007) on the 'real level of unemployment' has used control measures for differences in health among the general population to demonstrate that the spatial inequalities in disability benefit claiming cannot be understood solely as a function of the geography of health. Although industrial districts have higher rates of disability and poor health, it is job loss that has moved disabled people from employment to benefits.

However, policy makers should not conclude that malingering is at the root of the disability benefits problem. Rather, it is important to remember that Beatty et al.'s (2000, 2009) theory of 'employment, unemployment and sickness' did not merely identify 'hidden unemployment' as a component of rising disability benefit numbers, but also that 'hidden sickness' plays a key role – that is, those who claim disability benefits tend to have experienced ill-health while in work, and it is merely that there are fewer opportunities to cope with sickness in the workplace (and fewer jobs in general) in depressed labour markets. Beatty et al. (2009) argue that long-term sickness is widespread throughout the labour market, among those coping in the workplace, the unemployed and those claiming benefits. In 'full employment' labour markets, people with health conditions are more likely to sustain their employment, while in depressed labour markets people with similar ill-health face increased risk of labour market exclusion (Lindsay and Houston, 2011).

There is a substantial evidence base to support this argument. Survey research with disability benefits claimants has found that many left their previous job owing to ill-health (Beatty et al., 2010); most consistently identify health/disability limitations as a key barrier to work (Green and Shuttleworth, 2010); and the number and severity of these limitations has been shown to be a significant predictor of claimants' chances of returning to employment (Kemp and Davidson, 2010). Analyses of national datasets have demonstrated that ill-health and disability significantly affect long-term employment outcomes (Berthoud, 2011); and clinical professionals providing services for disability claimants have confirmed the presence of a range of work-limiting conditions (Lindsay and Dutton, 2010).

Jon Warren, Kayleigh Garthwaite, and Clare Bambra (Chapter 6) report on in-depth research to confirm as real the health problems faced by disability benefits claimants. Clinical measures (validated in other mental health settings) are used to expose the severity of the psychological and other health problems faced by many, adding to a growing evidence base that spatial health inequalities, and perhaps worsening health as a result of unemployment and deprivation, are important (Bambra, 2011). If we want to understand factors limiting disability claimants' employability in depressed labour markets, then we must not lose sight of the range and complexity of health problems that explain 'how they got there' in the first place.

David Webster, Judith Brown, Ewan B. Macdonald, and Ivan Turok (Chapter 7) acknowledge the need for more detailed population health data if we are to fully understand how place, employability, and wellbeing interact to exclude some people from the labour market. Building on their previous case study research centred on Glasgow in the UK (Webster et al., 2010), they note that both health and labour market inequalities explain the high levels of disability benefits claiming in that city. Responding directly to the remit of the 'health' strand of this book, Webster and his colleagues also argue that the experience of long-term labour market exclusion may shape attitudes towards health and disability.

## Implications for the policy in the UK

Christina Beatty, Steve Fothergill, and Donald Houston (Chapter 8) then take us full circle by returning to lessons for the current UK welfare reform agenda. They consider an emerging policy agenda that is based on a tightening of eligibility criteria for the new benefit, Employment and Support Allowance; increased compulsory work-related activity; and the introduction of means-testing for those claiming benefits for more than a year. They conclude that the current punitive welfare reform agenda may well achieve the previous government's target of getting 'a million people off benefits'

(Beatty and Fothergill, 2012), but that many of these people will not find employment. Instead, the risk of poverty and long-term labour market exclusion will be exacerbated for the least employable, those with complex health problems and people residing in depressed regions.

Some will argue that it is unrealistic for Beatty and colleagues to call for a dramatic recalibration of policy towards integrated health and employment services and demand-side regional economic development. Yet these suggestions should find favour with those who claim to be concerned about delivering value for money in public services. We know that previous 'Work First' active labour market programmes have failed to deliver significantly better employment outcomes for people on disability benefits (National Audit Office, 2010). If imposing compulsory 'Work First' activation on a client group facing complex barriers to work has been shown to offer poor value for money, then policy makers need to consider the evidence on the true nature of the problems faced by those trapped on disability benefits in order to identify effective solutions.

## The need for interdisciplinary and cross-national research

Another way to seek a deeper understanding of the UK's disability benefits crisis is to examine experiences in other welfare states. The chapters contributed to this book by experts on the situation in Germany, Sweden, The Netherlands and New Zealand highlight some similarities with the problems faced by UK policy makers, but also how distinctive welfare state and labour market features shape different experiences. Martin Brussig and Matthias Knuth (Chapter 9) note that there is no direct equivalent of the UK crisis in Germany, where the numbers on long-term disability benefits remain low by comparison, reflecting strict gatekeeping rules that restrict access to payments, and that social assistance is paid at a level that is relatively unattractive for claimants. Yet there are similarities with the UK, in terms of a substantial problem of ill-health and disability among those claiming unemployment benefits, an increased risk of poverty among these individuals, and spatial inequalities limiting labour market opportunities for some. Germany is arguably leaning towards an increasingly 'Work First'-type model of active labour market policy, again suggesting some shared thinking with the UK. However, Brussig and Knuth describe a more sophisticated understanding of variations in individuals' work capacities, with health assessments seeking to capture whether claimants are capable of full-time, part-time or no work at all.

Some similar and distinctive themes emerge from Rickard Ulmestig's discussion of the situation in Sweden (Chapter 10). Once again, the problem is less 'unemployment hidden as sickness' than that many people with health problems have found themselves directed towards an activating employability regime in order to restrict access to disability benefits, in

Ulmestig's words 'without any visible change in capacity for work'. Recent attempts to reduce Swedish disability claiming may reflect legitimate concerns that these benefits had become an early retirement tool for older workers, and Rik van Berkel identifies similar issues underlying the welfare reform agenda in the Netherlands (Chapter 11).

From the 1990s into the 2000s, the Dutch disability benefits crisis was seen as being more severe than the UK's. For van Berkel, there was clear evidence that government and social partners were complicit in using disability benefits to mitigate the social consequences of job losses during this period. Policy responses that have since stemmed the flow on to benefits share some similarities with the UK welfare reform agenda – eligibility requirements have been tightened; health assessments made more stringent; and the 2006 WIA reform (presaging the UK's Employment and Support Allowance) created dichotomous groups judged permanently disabled and fit for activation. However, an important lesson from the Netherlands is that part of the solution has involved placing additional requirements on employers, who are responsible for providing sick pay for, and the reintegration of, many employees reporting health and disability problems.

Neil Lunt and Daniel Horsfall's chapter on New Zealand (Chapter 12) identifies striking commonalities with the UK policy agenda on disability benefits. The seemingly contradictory themes of empowering individuals with health/disability limitations while also increasing conditionality and activation in the welfare state were common to the 'Third Way' (UK) and 'social development' (New Zealand) reform agendas of the early 2000s. Like the UK, New Zealand has more recently seen a shift away from a more progressive policy agenda, with a greater focus on restricting access to benefits through stricter capability assessments and an 'end to macro-level ambitions' to improve job availability for all citizens.

## Towards an evidence-based welfare reform agenda

There is a need for better-informed policy and a commitment to use the evidence in order to avoid the mistakes of the past. Indeed, elsewhere we have discussed how weak and inappropriate policy responses have contributed to – or at the very least exacerbated – the disability benefits crises experienced by the UK and other countries (Lindsay and Houston, 2011).

The authors gathered for this publication are drawn from the disciplines of economic geography, social policy, sociology, occupational medicine, and public health studies. We have come together in order to share evidence from across different labour market and welfare state contexts, and to attempt to move towards an interdisciplinary approach to understanding the problems faced by those on disability benefits for long periods. Crucially, we want to move the debate beyond simplistic constructions of a disability benefits crisis rooted in a mythical dependency culture and a supposedly passive welfare system. Our reading of the evidence is that the disability benefits crisis can only be understood as a function of the interaction of labour market, employability, and health problems. The chapters that follow present evidence on how these factors contribute to the disadvantage experienced by those on disability benefits, and lead us towards an understanding of 'what's needed' in terms of policies to facilitate sustainable transitions from welfare-to-work.

## Bibliography

Autor, D. and Duggan, M. (2006) 'The Growth in the Social Security Disability Rolls: A Fiscal Crisis Unfolding', *Journal of Economic Perspectives*, 20 (3), 71–96.

Baumberg, B. (2012) 'Re-evaluating Trends in the Employment of Disabled People in Britain' in S. Vickerstaff, C. Phillipson and R. Wilkie (eds) *Work, Health and Wellbeing* (Bristol: Policy Press).

Beatty, C. and Fothergill, S. (1997) *Unemployment and the Labour Market in Rural Development Areas* (London: Rural Development Commission).

Beatty, C. and Fothergill, S. (2004) 'Economic Change and the Labour Market in Britain's Seaside Towns', *Regional Studies*, 38 (5), 461–480.

Beatty, C. and Fothergill, S. (2005) 'The Diversion from Unemployment to Sickness across British Regions and Districts', *Regional Studies*, 39 (7), 837–854.

Beatty, C. and Fothergill, S. (2012) 'The Changing Profile of Incapacity Claimants' in S. Vickerstaff, C. Phillipson and R. Wilkie (eds) *Work, Health and Wellbeing* (Bristol: Policy Press).

Beatty, C., Fothergill, S., and Macmillan, R. (2000) 'A Theory of Employment, Unemployment and Sickness', *Regional Studies*, 34 (7): 617–630.

Beatty, C., Fothergill, S., Gore, T., and Powell, R. (2007) *The Real Level of Unemployment* (Sheffield: Sheffield Hallam University).

Beatty, C., Fothergill, S., Houston, D., Powell, R., and Sissons, P. (2009) 'A Gendered Theory of Employment, Unemployment and Sickness', *Environment and Planning C: Government and Policy*, 27 (6), 958–974.

Beatty, C., Fothergill, S., Houston, D., Powell, R., and Sissons, P. (2010) 'Bringing Incapacity Benefit Numbers Down: To What Extent Do Women Need a Different Approach?', *Policy Studies*, 31 (2), 143–162.

Beck, U. and Beck-Gernsheim, E. (2002) *Individualization: Institutionalized Individualism and its Social and Political Consequences* (London: Sage).

Berthoud, R. (2011) 'Trends in the Employment of Disabled People in Britain', Institute for Social and Economic Research Working Paper No. 2011-03 (Colchester, UK: University of Essex).

Brown, J., Hanlon, P., Turok, I., Webster, D., Arnottand, J., and Macdonald, E. (2009) 'Mental Health as a Reason for Claiming Incapacity Benefit – A Comparison of National and Local Trends', *Journal of Public Health*, 31 (1), 74–80.

Davidson, J. and Kemp, P. (2008) 'Sickness Benefits in a Polarised Labour Market', *Benefits*, 16 (2), 225–233.

DWP (2008) *No-One Written Off: Reforming the Welfare State to Reward Responsibility* (London: DWP).

DWP (2010) *Universal Credit: Welfare that Works* (London: DWP).

Freud, D. (2007) *Reducing Dependency, Increasing Opportunity: Options for the Future of Welfare to Work* (Leeds: Corporate Document Services).

Green, A. and Shuttleworth, I. (2010) 'Local Differences, Perceptions and Incapacity Benefit Claimants: Implications for Policy Delivery', *Policy Studies*, 31 (2), 223–243.

Halvorsen, K. (1998) 'Symbolic Purposes and Factual Consequences of the Concepts "Self-Reliance" and "Dependency" in Contemporary Discourses on Welfare', *Scandinavian Journal of Social Welfare*, 7 (1), 56–64.

Hytti, H. (2006) 'Why Are Swedes Sick but Finns Unemployed?', *International Journal of Social Welfare*, 15 (2), 131–141.

Kemp, P. and Davidson, J. (2010) 'Employability Trajectories among New Claimants of Incapacity Benefit', *Policy Studies*, 31 (2), 203–221.

Koning, P. and Van Vuuren, D. (2007) 'Hidden Unemployment in Disability Insurance', *Labour*, 21, 611–636.

Lindsay, C. and Dutton, M. (2010) 'Employability through Health? Partnership-Based Governance and the Delivery of Pathways to Work Condition Management Services', *Policy Studies*, 31 (2), 245–264.

Lindsay, C. and Houston, D. (2011) 'Fit for Purpose? Welfare Reform and Challenges for Health and Labour Market Policy in the UK', *Environment and Planning A*, 43 (3), 703–721.

Loretto, W., Platt, S., and Popham, F. (2010) 'Workplace Change and Employee Mental Health: Results from a Longitudinal Study', *British Journal of Management*, 21 (2), 526–540.

Loretto, W., Vickerstaff, S., and White, P. (2007) *The Future for Older Workers: New Perspectives* (Bristol: Policy Press).

McVicar, D. (2008) 'Why Have UK Disability Rolls Grown So Much?', *Journal of Economic Surveys*, 22 (1), 114–139.

Mead, L. (1986) *Beyond Entitlement* (New York: Free Press).

National Audit Office (2010) *Support to Incapacity Benefit Claimants through Pathways to Work* (London: National Audit Office).

OECD (2010) *Sickness, Disability and Work: Breaking the Barriers* (Paris: OECD).

Peck, J. (2001) *Workfare States* (New York: Guilford).

Waddell, G., Burton, K., and Aylward, M. (2007) 'Work and Common Health Problems', *Journal of Insurance Medicine*, 39 (2), 109–120.

Webster, D. (2005) 'Long-Term Unemployment, the Invention of Hysteresis and the Misdiagnosis of Structural Unemployment in the UK', *Cambridge Journal of Economics*, 29 (6), 975–995.

Webster, D., Arnott, J., Brown, J., Turok, I., Mitchell, R., and Macdonald, E.B. (2010) 'Falling Incapacity Benefit Claims in a Former Industrial City: Policy Impacts or Labour Market Improvement?', *Policy Studies*, 31 (2), 163–185.

# 2
# Disability Benefits in the UK: An Issue of Health or Jobs?

*Christina Beatty and Steve Fothergill*

## Introduction

The UK has 2.6 million men and women of working age out-of-work on disability benefits, far more than the number on unemployment benefits even in the wake of recession. While not unique in this respect, the 7% of the working age population out-of-work on disability benefits places the UK well towards the upper end of the range in Europe (Kemp, 2006).

This chapter considers the extent to which the high numbers on disability benefits in the UK are an *employment* problem, rooted in either a shortfall in job opportunities or shortcomings in employability, or whether they are essentially a problem of *ill-health and disability*.

The large numbers on disability benefits have typically been characterised by the UK government as an *employment* problem, or more specifically as a problem of low skills, low motivation and disengagement from the labour market rather than an absolute shortage of jobs. This view finds its clearest expression in policy statements from the Department for Work and Pensions (DWP) (2006, 2008, 2010). The underpinning assumption of the government's welfare reforms, both under Labour and its Coalition successor, has been that if disability claimants look for work, and equip themselves for work, they will find work. When the present reforms reach full fruition all but the most severely ill disability claimants will have to attend compulsory 'work-focussed interviews' and engage in 'work-related activity'. This does not rule out addressing health problems at the same time, but it would be fair to say that medical issues are not centre-stage in current thinking.

Yet *ill-health and disability* have clearly always been part of the mix. In order to qualify for disability benefits a degree of ill-health or incapacity is mandatory, and there are checks to make sure that claimants meet the relevant medical criteria. Disability claimants are initially 'signed off' by their own doctor. After six months, and sooner in the case of more recent claimants, their entitlement to benefit has to be confirmed by medical

15

practitioners working on behalf of the government agency Jobcentre Plus. The medical test – these days known as the Work Capability Assessment (WCA) – was toughened in 2008. Claimants do not have to prove that they are incapable of all possible work in all possible circumstances, but in view of the independent medical testing it is a reasonable assumption, especially for those who have passed through the WCA, that the health problems and/or disabilities are real enough.

So to what extent can the UK's high disability numbers be characterised as an issue of jobs or of health? Curiously, ill-health and disability have rarely been central to socio-economic research on disability benefits. Notable exceptions are studies by Anyadike-Danes (2010) on the distribution of claimants' conditions across the UK regions; by Lindsay and Dutton (2010) on the delivery of condition management services by the National Health Service and private contractors; and by Kemp and Davidson (2007, 2010) on the impact of health and disability on the trajectories of new incapacity claimants. More commonly, health issues are mentioned only in passing, for example while the discussion focuses on the impact of low wages and the falling demand for manual labour (Bell and Smith, 2004).

This chapter bridges the gap between 'health' and 'jobs' in understanding benefit numbers. It begins by setting out the classic evidence on the geography of claims and on the trends through time that point firmly towards the labour market as the root cause of the UK's high disability claimant numbers. The chapter then interrogates survey data on Incapacity Benefit claimants to shed greater light on the role of employability and then on the role of ill-health and disability. The evidence here is that employability and health are also central to an understanding of the numbers. The final part of the chapter then seeks to reconcile the competing perspectives, explaining the interaction between ill-health, employability and the difficult labour market that continues to be found in substantial parts of the UK.

Throughout the chapter the term 'disability benefits' is used to refer to a family of four social security benefits whose claimants add up to the headline figure of 2.6 million. These are:

- **Incapacity Benefit (IB)**. This dates back to 1995 when it replaced Invalidity Benefit. IB is not means-tested except for a small number of post-2001 claimants with significant pension income.
- **National Insurance credits-only IB claimants.** These are the disability claimants who fail to qualify for IB itself because they have insufficient National Insurance (NI) credits. The government counts these as IB claimants but most actually receive means-tested Income Support, usually with a disability premium.
- **Severe Disablement Allowance (SDA).** SDA is paid to a small number of pre-2001 claimants with a high level of disability and a poor NI contributions record.

- **Employment and Support Allowance (ESA)**. ESA replaced IB (including the NI credits-only variety) for new claimants in October 2008. By 2014 all existing IB and SDA claimants will have been moved over to ESA, subject to the appropriate medical test.

Approaching half the 2.6 million non-employed disability claimants of working age also receive a further disability benefit, **Disability Living Allowance (DLA)**, intended to offset the additional costs of disability, which is also paid to around 300,000 men and women in employment and to 1.4 million over state pension age.

The important point about the first four of these benefits is that claimants are not required to look for work as a condition of benefit receipt. This differentiates them sharply from the claimant unemployed in receipt of **Jobseeker's Allowance (JSA)**. The two groups of claimants are also mutually exclusive: it is not possible to claim any of these four disability benefits at the same time as JSA.

## Trends and geography

Two pieces of evidence point strongly to the role of the labour market, and more specifically a deficient demand for labour, as lying at the root of the UK's high disability benefit numbers.

The first is the very large increase through time in the number of claimants. Figure 2.1 takes a long view, from the early 1960s through to 2009. This shows the number of non-employed men and women of working age

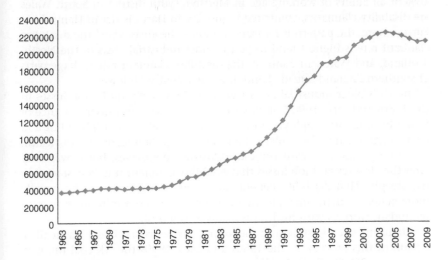

*Figure 2.1*  Disability claimants (6 months+) of working age*, GB, 1963–2009
*excluding SDA claimants.
*Source*: Webster (2004) based on DWP, and authors' update.

claiming disability benefits (including predecessors to the current benefits) for six months or more. Data on sub-six month claimants is not available on a consistent basis over this long period, but most disability claims are anyway long term. The striking feature here is the huge increase, from below half a million to in excess of 2 million.

It is impossible to explain this increase in health terms alone. If anything, trends in the underlying health of the working age population have moved in the opposite direction, which might have pointed to fewer disability claimants, though the improvements in health have arguably been slowest for some of the most disadvantaged groups in society. The UK government's General Household Survey provides a consistent measure through time of self-assessed health among the working age population. This shows that limiting longstanding illness is quite widespread but that there has been no great increase in the proportion of men and women affected – up from 16.1% to 16.7% of working age women between 1980 and 2006, but down from 17.4% to 15.5% for working age men over the same period (Beatty et al., 2009).

The timing of the large increase in disability claims does however coincide with a difficult period for the UK labour market, from the mid-1970s through to the 1990s, when the economy operated at well below full employment and claimant unemployment (that is, the number out-of-work on unemployment benefits) twice rose over 3 million.

The other piece of evidence that points powerfully to the labour market as an explanation for the UK's high disability benefit numbers is the distribution of claimants across the country, shown in Figures 2.2 and 2.3. Disability claimants are far from evenly spread across the country. At the extremes, 16% of all adults of working age in Merthyr Tydfil district in South Wales are disability claimants, compared to just 2% in Hart district in Hampshire. Furthermore, the pattern is far from random. The areas where the disability claimant rate is highest tend to be the older industrial areas of the North, Scotland, and Wales. In contrast, the disability claimant rate in large parts of southern England outside London is consistently far lower.

The UK's older industrial areas were especially badly hit by job losses in the 1980s and early 1990s, often witnessing the complete disappearance of formerly dominant employers in sectors such as coal, steel, shipbuilding and heavy engineering. These places had long had poorer standards of health, sometimes associated with the old industries themselves, but it was only after the closures and job losses that disability claimant numbers started to rise steeply. That disability benefits are in most circumstances financially more generous than unemployment benefits was a powerful incentive for redundant workers with health problems to claim IB.

Labour market adjustment in the former coalfields provides a classic illustration of this process. In the 1980s and early 1990s the UK coal industry shed some 250,000 jobs. Nearly all these jobs had been held by men, and a great many of the job losses occurred in places where the coal industry

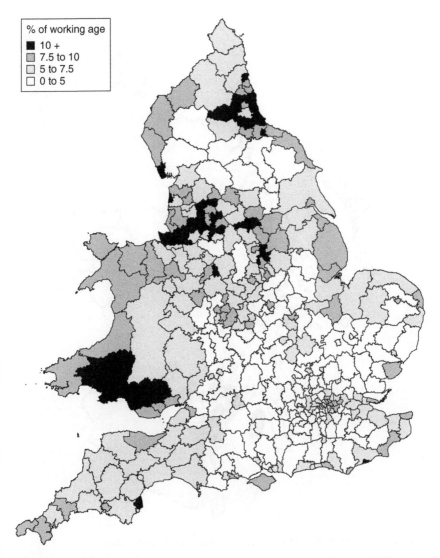

*Figure 2.2* Disability benefit claimant rate, England and Wales, February 2009
*Source*: DWP, ONS.

had been far and away the dominant male employer. Yet in response to the pit closures and redundancies, recorded unemployment among men in the coalfields rose little if at all. Instead, as Beatty and Fothergill (1996) and Beatty et al. (2007) document, the main labour market adjustment was a withdrawal of working age men from the labour market into 'economic inactivity'. This in turn was underpinned by a huge increase in the numbers

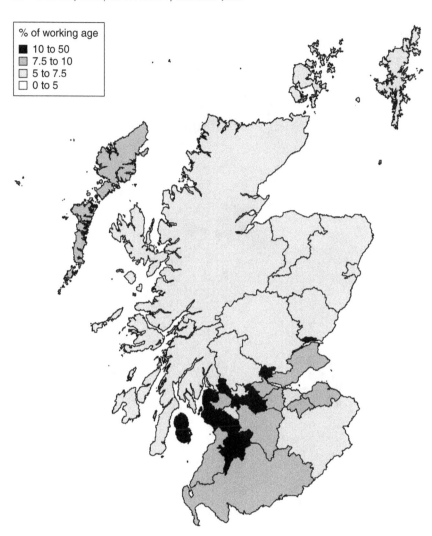

*Figure 2.3*   Disability benefit claimant rate, Scotland, February 2009
*Source*: DWP, ONS.

claiming disability benefits. Much of the increase in disability numbers, it could be argued, represented a form of 'hidden unemployment'. Newer evidence has also shown how job loss among men, in the coalfields and elsewhere, has eventually been transmitted via competition in local labour markets to higher disability claimant rates among women in the same places (Beatty et al., 2009).

More generally, the present authors have argued that there has been a large diversion from 'unemployment' to 'sickness' across Britain as a whole, and that up to a million disability claimants could be regarded as 'hidden unemployed' in that they would probably have been in work in a genuinely fully employed economy. The basis of these estimates is a comparison between the disability benefit claimant rate in each local authority district and a 'benchmark' for that district that reflects what should have been possible in a fully employed economy. The difference between the two is the estimated 'hidden unemployment'. In these calculations the benchmark is made up of two elements: the disability claimant rate in the parts of the country where the economy is operating at or close to full employment; and an adjustment for underlying differences between places in the extent of incapacitating ill-health. The methods have been set out in full on a number of occasions, notably in Beatty and Fothergill (2005).

The most recent application of these methods, reported in Beatty et al. (2010), suggests that across Great Britain as a whole in February 2009 510,000 men and 430,000 women on disability benefits could be considered to be 'hidden unemployed'. That does not mean that their disability claims were in any way fraudulent or that their health problems were anything less than real. The point is that ill-health or disability is not necessarily an absolute bar to working, and in the parts of the country where the economy is strong enough many people with long-term health problems do hold down a job. The hidden unemployed are the men and women who could have been expected to have been in work if there had been full employment in all parts of Britain.

A key aspect of hidden unemployment on disability benefits is that it is geographically concentrated. Just as disability claimants as a whole are unevenly spread across the country, the hidden unemployed within this group are unevenly spread too. As Beatty and Fothergill (2005) showed, there is no evidence of significant hidden unemployment in large swathes of southern England outside London, where the economy has been strong for many years. In these parts of the country the modest numbers on disability benefits are likely to be dominated by men and women with formidable obstacles to working. In contrast, the areas with the highest disability claimant rates nearly all have the highest estimated hidden unemployment. This is the case even after adjusting for underlying differences in the extent of incapacitating ill-health. It is in Britain's older industrial areas, plus a handful of seaside towns and inner urban areas, that the highest rates of hidden unemployment on disability benefits are to be found.

The view that there is extensive hidden unemployment on disability benefits has never been formally accepted by the UK's Department for Work and Pensions, even though many other commentators share the assessment that a weak demand for labour underpins the high disability claimant numbers in large parts of Britain (see, for example, Armstrong, 1999; MacKay, 1999; McVicar, 2006; Webster et al., 2010). There is however an uncanny symmetry between the Beatty–Fothergill estimates of around 1 million hidden unemployed on disability benefits and the target of a 1 million reduction in IB claimant numbers within ten years, set by the UK government in 2006 (DWP, 2006). On the other hand, even if up to 1million disability claimants are best regarded as hidden unemployed that still leaves 1.6 million claimants who might still be expected to claim disability benefits even if there were full employment in all parts of Britain. In effect, the calculations tell us that the benefit status of this 1.6 million is driven first and foremost by their health and, accordingly, to reduce the size of this group would require an improvement in underlying standards of health, a greater willingness among employers to take on and retain people with health problems or disabilities, or a tightening of the criteria allowing disability claims.

## Survey evidence

Let us now turn to a different source of evidence on disability claimants – a large-scale face-to-face survey – that at first sight provides very different explanations for Britain's high disability numbers.

The data reported here is taken from a survey of more than 3,600 IB claimants (including National Insurance credits-only claimants and those receiving Income Support on the grounds of incapacity) carried out in 2006 and 2007 in eight local authority districts spread across five UK regions. The survey covered a range of different types of locality but was structured to focus on areas where the incapacity claimant rate is relatively high, since it is the high claimant rate in these places that is most in need of explanation. A full description of the technical aspects of the survey is published elsewhere (Beatty et al., 2009). What should be noted here is that it achieved a high response rate, and cross-checking against DWP data on age and duration on benefit confirms that the survey sample is highly representative.

Let us begin with the evidence on the *employability* of IB claimants. Table 2.1 presents a range of indicators from the survey. In broad terms, it paints a

*Table 2.1*   Indicators of employability of IB claimants

|  | Women (%) | Men (%) |
| --- | --- | --- |
| Age 45+ | 60 | 68 |
| At least 5 years since last regular paid job* | 70 | 71 |
| No formal qualifications | 60 | 61 |
| Manual occupation | 79 | 85 |
| Would like a job | 17 | 15 |
| Might like a job further into future | 12 | 9 |
| Looking now | 4 | 4 |

*includes small numbers who have never had regular paid employment.
*Source*: IB survey data.

picture of a claimant group that is unlikely to be attractive to employers and one that displays considerable detachment from the labour market.

The first two lines of Table 2.1 show that IB claimants are a predominantly older group and a high proportion had not been in regular paid employment for at least five years. Indeed, these statistics probably understate the full extent of the problem: there is a clear tendency for the likelihood of claiming IB to rise with age, and nearly half of IB claimants in the survey had not had a job for at least ten years. If we assume that employers discriminate against older job applicants (which is almost certainly true but hard to prove) and that they prefer those with recent work experience, it seems that many IB claimants are in a weak labour market position. Likewise, the high proportions with no formal qualifications and with primarily manual work experience (in the third and fourth lines of Table 2.1) will compound the potential unattractiveness to many employers.

The final three lines of Table 2.1 illustrate the formidable labour market detachment that has developed among IB claimants. Less than one in five say they would like a job, and adding in those who say they 'might like a job further into the future' only raises the proportion to around 30% of women and a quarter of men. Hardly any IB claimants – around 4% – were actively looking for work at the time they were surveyed.

Taken as a whole, this evidence points to low levels of employability among claimants. Putting aside the demand for labour, this is not a group that is going to find work easily, and is disinclined to try to do so.

But what of the survey evidence on the role of *ill-health and disability*? Table 2.2 begins by showing the medical conditions affecting IB claimants. This information here refers to the official medical reason for the claim, recorded in DWP files, not the claimant's own assessment. Comparisons with official data for Great Britain as a whole confirm that in terms of the mix of health problems and disabilities the survey sample differs only marginally from the national average. The DWP records a single, primary reason for each IB claim. In practice, many incapacity claimants are affected by

*Table 2.2* Medical diagnosis of IB claimants

|  | Women | Men |
| --- | --- | --- |
| Mental, behavioural | 41 | 34 |
| Musculoskeletal | 22 | 22 |
| Injury, poisoning | 5 | 5 |
| Circulation | 3 | 8 |
| Nervous system | 7 | 6 |
| Respiratory | 3 | 3 |
| All other | 20 | 21 |
| Total | 100 | 100 |

*Source*: IB survey data.

more than one illness or disability, and there can be a tendency for health problems to multiply the longer that claims last.

'Mental and behavioural problems' account for the largest single group of both men and women claiming IB. This is a broad category that includes stress and depression as well as other forms of mental illness, and also includes drug and alcohol problems. The other large medical category is 'musculoskeletal problems', which includes bad backs and other movement difficulties. DWP statistics show that over time the share of IB claimants with mental or behavioural problems has been increasing while the share with musculoskeletal problems has fallen.

The survey data highlights differences between IB claimants with mental or behavioural problems and those with musculoskeletal problems. The claimants recorded as suffering from mental or behavioural problems are a notably younger group – just 33% of the men and 30% of the women are aged 50-plus, compared to 71% of the men and 54% of the women with musculoskeletal problems. There is evidence here, perhaps, of an older generation of former industrial workers with physical problems gradually being replaced by a younger generation with a different portfolio of health problems.

Table 2.3 shows the reasons men and women give for the loss of their last job. An important point to bear in mind here is that the reasons why an individual leaves a job can be complex. Sometimes there is a single, clear-cut cause. On other occasions job loss is the result of the interaction of a number of factors – for example, cuts in a firm's workforce combined with personal ill-health, domestic responsibilities and maybe even a bullying or unsympathetic boss. The survey asked men and women to identify the *principal* reason for leaving their last regular paid job, and the answers presented here exclude the very small number of claimants (5% of men and 9% of women) who have never had a job.

The key feature is the importance of illness or disability as the trigger of job loss. This is cited by 74% of men and 70% of women. This is clear evidence

*Table 2.3*   Principal reason for job loss

|  | Women (%) | Men (%) |
| --- | --- | --- |
| Compulsory severance* | 10 | 16 |
| Voluntary – redundancy/retirement | 1 | 3 |
| Voluntary – pregnancy/baby | 8 | n.a. |
| Voluntary – to look after children/others | 4 | 1 |
| Voluntary – other reasons | 5 | 4 |
| Illness or injury | 70 | 74 |
| Other | 1 | 1 |
| Total | 100 | 100 |

*compulsory redundancy, dismissal, end of contract.
*Source*: IB survey data.

that ill-health, injury, and disability play a powerful role in triggering individuals' exit from the labour market, even if the aggregate numbers point strongly to labour market processes. The importance of ill-health, injury, or disability in the job loss process is underlined by the further 8% of men and 7% of women who say that this was a *contributory* factor, even where they cited other factors as the main reason.

By contrast, compulsory severance – mainly redundancy but also dismissal and the end of a short-term contract – accounts for just one in six men and one in ten women. There is little evidence here that redundant industrial workers make up the bulk of incapacity claimants, but it is worth underlining that this survey data is for late in the first decade of the 2000s. Further back in time, in the 1990s, similar surveys used to find that between a third and a half of male IB claimants had lost their last job through redundancy (Alcock et al., 2003).

Table 2.4 shows individuals' assessment of the severity of their health problems or disability at the time they were working in their last job. Over half of all men, and over half of all women, say that their difficulties at that time were either less severe, barely an issue or not a problem at all. What this suggests is that for many men and women there has at some point been a deterioration in health, either gradual or sudden, and this may help account for the high proportion who say they lost their last job because of ill-health, injury, or disability.

Table 2.5 shows claimants' own assessment of the influence of health on their ability to work. A degree of self-reported health limitation is nearly universal among both men and women – fewer than 5% say there is no limitation on the work they can do. Also, relatively few report only modest limitations. On the other hand, only around a quarter say they 'can't do any work'. What needs to be kept in mind here is that eligibility for IB never depended on being unable to do any type of work in any circumstances. To qualify for IB, a claimant had to demonstrate a sufficient degree of ill-health or disability to be not required to look for work.

*Table 2.4* Severity of health problems/disabilities while in last job

|  | Women (%) | Men (%) |
| --- | --- | --- |
| Not a problem/barely an issue | 16 | 15 |
| Less severe | 42 | 44 |
| About the same as at present | 15 | 16 |
| More severe | 12 | 13 |
| Fluctuating | 11 | 10 |
| Don't know/can't remember | 3 | 3 |
| Total | 100 | 100 |

*Source*: IB survey data.

*Table 2.5*   Self-assessment of influence of health on ability to work

|                       | Women (%) | Men (%) |
|-----------------------|-----------|---------|
| 'Can't do any work'   | 23        | 26      |
| 'A lot' of limitation | 57        | 56      |
| Some limitation       | 16        | 15      |
| No limitation         | 4         | 3       |
| Total                 | 100       | 100     |

*Source*: IB survey data.

*Table 2.6*   Expectations about current health problems/disabilities

|                    | Women (%) | Men (%) |
|--------------------|-----------|---------|
| Get better         | 5         | 5       |
| Stay much the same | 13        | 15      |
| Fluctuate          | 24        | 21      |
| Get worse          | 52        | 54      |
| Don't know         | 6         | 6       |
| Total              | 100       | 100     |

*Source*: IB survey data.

Table 2.6 presents claimant's expectations about their health or disabilities. Pessimism is the norm. Half of all the men, and half of all the women, expect their problems to worsen. Far fewer men or women expect their health problems to ease, though between a fifth and a quarter think their problems will fluctuate. Here is evidence that in the eyes of claimants their health problems or disabilities are not only an important obstacle to working but in many cases are likely to get worse.

Unsurprisingly, perhaps, in the light of this evidence, poor health dominates the list of reasons given for not wanting a job – more than 90% of men and women cite their poor health or disability as one of the main reasons. No other factor accounts for even 10% of claimants. The next most important reason for not wanting a job – 'too much uncertainty' – comes a very poor second, cited by just 5% of survey respondents.

Likewise, even among those who say they would like a job or might like a job in future, ill-health, injury, or disability dominates the list of perceived obstacles – more than nine out often cite this factor. There is clearly a major issue here. Whatever the objective reality of men and women's health, or indeed the true opportunities in the labour market, the *perception* has unquestionably taken root even among those closest to the labour market that their health or disability is a stumbling block to employment.

And the stumbling block is not simply about what IB claimants think about themselves. It also applies to their views on potential employers. In response to the question 'What do you think potential employers would think about you?' hardly any men or women – fewer than 10% of all IB claimants – are confident that an employer would think them 'a pretty good bet' or 'worth a try'. More than half think they would be viewed as 'too ill or disabled'. A further quarter think they would be seen as 'too big a risk', no doubt in most cases because of their health problems or disabilities.

The survey data therefore provides compelling evidence not only that *employability* is a key issue but also that *health* is central to an understanding of disability claims. In summary:

- Illness, injury, or disability is the principal reason for job loss in at least 70% of cases.
- Claimants mostly see their health problems or disabilities as worse now than when they were working.
- Virtually all claimants see their health problems or disabilities as limiting the work they could do.
- Far more claimants expect their health problems or disabilities to worsen rather than ease.
- Ill-health or disability is by far the most important reason for not wanting a job.
- Ill-health or disability is seen as by far the most important obstacle to finding work, even by those who would like to work again.
- Many IB claimants who would like work think that potential employers would see them as too ill or disabled.

To underline the extent to which ill-health or disability is a powerful factor detaching IB claimants from the labour market, Table 2.7 presents the results of a logistic regression analysis using the survey data. The dependent variable in this analysis is the likelihood of an IB claimant saying that they would like a job or might like one in the future. The factors assessed as potentially relating to wanting to work are age, qualifications, duration claiming IB, health, and whether or not the individual also claims Disability Living Allowance.

For those unfamiliar with logistic regression, the key statistic is the 'odds ratio'. This expresses the strength and direction of any given factor's association with the dependent variable (in this case an interest taking up employment). Each odds ratio is expressed relative to a base line (for example, for age, relative to the 16–34 year old group). An odds ratio of 0.50, for example, in this context indicates that an interest in taking up employment is half as likely in comparison to the base line. The statistical significance of each odds ratio is also calculated. A significance of less than 0.05 indicates that the variable is statistically significant at a confidence level of more than

95%. Logistic regression measures the strength of association of each factor *simultaneously*, in other words taking all the other factors into account at the same time.

Table 2.7 shows that age, qualifications and duration on benefit are all statistically significant factors related to the likelihood that an IB claimant wants a job. The older a claimant, the poorer their qualifications and the longer their duration on IB, the less likely they are to be interested in working again. But over and above these factors the logistic regression shows that self-assessed health is also an important and statistically significant factor. Claimants who say they 'can't do any work' are 87% less likely to want a job than those who report 'no limitation' or only 'some limitation'. Claimants reporting 'a lot of limitation' are also 58% less likely to want a job than those with no/some limitation.

The analysis also shows that, over and above the other factors, being a DLA claimant is a statistically significant factor associated with the likelihood of wanting work – DLA claimants are 37% less likely to want a job. This may reflect the additional financial cushion provided by DLA, which may reduce the incentive to return to work. It may however indicate that even over and above self-assessed heath, the particular health problems and disabilities of DLA claimants add a further obstacle to re-engagement with the labour market.

*Table 2.7*  Logistic regression of factors explaining variance in whether IB claimants would like a job now or in the future

|  | Odds ratio | Significance |
|---|---|---|
| Age |  |  |
| 16–34 | 1.00 | 0.000 |
| 35–49 | 0.63 | 0.001 |
| 50+ | 0.20 | 0.000 |
| Formal qualifications |  |  |
| Yes | 1.00 | 0.000 |
| None | 0.60 | 0.000 |
| Duration on incapacity benefit |  |  |
| Less than 2 years | 1.00 | 0.000 |
| 2–5 years | 0.72 | 0.016 |
| 5–10 years | 0.42 | 0.000 |
| 10 years or more | 0.36 | 0.000 |
| Self-assessed health |  |  |
| No/some limitation | 1.00 | 0.000 |
| A lot of limitation | 0.42 | 0.000 |
| Can't do any work | 0.13 | 0.000 |
| DLA claimant |  |  |
| No | 1.00 | 0.000 |
| Yes | 0.63 | 0.000 |

*Source*: IB survey data.

## Reconciling health and labour market issues

We face apparently contradictory perspectives on the high numbers claiming disability benefits in the UK. On the one hand, the aggregate statistics on the increase through time and on the location of claimants around the country point firmly to a *labour market* explanation. On the other hand, the survey evidence points unequivocally to severe shortcomings in *employability* and to *health* issues as lying at the core of why individuals have fallen out of employment and then become thoroughly marginalised from the world of work. Can these competing perspectives be reconciled?

The starting point has to be the underlying weakness of the local economy in the areas – principally older industrial Britain – where disability claimants are concentrated. These areas were all to a greater or lesser extent badly affected by job losses in the 1980s and early 1990s. The long economic recovery from the mid-1990s onwards helped plug the gap but never completely. In these circumstances there have never been quite enough jobs to go around. With a continuing imbalance in the local labour market, with the local demand for labour still running behind the potential local labour supply, it was therefore inevitable that some individuals would be squeezed out.

In the first instance it was often the newly redundant industrial workers themselves – the ex-miners and ex-steelworkers, for example – who were squeezed out. Many of them accessed disability benefits rather than unemployment benefits because they carried forward ill-health and injuries from their former employment and because they were mostly financially better off claiming disability benefits. As time has passed, they have either found work again (in the case of the younger and more dynamic claimants) or dropped off disability benefits onto a state pension.

More recently, in a competitive labour market it has been those who are least able or least willing to keep a foothold in the labour market that have been marginalised in the places where there have never been enough jobs for everyone. These men and women are typically the poorly qualified, low-skill manual workers in poor health, whose alternative would at best be unrewarding work at or close to the national minimum wage.

As a result, the composition of the UK's stock of incapacity claimants has changed quite radically over the last decade, even though the headline total has altered relatively little. In Barrow-in-Furness in the North West of England, a shipbuilding town hit by job losses, two comparable surveys of male IB claimants in 1999 and 2006/7 found that the redundant, craft-trained shipyard worker with a strong residual desire to return to work had by 2007 been almost entirely replaced by the low-skill, poorly qualified worker who had dropped out of their last job for health reasons and was now disenchanted with the idea of ever returning to work (Beatty and Fothergill, 2007).

For the men and women excluded from employment in this way, Incapacity Benefit offered a more satisfactory way forward than Jobseeker's Allowance. In most circumstances IB is more generous and there is no requirement to look for work – work that anyway may be unattractive, low-paid and (bearing in mind issues of age, health and poor qualifications) difficult to obtain. Those who are excluded from employment and have health problems or disabilities have normally been entitled to IB and almost always therefore claimed IB in preference to JSA.

Added to this, the effect of lengthening durations on disability benefits saps the enthusiasm of many to re-engage with the labour market. Long-term IB claimants adjust their lifestyle and aspirations to fit with the diminished job opportunities they perceive as available to them, lowering their standards of consumption to fit with ongoing benefit dependency. Their 'fitness to work' often declines as despondency sets in and disabilities worsen with age. An initial willingness to consider new employment is thus gradually replaced by a complete detachment from the world of work, rationalised in terms of largely insurmountable health obstacles.

None of this indicates that the health problems and disabilities affecting the men and women who claim IBs are anything less than real, or that the older industrial areas where disability claimant rates are highest do not have higher underlying levels of ill-health. What seems to be happening is that in areas where there is a surplus of labour, employers have less incentive to hold on to staff in poor health, for example by moving them on to lighter duties. In these places staff can always be replaced, so the individual is less likely to be supported in trying to maintain their job. Equally, once an individual has lost their job because of ill-health or disability, in a difficult local labour market they are less likely to find a way back into work. Employers have the option of taking on the fit and healthy instead – and the men and women on disability benefits know that is how the labour market works. In a weaker labour market even a modest degree of ill-health or disability is likely to prejudice an individual's chances of gaining and holding down employment. In essence, their *employability* is low. Bear in mind too that given the low-skill, manual background of so many disability claimants, the jobs for which they might compete often require a degree of physical robustness and a mental resilience to cope with mundane and repetitive tasks.

So even though ill-health or disability is rarely an absolute obstacle to all employment in all circumstances, even in the eyes of disability claimants themselves, in practice even modest incapacities can prove to be a formidable obstacle, especially if an individual has no special qualifications or training to offer. Bearing in mind their official status as a 'disability claimant' it is perhaps hardly surprising that for many individuals their health or disability becomes part of their identity and, in their view, an explanation for their exclusion from the labour market.

In other words, the UK's high incapacity claimant numbers are an issue of jobs *and* of health. Where there are plenty of jobs – a situation that characterised much of southern England up until the 2008 recession – large numbers of men and women with health problems or disabilities do not hang around on disability benefits. They either stay in work or, if they lose their job, find new work again. Where labour supply continues to exceed labour demand, as in so much of older industrial Britain, ill-health or disability acts as one of the great discriminators in determining who works and who doesn't. In these places, if an individual has not only poor health but also poor qualifications and low-grade manual work experience, and is perhaps over 50, their chances in a competitive labour market are slim indeed.

## Policy implications

It once suited almost everyone to turn a blind eye to the scale of this process. The government liked disability benefits because they hid the true scale of joblessness, employers liked them because they were freed from an obligation to take on workers in poor health, and claimants liked them because as long as they were going to be jobless they might as well be on the most generous benefit. Welfare reform has shattered the cosy consensus.

What the evidence shows is that if disability numbers are to be brought down other than by just a tightening of eligibility criteria (something that is actually already well underway) there will need to be a focus not only on jobs but also on health. A growing economy, with rising employment, is arguably a prerequisite. The evidence shows that in the parts of Britain where the economy is strong enough for long enough it is possible to achieve disability claimant rates far below those currently prevailing in many parts of the country.

But the evidence also shows that existing disability claimants are unlikely to be moved quickly back towards the labour market even in favourable economic circumstances. Their problems are multiple and entrenched and, crucially, include poor health or disability alongside more traditional concerns of poor qualifications and low motivation. If the survey evidence is any guide, perhaps the majority of disability claimants will require physical or mental rehabilitation of some kind. It is not at all clear that the UK's Department for Work and Pensions has recognised the importance of this point.

## Bibliography

Alcock, P., Beatty, C., Fothergill, S., Macmillan, R., and Yeandle, S. (2003) *Work to Welfare: How Men Become Detached from the Labour Market* (Cambridge: CUP).

Anyadike-Danes, M. (2010) 'What Is the Problem, Exactly? The Distribution of Incapacity Benefit Claimant's Conditions across British Regions', *Policy Studies*, 31 (2), 187–202.

Armstrong, D. (1999) 'Hidden Male Unemployment in Northern Ireland', *Regional Studies*, 33 (6), 499–512.

Beatty, C. and Fothergill, S. (1996) 'Labour Market Adjustment in Areas of Chronic Industrial Decline: The Case of the UK Coalfields', *Regional Studies*, 30 (7), 637–650.

Beatty, C. and Fothergill, S. (2005) 'The Diversion from Unemployment to Sickness across British Regions and Districts', *Regional Studies*, 39 (7), 837–854.

Beatty, C. and Fothergill, S. (2007) 'Changes in the Profile of Men Claiming Incapacity Benefit – A Case Study', *People, Place and Politics*, 1 (3), 136–148.

Beatty, C., Fothergill, S., and Powell, R. (2007) 'Twenty Years On: Has the Economy of the UK Coalfields Recovered?', *Environment and Planning A*, 39 (7), 1654–1675.

Beatty, C., Fothergill, S., Gore, T., and Powell, R. (2010) *Tackling Worklessness in Britain's Weaker Local Economies* (Sheffield: Sheffield Hallam University).

Beatty, C., Fothergill, S., Houston, D., Powell, R., and Sissons, P. (2009) *Women on Incapacity Benefits* (Sheffield: Sheffield Hallam University).

Bell, B. and Smith, J. (2004) *Health, Disability Insurance and Labour Force Participation, Bank of England Working Paper No. 218* (London: Bank of England).

DWP (2006) *A New Deal for Welfare: Empowering People to Work* (London: DWP).

DWP (2008) *No-One Written Off: Reforming the Welfare State to Reward Responsibility* (London: DWP).

DWP (2010) *Universal Credit: Welfare that Works* (London: DWP).

Kemp, P. (2006) 'Comparing Trends in Disability Benefit Receipt', in P. Kemp, A. Sunden, and B. Bakker Tauritz (eds) *Sick Societies? Trends in Disability Benefits in Post-industrial Welfare States* (Geneva: International Social Security Association).

Kemp, P. and Davidson, J. (2007) *Routes onto Incapacity Benefit: Findings from a Survey of Recent Claimants, DWP Research Report 469* (Leeds: Corporate Document Services).

Kemp, P. and Davidson, J. (2010) 'Employability Trajectories among New Claimants of Incapacity Benefit', *Policy Studies*, 31(2), 203–221.

Lindsay, C. and Dutton, M. (2010) 'Employability through Health? Partnership-Based Governance and the Delivery of Pathways to Work Condition Management Services', *Policy Studies*, 31 (2), 245–264.

MacKay, R. (1999) 'Work and Nonwork: A More Difficult Labour Market', *Environment and Planning A*, 31, 919–934.

McVicar, D. (2006) 'Why Do Disability Benefit Rolls Vary Between Regions? A Review of Evidence from the US and UK', *Regional Studies*, 40, 519–533.

Webster, D. (2004) *Sickness, Invalidity and Incapacity Benefit Claimants over Six Months 1963–2004*, based on calculations using *Social Security Statistics*, personal communication.

Webster, D., Arnott, J., Brown, J., Turok, I., Mitchell, R., and Macdonald, E.B. (2010) 'Falling Incapacity Benefit Claims in a Former Industrial City: Policy Impacts or Labour Market Improvement?', *Policy Studies*, 31 (2), 163–185.

# 3
# A History of Work-Disability

*John Macnicol*

## Introduction: The present debate

Since the early 1970s, there have been marked improvements in the aggregate health status of the UK population. Between 1980/2 and 2008/10, life expectancy at birth increased from 70.81 years to 78.05 years for males, and from 76.80 years to 82.12 years for females. Life expectancy at age 65 also increased over the same period – by 4.3 years for males and 3.5 years for females. Between 1968 and 2008, age-standardised mortality rates for men and women declined by 51% and 43% respectively, and now stand at their lowest-ever recorded level. Strikingly, coronary deaths have halved in the last ten years.

This success story does need to be tempered by three reservations. First, there are substantial social class differentials in mortality. Second, since the 1970s self-reported health appears to have worsened and health care utilisation rates have risen (a result of rising expectations, an increasing supply of resources, improved diagnostic techniques, earlier diagnosis and new technology). Third, disability-free life expectancy has become a smaller proportion of total life expectancy. There is also much debate about whether these health gains at older ages will continue in the future (Olshansky et al., 2005; Oeppen and Vaupel, 2002). Nevertheless, we can conclude with reasonable confidence that, since the early 1970s, the aggregate health of the UK population has improved markedly.

Yet concurrent with these improvements there has occurred a remarkable counter-trend: the number of people claiming disability-related benefits of all kinds has almost tripled since the 1970s, reaching a high point of 2,740,000 in May 2005, and then slightly declining to c.2,500,000 in 2010. Controversially, this level of claims was unaffected by the employment growth of 1992–2008, which caused other claimant groups – notably, lone parents and older people – to return to work in increasing numbers. (Of course, without this aggregate employment growth claims to disability-related benefits might have risen even higher.) On the face of it, therefore, there has been a threefold increase in the number of people considering themselves too sick to work. How is this paradox to be explained?

The causes are complex and interrelated, but essentially four principal ones can be considered. First, it has been argued that, compared with Jobseeker's Allowance, the higher monetary value and easier eligibility conditions for the total package of incapacity benefits have acted as an incentive to remain out of the labour market, particularly in areas where job offerings are scarce. However, the rise in work-disability did not coincide with an increase in the relative value of incapacity benefits, or a relaxation of eligibility conditions. In addition, levels of work-disability have increased since the 1970s in most comparable industrialised societies, regardless of benefit regime (Aarts et al., 1996). Second, claimants to all disability benefits tend to be poorly qualified – some 60% possess no formal qualifications at all – and thus have sub-optimal employability, which makes them less attractive to employers. As Richard Berthoud observes, in recent years disability and disadvantage have become increasingly concentrated within a dwindling group at the bottom of society (Berthoud, 2011, p. 50). Third, there are issues of health: long-term joblessness undoubtedly worsens health status, and renders individuals less likely to be reabsorbed into employment once economic conditions improve. However, such health deteriorations are secondary consequences of joblessness, and not prime causes of it. It is unconvincing to argue that health would suddenly worsen for a population sub-set within one particular generation. The fourth and final factor is the one that will form the basis for this chapter: that lack of regional and sectoral labour market demand has created 'hidden unemployment' in which there is a complex overlap between sickness and joblessness. Of course, all of these broad causal factors interact: for example, the problem may have originated in sluggish labour market demand but it has been intensified by the corrosive effects of long-term joblessness on health and motivation; again, those with the lowest skills are the first to be shaken out of the labour force during a recession.

Contextual factors are all-important. The rise in work-disability is a product of the profound economic changes that have affected all western economies since the early 1970s. There has been a massive 'redistribution of work' – from older men to women of all ages, from heavy industry to service jobs, from full-time jobs to part-time, from old industrial regions to new centres of economic growth, and so on. Hence between 1981 and 2006 in the UK the proportion of all jobs in manufacturing declined from 31% to 17% (men) and from 18% to 6% (women); and those in banking and finance rose from 11% to 21% (men) and from 12% to 19% (women). Virtually all net job growth in the UK economy has been via part-time jobs, which have increased tenfold since 1951 (from 831,000 jobs to nearly 8,000,000 now). Qualitatively, job growth has also been in the shape of an hour-glass, with expansion at the top and at the bottom. All of this has led to a polarisation between 'work-rich' households (where at least two adults have jobs) and 'work-poor' households (where nobody has a job).

These collective changes have impacted devastatingly on older men in the UK's traditional industrial heartlands, and at the same time the developing service-based jobs (often part-time, feminised, low-paid and insecure) have presented new social and psychological challenges. In essence, there are two distinct problems in modern labour markets: deindustrialisation and worklessness, which have left whole communities with reduced opportunities for waged employment; and the growth of new jobs which, being low-paid and insecure, are inadequate to support a family and symbolise the slow shift from the male breadwinner model to the adult breadwinner model.

The story of work-disability since the 1970s is in many ways a metaphor for these changes. It also symbolises other broad themes. One is the whole question of how far economically inactive citizens should be forced, by a withdrawal of benefits, to take any job, at any wage – or to perform, long term, those low-paid, unattractive jobs that migrant workers are prepared to do in the short term. This in essence is what 'employability' really means in the present economic climate. Since the recession and stagflation of the 1970s and early 1980s, successive UK governments have adopted a neo-classical macroeconomic strategy of expanding labour supply in order to achieve steady, non-inflationary economic growth by exerting downward pressure on wages. In part, this has been a rationalisation of the growth of part-time jobs: there has emerged a prescriptive ideology that all citizens of working age should support themselves through paid labour. But even more important is the fact that the control of inflation has been absolutely central to neoliberal economics ever since monetarism in the early 1980s: low inflation creates a stable, predictable world in which finance capital can flourish (Harvey, 2007, pp. 22–7). A major purpose of activation policies is therefore to control inflation.

Activation discourses are multi-layered and complex, and this underlying macroeconomic motive tends to be hidden beneath a rhetoric on 'rights and responsibilities', with an increasingly hostile condemnation of 'welfare dependency' and rather simplistic exhortations about the beneficial effects of paid work on individuals. This was strikingly illustrated in the way that the New Labour government (1997–2010) deployed the emancipatory, post-civil rights social model of disability to justify the labour market activation of disabled people, and a tightening up of benefit conditionality: pushing more disabled people into jobs was beguilingly presented as 'empowerment' via a removal of the 'discriminatory barriers' that were said to prevent them from working (DWP, 2006, p. 15).

Another theme is that in western societies there has been a growing propensity to define minor health conditions as disabling – often termed 'the medicalisation of everyday life' or the 'cultural inflation' of sickness.

However, now the opposite is taking place, and disability is being defined down. It is important to bear in mind that categories like 'retirement', 'unemployment' or 'disability' are essentially constructs of twentieth-century welfare states: in the nineteenth century, there were no clear-cut distinctions between them. Now, as welfare states are being cut back, these categories are being eroded. Welfare discourses are moving 'back to the future' (Macnicol, 2010).

Welfare benefit caseloads in modern societies are complex, reflecting the fact that postindustrial labour markets are highly variegated, with cross-cutting divisions of gender, age, region, skill, sector and so on. Before the current recession pushed formal ILO (International Labour Organization) unemployment up to c.2,500,000, joblessness in the UK was the product of supply–demand mismatches between these many headings. All activation programmes thus face the problem that they have to be precisely tailor-made and personalised to fit the unique combination of factors that constitute the individual circumstances of each client.

Generalisations are therefore hazardous, but it can be analytically useful to divide the population on all incapacity benefits into two categories: first, deindustrialised older men, concentrated in those regions that led the industrial revolution; second, a diverse and growing group suffering mental and behavioural disorders – more feminised and located in areas where aggregate economic growth is reasonably sustained.

Members of the first group are suffering because of a lack of suitable jobs. Their age-profile is older and therefore many might reasonably be expected to have moved into retirement or death in ten years: since c.850,000 of all claimants to incapacity benefits were aged 55+ in 2006, New Labour's ten-year target of getting 1,000,000 of them 'off benefit' – but not necessarily into jobs – by 2016 was in many ways a rationalisation of the inevitable. With this group, the problem is one of programme duration and lack of outflows from benefit (Anyadike-Danes and McVicar, 2008): hence the dramatic, if misleading, soundbite that, after being on incapacity benefits for two years, a person is 'more likely to die or retire than get a job'.

The second group are suffering because of the nature of the new jobs and because an increasingly competitive society and labour market has created more social casualties suffering from varieties of alienation. This has affected people at every level in society and has attracted widespread comment: the fact that some 40% of claimants to disability benefits are suffering from mental and behavioural disorders is paralleled by the rising use of antidepressants in the population at large (prescriptions for which rose 43% between 2006 and 2010) (Evans, 2011). However, it is most pathologised when those at the bottom of society are under consideration. There is also the problem that younger men are now in competition with women for low-grade, service jobs – and, in consequence, women so displaced from the labour market are claiming incapacity benefits (Kemp and Davidson, 2009;

Beatty et al., 2009). Interestingly, in its last years of office the New Labour government, anxious not to emphasise labour market demand as a causal factor, focused more on this second group: the new trend in claimants, it argued, was 'away from the stereotype of middle-aged men in the industrial heartlands and towards a new generation with manageable mental health or musculo-skeletal conditions' (Freud, 2007, p. 28).

Under New Labour, welfare reform was pursued with renewed vigour after 2006, particular attention being paid to the stubborn problem of long-term disability. The new Pathways to Work scheme was begun on a trial basis in 2003 and made mandatory for all new claimants from 2008, Incapacity Benefit is being replaced by the Employment and Support Allowance, and a stricter work capability assessment has been introduced. All of this has occurred against a background of growing press criticism of work-disabled people, with claims that a majority of them (indeed, two-thirds or more) are capable of work (Walker, 2011). On the other side have been numerous complaints about the severity of the new privately adminis-tered medical assessments. The Conservative–Liberal Democrat government has intensified conditionality, with the aim of pushing as many of the long-term disabled as possible onto Jobseeker's Allowance (where they will be pressurised much more to accept any job or lose their right to benefit). A major driver behind this has been the perceived need to reduce public expenditure.

## Defining work-disability

How should work-disability be defined? It is a truism that all disability is an interaction between person and environment. It is equally a truism that sickness is a multidimensional phenomenon, influenced by many contex-tual and psychosocial factors – of which labour market demand will be an important one. Work-disability therefore involves a complex interaction between an individual's self-defined state of health and their working envi-ronment. It is a phenomenon often dismissed pejoratively as 'malingering' (originally used by military doctors to denote the use of feigned sickness to evade combat duties) (Collie, 1913). However, malingering is better understood as a conscious and calculated attempt at deception, whereas the phenomenon under study here is a much more subtle and complex process whereby reduced labour market demand and/or greater job insecurity causes individuals to take a more pessimistic view of their own health status. Poor health becomes a socially acceptable reason for joblessness. Whether or not this amounts to a deliberate act of deception is a moot point. Individuals may or may not be aware that the perceived severity of their work-disabling condition is relative to prevailing job opportunities: unravelling the complex layers of conscious and unconscious motivation involved would be a chal-lenging task. Quite possibly there is much to be learned from ethnographic studies of how low-income populations decide between the very restricted range of choices available to them as a result of severe economic constraints (Smith, 2005).

Work-disability can therefore be envisaged as having a hierarchy of component parts on each side of the equation, and the interaction between these is complex:

| Individual | Workplace |
| --- | --- |
| Prevailing health expectations | New technology |
| Doctors' definitional thresholds | Stress of work |
| Self-referral thresholds | Demand for product |
| Medical technology | Local economy |
| Diagnostic techniques | Globalisation |
| Timing of medical intervention | Workforce downsizing |
| Functional ability | The existence of a job |
| Availability of benefits | |

With this in mind, we need to look backwards at how this problem was discussed in the past. Adopting this perspective, it can be seen that the boundaries between 'unemployment' and 'sickness' have always been blurred, that the labour market has always exerted a powerful influence on self-defined work-disability and that there have been two previous versions of today's debate. There are extraordinary similarities between all three iterations.

## From the late nineteenth century to the First World War

The 1880s marked a turning-point in the economic and social development of the UK. There occurred a number of important structural changes, which interacted in a highly complex way: the amalgamation of firms into larger units of production; increasing international economic competition; a growing emphasis on individual workplace productivity; an intensification of work for all urban workers and, as a consequence, an increasing displacement of older male workers from the workforce. Modern 'jobless' retirement began in the 1880s: whereas in 1881 73.6% of UK males aged 65 and over had been recorded by the census as 'gainfully occupied', by 1931 this had fallen to 47.9%, by 1971 it was 23.5% and now it is just under 12%. Before the 1880s, retirement had been intimately associated with disability, as the Poor Law category 'aged and infirm' demonstrated. Most workers moved to progressively lighter tasks as they aged and became less physically capable, their diminishing incomes often supplemented by Poor Law outdoor relief. As E.H. Hunt puts it, such payments were 'not old age pensions as such but disability supplements intended to offset the diminishing market value of men no longer able to earn their keep but not yet sufficiently feeble to warrant full support' (Hunt, 1990, p. 415). The social security system of the day therefore recognised that work-disability increased with age.

By the 1890s, these displaced older workers were attracting much attention. The social literature of the time is littered with concerns that older workers were not sharing in the general improvement in living standards and real wages: economic progress appeared to be passing them by. As one commentator argued in 1896, it was now 'recognised by all students of industry' that 'improved methods of production, the introduction of machinery, the competitive stress involved in the fight for the world's markets, have placed old age, inconvenienced already by its natural disadvantages, at an ever-increasing discount' (Turner, 1896, p. 271). Modern urban industry appeared to 'age' workers more rapidly than did traditional rural society. As Charles Booth graphically put it, 'In one way or another effective working life is ten years longer in the country than in the town, or, speaking generally, is as seventy to sixty' (Booth, 1894, p. 321).

The most interesting source of contemporary evidence is to be found in the oral sessions held in front of the 1893–5 Royal Commission on the Aged Poor (the Aberdare Commission). Witness after witness testified to the fact that older urban male workers were 'worn out' at progressively earlier ages compared with those working in the rural economy. For example, a wire-worker from Finsbury, London, testified that, in his own trade, new technology (in the form of tools) had increased the pace of work compared to his father's day; another witness, a carpenter from Birmingham, claimed that in large towns a man of only 55 'is looked upon as almost played out, and the competition of younger men is so great that he has very little chance if he gets out of employment at that period of life of ever getting on again at his own trade' (Royal Commission on the Aged Poor, 1895, pp. 742, 880).

Before the commencement of the National Health Insurance scheme in 1912, records of sickness in the British population were few and far between, being limited to the notification of certain diseases, the school medical service and the medical inspection of recruits to the army and navy (Newman, 1939, p. 408). Some tantalisingly incomplete but nevertheless indicative sources for the sickness experience of workers (largely men) in the nineteenth century are the records of the friendly societies. These mutual self-help bodies drew their membership predominantly from the skilled, male working class, and their membership was growing in the late nineteenth century, reaching 4,200,000 in registered societies in 1898, with perhaps another 4,000,000 in unregistered ones. The two big federal organisations, the Manchester Unity of Oddfellows and the Ancient Order of Foresters, consisted of many branches spread all over the UK. Coverage for old age per se (via superannuation schemes) was uncommon, but the societies paid benefits to those of their members unable to work through sickness or infirmity. By the end of the nineteenth century sickness benefit was increasingly becoming a surrogate old age pension for older members in response to rises in a range of medical conditions. Sickness benefit claims rose at all ages, but particularly so for older members, who also experienced a higher duration of claims ('protracted sickness').

The finances of friendly societies were closely monitored and regulated by the state: their financial soundness was in the hands of consultant actuaries, who were not loath to dispense rigorous advice. However, various factors inclined the societies towards an increasingly elastic definition of sickness in the last decades of the nineteenth century. Modern scholars have discussed the possible causal factors, such as age compositional changes in membership, more liberal definitions of sickness, the survival of members with more health-impaired lives, different administrative practices, changes in sickness recording, or the fact that the societies' driving-down of doctors' fees (in the interests of cost-cutting) resulted in more perfunctory medical assessments (Harris et al., 2011). One factor – stressed elsewhere by this author (Macnicol, 1998, ch.5) – was the changing labour market. The friendly society definition of sickness was 'inability to work': as the actuary Francis Neison observed in 1849, 'the sickness of friendly societies … is not sickness as medically viewed; it is incapacity from labour' (quoted in Harris et al., 2012, p. 739). Conversely, as James Riley puts it, 'wellness … was the ability to work' (Riley, 1997, p. 127). It will here be argued that the societies were forced to become more generous in their interpretation of sickness when faced with growing job insecurity experienced by their older members.

There were several reasons for this. First, the fraternal ethos of the societies, plus the fact that their internal workings were closely monitored by their members, especially in the smaller branches, disinclined them to be anything less than generous with their older members who had long records of contributions. Blatant malingering was held in check by the observations of fellow members and quite strict medical assessments. Providing that sickness was certified by a society doctor and a sick visitor (who conducted home inspections), payment of benefits was a contractual right. As friendly society leaders frequently stressed, 'the human element' had to take precedence wherever possible over the impersonal constraints of actuarial science (Moffrey, 1900). Those outside the societies – often motivated by class distancing – claimed that malingering was widespread, but insiders knew that it was not (Cordery, 2003, pp. 26–7, 125, 129, 150).

However, the adverse effects of labour market changes at a local level would be well known and would encourage a more elastic definition of what constituted work-disabling sickness. Doctors would have intimate knowledge of local labour markets and would be sympathetic towards those long-serving older society members whose sickness masked de facto unemployment. Again, competition for new members meant that the societies had to appear to be generous in dispensing benefits: it would look bad if older society members were forced to have recourse to the Poor Law, and the societies prided themselves on how few actually did. As one perceptive observer put it, 'When the period of loss of wages arising from the disability of old age and worn-out working powers arrives, the society's doctor in many cases feels compelled to stretch a point and, rules notwithstanding, to judge cases brought to his notice by the heart rather than the head, lest the old folk become altogether destitute and fall on the poor-rate' (Wilkinson, 1892, pp. 725–6).

As is well known, the friendly societies faced something of a financial crisis at the end of the nineteenth century owing to this rise in protracted sickness. Bentley Gilbert's famous verdict that the unfolding of the epidemiological transition, compounded by their use of outmoded life tables, was bankrupting the societies (Gilbert, 1966, pp. 165–80) has been substantially moderated by subsequent historians: the 'crisis' was manageable, and was dealt with by a number of means, notably by raising weekly subscriptions. A steady influx of new members kept contribution income buoyant. Nevertheless, the rise in protracted sickness aroused much comment at the time, and it is well worth considering because in many ways it was a rehearsal for the debate one hundred years later.

The apparent rise in sickness was, of course, counter-intuitive, in that it had occurred alongside great improvements in real wages and the built environment, reductions in mortality, and so on. In short, it seemed puzzling to many contemporaries that one section of society should be falling behind the overall increase in material prosperity. The rise in long-term sickness was also occurring among the labour aristocracy – exactly those men most deeply imbued with Smilesean virtues, and the least likely to be work-shy malingerers.

The most systematic and important contemporary investigation was by Alfred Watson, consultant actuary to the Manchester Unity of Oddfellows. This showed that sickness benefit claims had risen at all ages in the Manchester Unity between 1846–8 and 1893–7, but the highest rate of increase had occurred among those members aged 65+. Thus the 'weeks of sickness' experienced by those aged 65+ had risen from 1.8% of the total weeks of sickness to 31.6% over that period. The most striking feature was the increase in protracted sickness (that is, more than two years' duration) and permanent sickness (Watson, 1903). Watson's classic study was methodologically imperfect and has been criticised by modern historians (Riley, 1997, p. 173), but his evidence regarding protracted sickness among older society members stands largely unchallenged.

From this brief exploration we can see that the late nineteenth century debate on work-disability was extraordinarily similar to that of today – most strikingly, in the widespread suspicion that both friendly society members and their doctors had inflated their definitions of what constituted work-disabling sickness. What was less frequently mentioned – except by a few contemporaries (Turner, 1896, p. 271) – was the fact that both increasing job insecurity and the disappearance of jobs were major drivers behind the rise in long-term sickness benefit claims.

An interesting and prescient commentary on this phenomenon was provided by the economic historian T.S. Ashton in 1916, based on his study of the sickness records of Amalgamated Society of Engineers members before and during the First World War. It might be intuitively assumed, suggested Ashton, that 'when earnings are high, and employment good, the numbers on sick benefit would grow, because men would be able to afford an illness'. Conversely, in times of economic depression recorded sickness rates would fall: workers would try to remain in work, for fear of losing their jobs to others. In fact the reverse was true, and Ashton's research showed that there was a correlation between unemployment among engineers and sickness benefit claims by them: when the former rose, the latter also rose (Ashton, 1916).

## From the First World War to the 1950s

Between 1912 and the launching of the National Health Service in mid-1948, the principal source of health care for the majority of the population in the UK was National Health Insurance (NHI). Originally introduced as something of a partial measure, NHI appeared more radical than it actually was because of the controversies that attended its passage through Parliament in 1911. Indeed, such was the opposition of the British Medical Association and other vested interests that the Act nearly proved unworkable. Only an immense amount of hard work by the specially convened and exceptionally able team of civil servants charged with framing the Act, plus the political courage of the politicians in charge, saved it.

Given that they were breaking new ground, the planners of the new scheme could not predict the likely adverse consequences. The official most closely involved with the framing of the Act, W.J. Braithwaite, recorded in his famous contemporary account that there were three risks: 'the risk of discovering that sickness was much greater than supposed, the risk of malingering, and the Parliamentary risk of greater and greater demands' (Bunbury, 1957, p. 127). Braithwaite considered that outright malingering was unlikely, given the low monetary level of sickness benefit. However, he made an interesting conceptual distinction between 'conscious swindling' on the one hand, and, on the other, a more subtle kind of psychosis, comprising an unconscious tendency to sickness better described by the German word 'rentenhysterie' (Bunbury, 1957, pp. 94–5).

Some opponents of the Act played upon this point. 'I fear the growth of malingering,' wrote Beatrice Webb in her diary (Webb, 1948, p. 474). Although Sidney Webb was not so implacably opposed, the Webbs both disliked the Act for falling too far short of the fully preventive and curative state medical service they sought and had recommended in the famous Minority Report of the 1905–9 Royal Commission on the Poor Laws. Convinced that the German scheme of health insurance had encouraged fraudulent claims, they pointed to the late nineteenth-century paradox of falling death rates yet rising friendly society sickness benefit claims and argued that an insurance-based scheme inevitably encouraged moral hazard among its users via 'the half-conscious determination to get value for their money by drawing out in benefits the full measure of their own contributions' (Webb and Webb, 1911, pp. 160–7). Similar fears were occasionally expressed during the Parliamentary debates on the Act: most notably, Sir Thomas Whittaker MP warned that 'malingering and slackness' were the great dangers and would increase, especially as there would henceforth be included people of 'a less satisfactory character'. Another MP, Theodore Taylor, also viewed malingering as the greatest danger but was confident that the friendly societies' experience in dealing with this problem would minimise it (*H of C Deb*, 1911, cols 331, 551). Once the scheme commenced, the higher-than-expected level of sickness benefit claims raised questions of lax certification procedures by doctors. Others argued that this merely revealed a submerged mass of hidden, untreated sickness.

Estimates vary, but one authoritative source records that, two years after its inception (in late 1914), NHI covered 13,689,000 manual workers and other employees earning less than £160 per annum (the income tax limit). This number had risen to 19,706,000 by late 1938 (with overall population growth, and a raising of the eligibility income limit in 1920 to £250 per annum) (*Social Insurance and Allied Services*, 1942, p. 213). Initially, sickness benefit of 10s0d (50p) per week was paid to men and 7s6d (37p) per week to women for six months, followed by disablement benefit of 5s0d (25p) per week for an indefinite duration. These benefit rates were raised in 1920 to 15s0d (75p), 12s0d (60p) and 7s6d (37p) respectively, and then reduced slightly (in the case of married women) as an economy measure from January 1933. Maternity benefit was also paid. The scheme was funded by state-supervised contributory insurance and administered through the 'approved societies' (basically, friendly societies and industrial insurance companies).

Notoriously, NHI had several glaring faults: the dependants of a wage-earner were not covered (which meant that the majority of working-class women and children had no guaranteed right to health care until 1948); self-employed working people were also excluded; treatment by GPs tended to be perfunctory and palliative – a 'bottle of medicine' approach; there was no routine access to specialist treatment in a hospital; additional benefits (mainly ophthalmic and dental) were patchily provided (depending on the solvency of the individual approved society); and the administrative structure was one of baffling complexity. These inherent deficiencies exacerbated all the usual problems of measuring the 'true' level of morbidity. NHI sickness records were therefore a less-than-perfect reflection of the health of the nation. For example, claim levels by region, spell duration and even total number were not routinely published (although the annual cost was).

Nevertheless, something interesting can be learned from the course of NHI sickness benefit claims in the inter-war years. For the purposes of this chapter, the focus will be on the way that unemployment and increased job insecurity pushed up claims, against a background of falling mortality and overall health improvements. Then, as now, this was a paradox to many contemporaries, especially those in the health-related professions who prided themselves on the improvements in public health that had taken place since the late nineteenth century (Wood, 1930, col. 83). Avowed opponents of state national insurance seized upon this paradox as evidence of the corrupting effect of all state-provided benefits (Ormerod, 1930), but the causal processes were much more complex.

The inter-war depression engendered an enormously wide-ranging debate on the effect of unemployment and low incomes on physical and mental health. After a brief postwar economic boom, unemployment started to rise in 1921, reaching 1,751,000 in June 1926, and falling slightly to 1,059,000 in May 1927; it then rose again, reaching just under 3,000,000 in January 1933. There then occurred a slow fall and stabilisation for the rest of the 1930s; but on the eve of the Second World War unemployment still totalled 1,232,000. Rarely in the inter-war years did unemployment fall below 10% of the insured population, and at its highest it reached 23%. As is well known, inter-war mass unemployment was a product of a worldwide recession bringing about a slump in demand for the products of the old 'staple' industries, exacerbated by changes in world markets induced by the First World War.

The human impact of unemployment was, of course, greatly exacerbated by its regional concentration in those 'depressed areas' that were centres of the recession-hit heavy industries (most notably, coal mining, shipbuilding, iron and steel production and heavy manufacturing) located in South Wales, the North West and North East of England, and central Scotland – precisely those regions that have high levels of claims to long-term sickness and disability benefits today. The inter-war economy experienced growth in some sectors and regions, and decline in others. In the 1930s, these depressed areas became the focus of numerous investigations into the effects of unemployment on child nutrition, maternal and infant mortality, life expectancy, psychological well-being, and so on. The public health controversy in the 1930s was a bitter and protracted one, not least because it was a cardinal principle of the National Government's neoclassical, deflationary economic strategy to keep wage and benefit levels low in order to cut production costs and render British-made goods more competitive on world markets. As in the 1980s, unemployment was a deflationary device. There were frequent accusations that this strategy was condemning the unemployed and their families to extreme poverty and even malnutrition.

The NHI scheme was tested to breaking point in the inter-war years. During the First World War, full employment increased NHI contribution income and decreased benefit claims, which boosted approved society funds and dispelled for a time concerns over malingering. But claims began to rise as unemployment rose from 1921 onwards. An official analysis by Sir Alfred Watson (now Government Actuary) showed that, between 1921 and 1927, claims to sickness benefit had risen by 41% for men, 60% for unmarried women and 106% for married women; for each of these groups, claims to disablement benefit had risen by 85%, 100% and 159% respectively (Government Actuary, 1930, pp. 5–6). Expenditure on sickness benefit increased from £8,010,000 in 1914–15 to £13,153,000 in 1921–2 and £20,482,000 in 1926–7 (partly owing to the General Strike); it then stabilised at just under £19,000,000 per annum (*Social Insurance and Allied Services*, 1942, p. 214). While a funding crisis never actually materialised, there was enough concern to cause some cuts and a tightening up of administration in the early 1930s.

NHI in the inter-war years was the subject of some controversy – admittedly, not as bitter as the controversies that bedevilled unemployment insurance – over issues like the administrative efficiency of the approved societies, the financial surpluses they had built up by the end of the 1930s, the question of what to do with contributors who became unemployed and fell into arrears, the treatment of married women (basically, whether maternity constituted 'sickness'), and so on. But for the purposes of this chapter, only one of these will be considered – the effect of unemployment on self-defined health, and the related accusation that a significant number of NHI claimants were malingering.

The NHI scheme contained within itself some contradictory incentives. On the one hand, sickness benefit was generally easier to claim than unemployment benefit, and was subject to less conditionality (for example, the 'genuinely seeking work' test in the latter). Unlike unemployment benefit, it could be received during a trade dispute, and sickness benefit claims rose temporarily during the General Strike of May 1926 and the subsequent miners' lock-out (Hohman, 1933, p. 172). Again, after January 1935, about 1,000,000 long-term unemployed were transferred to the Unemployment Assistance Board and subject to its controversial household means test. Sickness benefit had no equivalent, being a contributory entitlement (Whiteside, 1988, pp. 187–8). It was possible – and often desperately necessary – to supplement it with other sources of income.

On the other hand, there is powerful testimonial evidence that some sickness benefit claimants with families pressurised health insurance GPs (panel doctors) to certify them 'fit for work' so that they could move to unemployment benefit which, thanks to its dependants' allowances, was higher in value for a family man – a situation greatly welcomed by the approved societies, since it saved them money. For example, in 1936 a man with a wife and three children would have been able to claim 35s0d (£1.75p) per week in unemployment benefit, but only 15s0d (75p) per week if on sickness benefit. Unemployment benefit was on the margins of subsistence (as defined by the many inter-war poverty surveys), so sickness benefit was drastically below it: such a family would have required £2 per week to reach an agreed 1936 subsistence level – nearly three times the level of sickness benefit and six times the level of long-term disablement benefit. A very low urban wage in the 1930s would have been £2.10s0d (£2.50p) to £3 per week. The illogical variation in benefit levels had been discussed by the 1924–6 Royal Commission on National Health Insurance: the Minority recommended an equalisation of benefit levels, but the Majority could only support dependants' allowances. Many critics agreed that this only resulted in an unemployed person putting off seeking treatment for sickness for fear of being moved to the lower benefit – quite contrary to any rational public health policy (*Royal Commission on National Health Insurance*, 1926, pp. 144, 318–19).

It was clear, therefore, that the monetary level of sickness benefit was far too low to act as much of an incentive in anything other than the most desperate financial circumstances. An individual or family could only survive on it by utilising other sources of income – from savings, trade union benefit schemes, relatives, neighbours, moneylenders, pawnbrokers, the Poor Law or Public Assistance Committees, and so on. Such households would have had to reduce their expenditure to the lowest level possible in order to survive (Levy, 1944, pp. 77–8). Even more serious was the reduction of disablement benefit by half after six months, which was designed to sift out all but the most genuine cases. Critics argued that this reduction occurred exactly at that point when a claimant needed more financial support, not less, to help them through a period of convalescence; disablement benefit also carried no provision for occupational therapy or rehabilitation (Clarke, 1943, pp. 96–7). As one commentator put it, these low benefit levels could only be justified 'on the ground of deterrence' (Hohman, 1933, p. 180). Bentley Gilbert's accusation that a large number of working-class households were using sickness or disablement benefit 'as a supplement to ordinary family income' needs to be placed in this context (Gilbert, 1970, p. 290).

Were there other administrative factors that might have caused an upward rise in sickness benefit claims? Some argued at the time that the problem was compounded by lax administration in certain approved societies, the societies' reluctance to countenance any criticism of their workings, the tendency of would-be claimants to 'shop around' until they found a panel doctor willing to certify them as unfit to work, panel doctors being too anxious to attract new patients (and the related capitation fee) by appearing to be generous with sick notes, perfunctory diagnoses by panel doctors owing to overwork, or a general cynicism shown by panel doctors towards a system that they had never fully accepted (Hohman, 1933, p. 165).

However, these possible inflationary factors were more than counterbalanced by deterrent devices. Approved societies operated a system of domestic surveillance by 'sick visitors' who tested the authenticity of claims, and after 1930 these visits were increased. In general, societies did everything they could to get claimants back to work quickly, so that benefit expenditure was minimised: the more they amassed in their accumulated reserves, the more could they offer in the way of additional benefits and thereby attract new members (Clarke, 1943, pp. 101–2). Finally, any case of diagnostic disagreement could be referred to Regional Medical Officers (full-time salaried doctors employed by the Ministry of Health). At the time, much was made of the fact that only a small proportion of such referrals were allowed to continue on benefit: this was 34% in 1930 (for England and Wales), with 66% being judged 'fit for work' (Harris, 1946, p. 115) – a proportion nearly identical to today's. However, then, as now, being judged 'fit for work' was not the same thing as having a job. All in all, therefore, the financial and administrative incentives worked *against* the claiming of sickness benefit.

Intriguingly, in the inter-war years there were exactly the same allegations as there are today regarding the tendency of panel doctors who worked in the high-unemployment depressed areas to dispense sick notes too readily, out of misguided kindness. Such doctors would be aware of the devastation caused to local economies by the world recession, and would feel considerable sympathy for men thrown out of work as a result. A charge of malingering was therefore as much a charge against a doctor, who made the diagnosis, as against a patient.

It is clear that many contemporaries in the inter-war years realised that the labour market was having a profound effect on self-defined work-disability, even if they expressed this in guarded terms. Bentley Gilbert recounts a 1926 speech to the annual conference of panel doctors by Walter Kinnear, Controller of the Insurance Department of the Ministry of Health, expressing deep concerns about this and imploring them not to turn the NHI system into a form of the dole (Gilbert, 1970, pp. 289–90); in 1931, Kinnear again declared that 'a not unsubstantial proportion' of sickness benefit claimants were receiving benefits 'to which they had no legal or moral right' (quoted in Cohen, 1932, p. 14). There were also periodic warnings from the Ministry of Health about 'the doctor as relieving officer instead of physician' (Hohman, 1933, p. 174). However, the Ministry of Health tended to see the problem largely as a decline in health on the part of the long-term unemployed and emphasised administrative factors such as lax certification (for example, Ministry of Health, 1930, p. 189).

Finally, it is possible to view the inter-war rise in NHI claims as a much-exaggerated problem. To be sure, Watson's 1930 report did reveal a significant rise in claims between 1921 and 1927, but only for women were they markedly higher than the actuarial 'expectation' set by Watson himself on the basis of his 1903 study of the Manchester Unity – and arguably Watson had set the expectation for women too low, basing it on the small and unrepresentative number who were friendly society members. (Women – both married and unmarried – numbered only one-third of those covered by NHI.) If the increase for men had been caused by outright malingering, then claim duration would have increased much more rapidly than claim numbers. However, this was not the case: the essence of the problem in the 1920s was an increase in claims of short duration (Government Actuary, 1930, p. 14). Again, the level of disablement benefit claimed by men (the most likely recourse of the malingerer) was exactly at the actuarial expectation in 1927. In the 1930s, the number of claims to sickness benefit stabilised but claims to disablement benefit of longer duration continued to rise (Whiteside, 1987, pp. 233–5) – exactly what one would expect to find in a prolonged recession, with a large number of discouraged workers.

The whole question of incentives internal to the benefit system must therefore be placed in the much bigger context of the economic depression. As today, lack of labour market demand by sector and region encouraged the more infirm to self-classify themselves as too sick to work, rather than as unemployed (and fit enough to take any suitable job offered). Only a small part of the increase in recorded sickness can be attributed to improved medical diagnostic techniques, higher health expectations or a deterioration in the health of the long-term unemployed. Those who would be first displaced from the labour market by economic recession would be those with the most health-impaired lives. Once unemployed, with little prospect of regaining work, they would perceive their symptoms as work-disabling. It is clear, therefore, that sickness was being used to mask de facto unemployment. As in every recession, the boundary between 'sickness' and 'unemployment' became blurred – especially in the case of mental disorders, which in 1934–5 amounted to over one-third of 'chronic' disability cases (off work for one year or more) (Whiteside, 1988, p. 188). As Noel Whiteside observes, 'When unemployment rose in the 1930s, numbers of "impaired lives", with no hope of finding work, settled into semi-retirement on disability benefits and public assistance' (Whiteside, 1987, pp. 240–1).

Even Bentley Gilbert, whose somewhat stern account is entitled 'unemployment and malingering' and who views the whole problem as an 'abuse', nevertheless acknowledges that 'the line between sickness and well-being for a man suffering economic deprivation was likely to be unclear even to the individual, without taking into account any conscious efforts on the part of the claimant to dissemble' (Gilbert, 1970, pp. 285–6, 292). Gilbert appears to be arguing that the recession eroded standards of public honesty by making benefit income more attractive. He does not, however, draw the logical conclusion that economic conditions were the prime factor, and that such behaviour would not have occurred had there been full employment. A more obvious verdict – substantiated by today's situation – is that, in a recession, both employers and employees become more stringent in their assessment of what constitutes 'employability'.

In the late 1930s, there was a growing concern in governmental circles that long-term unemployment had eroded the will to work in the depressed areas and that the 'dole habit' might even become intergenerational. As today, a long period of economic restructuring had built up a large reserve army of labour, for whom there were no realistic jobs. Greater conditionality and even a compulsory work programme were being considered within the Ministry of Labour and elsewhere. Something of this mood was articulated in an editorial of 22 February 1938 in *The Times*, entitled 'Idle and Content', which claimed that there were 'hundreds and thousands of young men who do not show any disposition to bestir themselves to get out of unemployment into employment.... That salutary action is necessary is beyond dispute' (*The Times*, 1938). The problem was of course resolved, in somewhat spectacular fashion, by the Second World War. Unemployment fell significantly from mid-1940, with the enormous economic stimulus created by a war economy (assisted by military call-up removing from the civilian labour market many men and women of prime working age). During the War, groups who had previously been marginal to the workforce (including those judged to be 'unemployable') found jobs in a very tight labour market. Interestingly, sickness benefit claims rose for a time, probably because of the entry into the labour market of more health-impaired people (the long-term unemployed, older workers and less healthy women), plus the stresses and strains of wartime (Titmuss, 1950, pp. 527–9). However, from 1946 claims fell. It is significant that, in the full-employment 1950s and 1960s, claim levels remained roughly constant, at just under or just over 1,000,000 claims per annum at any one time (Central Statistical Office, 1960, p. 50; Central Statistical Office, 1971, p. 50) – although, interestingly, multiple spells increased. From the 1970s, however, things began to change once again.

Some caution must be exercised in drawing temporal conclusions from sickness benefit claim levels, since they were affected by more factors than just the labour market – for example, changing patterns of morbidity, higher expectations, greater availability of health care (most notably, with the introduction of the National Health Service), earlier and better diagnosis through technological improvements, benefit eligibility conditions, and so on. There were variations in claims by season, age, social class, gender and marital status (for example, in the 1950s two-thirds of married women who worked in the labour market were excluded because they did not pay full National Insurance contributions) (George, 1968, ch. 6).

Nevertheless, two reasonably robust conclusions can be drawn from this historical analysis. First, were the rise in sickness claims mainly the result of a 'cultural inflation' or a change in the propensity to claim benefits, then there would not have been a low level of claims in 1914–21 and in the 1950s and 1960s. Instead, recorded sickness would have steadily risen in both good times and bad. Second, had health worsened because of the adverse effects of heavy industrial working, or because of the survival to later ages of more people with health-impaired lives, then sickness benefit claims would also have been high in the full-employment 1950s and 1960s. In fact, the fluctuations in claim levels correlate closely with economic conditions.

## Conclusion

The history of work-disability has much to teach us regarding the present. From this backward gaze, we can see that over the past 130 years there have been three periods in which trends in mortality and recorded morbidity have followed divergent paths and levels of work-disability have risen. Despite overall improvements in population health, sickness has appeared to increase for a minority. In each period, there has been a vibrant debate over the many factors that might cause levels of recorded sickness to rise, and a recognition that sickness is a continuum that is subject to many contextual influences.

What light does the historical evidence throw on the four possible explanations outlined at the start of this chapter? First, the incentive effect of benefits was only minimal. Nineteenth-century friendly society payments were heavily policed by fellow members and society officials, who seem to have sanctioned the increasing subsidy of their older members in recognition of the fact that it was becoming progressively more difficult for them to hold on to jobs. Again, NHI sickness benefit was markedly lower in value than unemployment benefit, and was therefore only used as a desperate last resort (often as a supplement to other meagre sources of income). Second, the work-disabled certainly suffered from poor employability and were the first to be shaken out of the labour force during major economic restructuring, but this was primarily a consequence of diminished sectoral labour market demand. Third, deteriorating health among the long-term unemployed was a serious problem in the inter-war years, but it was much more a consequence of unemployment than a cause of it: once the UK labour market tightened up after 1940, even the most health-impaired found jobs. Finally, the one factor common to all three peaks in work-disability has been labour market restructuring, causing jobs to disappear and/or producing lower-quality replacement jobs. Conversely, sickness benefit claims went down when tight labour markets briefly existed in 1914–21 and in the 1950s and 1960s.

Over the past thirteen decades, therefore, there have only been three in which work-disability has *not* been a major social problem. The crisis in the late nineteenth century was ameliorated by the introduction of old age pensions and a growing acceptance of the inevitability of retirement. The crisis in the inter-war years was abruptly resolved by the Second World War and the subsequent 25-year postwar boom in manufacturing. It remains to be seen whether supply-side policies and a withdrawal of benefits will be able to resolve this latest crisis.

## Bibliography

Aarts, L.J.M., Burkhauser, R.V., and de Jong, P.R. (1996) *Curing the Dutch Disease. An International Perspective on Disability Policy Reform* (Aldershot: Avebury).

Anyadike-Danes, M. and McVicar, D. (2008) 'Has the Boom in Incapacity Benefit Claimant Numbers Passed Its Peak?', *Fiscal Studies*, 29 (4): 415–34.

Ashton, T.S. (1916) 'The Relationship between Unemployment and Sickness', *Economic Journal*, 26: 396–400.

Beatty, C., Fothergill, S., Houston, D., Powell, R., and Sissons, P. (2009) *Women on Incapacity Benefits* (Sheffield: Sheffield Hallam University).

Berthoud, R. (2011) *Trends in the Employment of Disabled People in Britain* (Colchester: Institute for Social and Economic Research, University of Essex).

Booth, C. (1894) *The Aged Poor in England and Wales* (London: Macmillan).

Bunbury, H.N. (ed.) (1957) *Lloyd George's Ambulance Wagon: Being the Memoirs of William J. Braithwaite, 1911–1912* (Postway, Bath: Cedric Chivers).

Central Statistical Office (1960) *Annual Abstract of Statistics No. 97 1960* (London: HMSO).

Central Statistical Office (1971) *Annual Abstract of Statistics No. 108 1971* (London: HMSO).

Clarke, J.S. (1943) 'National Health Insurance', in William A. Robson (ed.) *Social Security* (London: George Allen and Unwin).

Cohen, P. (1932) *The British System of Social Insurance* (London: Philip Allan).

Collie, J. (1931) *Malingering and Feigned Sickness* (London: Arnold).

Cordery, S. (2003) *British Friendly Societies, 1750–1914* (Basingstoke: Palgrave Macmillan).

DWP (2006) *A New Deal for Welfare: Empowering People to Work*, Cm. 6730 (London: DWP).

Evans, M. (2011) 'Recession Linked to Huge Rise in Use of Antidepressants', *The Telegraph*, 7 April.

Freud, D. (2007) *Reducing Dependency, Increasing Opportunity: Options for the Future of Welfare to Work* (Leeds: Corporate Document Services).

George, V. (1968) *Social Security: Beveridge and After* (London: Routledge).

Gilbert, B. (1966) *The Evolution of National Insurance in Great Britain: The Origins of the Welfare State* (London: Joseph).

Gilbert, B. (1970) *British Social Policy 1914–39* (London: Batsford).

Government Actuary (1930) *National Health Insurance. Report by the Government Actuary on an Examination of the Sickness and Disablement Experience of a Group of Approved Societies in the Period 1921–27*, Cmd. 3548.

Harris, B., Gorsky, M., Guntupalli, A., and Hinde, A. (2011) 'Ageing, Sickness and Health in England and Wales during the Mortality Transition', *Social History of Medicine*, 24 (3), 643–65.

Harris, B., Gorsky, M., Guntupalli, A.M., and Hinde, A. (2012) 'Long-Term Changes in Sickness and Health: Further Evidence from the Hampshire Friendly Society', *Economic History Review*, 65 (2), 719–45.

Harris, R.W. (1946) *National Health Insurance in Great Britain 1911–1946* (London: George Allen and Unwin).

Harvey, D. (2007) *A Brief History of Neoliberalism* (Oxford: Oxford University Press).

Hohman, H.F. (1933) *The Development of Social Insurance and Minimum Wage Legislation in Great Britain* (Boston: Houghton, Mifflin).

Hunt, E.H. (1990) 'Paupers and Pensioners: Past and Present', *Ageing and Society*, 9 (4), 407–30.

Kemp, P. and Davidson, J. (2009) 'Gender Differences among New Claimants of Incapacity Benefit', *Journal of Social Policy*, 38 (4), 589–606.

Levy, H. (1944) *National Health Insurance. A Critical Study* (Cambridge: The University Press).

Macnicol, J. (1998) *The Politics of Retirement in Britain, 1878–1948* (Cambridge: Cambridge University Press).

Macnicol, J. (2010) 'Anti-ageism and the Neoliberalisation of Old Age', *Paper to the ISA World Congress of Sociology*, Gothenburg, Sweden, July.

Ministry of Health (1930) *Eleventh Annual Report of the Ministry of Health 1929–1930*, Cmd. 3667.

Moffrey, R.W. (1900) in 'Discussion', *Journal of the Institute of Actuaries*, XXXV, July, 323–32.

Newman, G. (1939) *The Building of a Nation's Health* (London: Macmillan).

Oeppen, J. and Vaupel, J.W. (2002) 'Broken Limits to Life Expectancy', *Science*, 296, 1029–1031.

Olshansky, S.J. et al. (2005) 'A Potential Decline in Life Expectancy in the United States in the 21st Century', *New England Journal of Medicine*, 325 (11), 17 March, 1138–45.

Ormerod, J.R. (1930) *National Insurance: Its Inherent Defects* (London: Stone and Cox).

Riley, J.C. (1997) *Sick, Not Dead. The Health of British Workingmen during the Mortality Decline* (Baltimore: Johns Hopkins University Press).

*Royal Commission on the Aged Poor*, 1895, C-7684-II, III, *Minutes of Evidence*.

*Royal Commission on National Health Insurance: Report*, 1926, Cmd. 2596.

Smith, D.M. (2005) *On the Margins of Inclusion. Changing Labour Markets and Social Exclusion in London* (Bristol: Policy Press).

*Social Insurance and Allied Services*, 1942, Cmd. 6404.

*The Times* (1938) Editorial: 'Idle and Content', 22 February.

Titmuss, R.M. (1950) *Problems of Social Policy* (London: HMSO).

Turner, G. (1896) 'State Pensions in Old Age', *Oddfellows' Magazine*, XXVII, 261, 271–4.

Walker, K. (2011) 'The Shirking Classes: Just 1 in 14 Incapacity Claimants is Unfit to Work', *Daily Mail*, 27 July.

Watson, A. (1903) *An Account of an Investigation of the Sickness and Mortality Experience of the I.O.O.F. Manchester Unity during the Five Years 1893–1897* (Manchester: Independent Order of Oddfellows, Manchester Unity).

Webb, B. (1948) *Our Partnership* (London: Longmans, Green).

Webb, S. and Webb, B. (1911) *The Prevention of Destitution* (London: Longmans).

Whiteside, N. (1983) 'Private Agencies for Public Purposes: Some New Perspectives on Policy Making in Health Insurance between the Wars', *Journal of Social Policy*, 12 (2), 165–94.

Whiteside, N. (1987) 'Counting the Cost: Sickness and Disability among Working People in an Era of Industrial Recession, 1920–39', *Economic History Review*, 40 (2), 228–46.

Whiteside, N. (1988) 'Unemployment and Health: An Historical Perspective', *Journal of Social Policy*, 17 (2), 177–94.

Wilkinson, J.F. (1892) 'Friendly Society Finance', *Economic Journal*, II, 8 December, 721–7.

Wood, K. (1930) *H of C Deb.*, 5s, 238, 29 April, col. 83.

# 4
# Are Incapacity Benefit Claimants beyond Employment? Exploring Issues of Employability

*Anne Green and Ian Shuttleworth*

## Introduction

The period since 2008 has seen considerable changes in the global political and economic environment as a consequence of the ongoing financial crisis that originated in the USA. Within individual nations, after a long period of expansion, economic and jobs growth has slowed or even reversed, the brakes have been put on public spending, risk and uncertainty in the labour market have increased, and austerity is the watchword across Europe for the foreseeable future. Despite these developments, which have radically changed the environment for job seekers, workers, benefit claimants and policy makers alike, there have been important continuities in labour market and welfare policy. The reintegration of economically inactive people with the world of work, for example, remains a stated aim of the UK government. The target of a reduction of one million in the number of Incapacity Benefit (IB) claimants by 2015 seemed ambitious (Houston and Lindsay, 2010) during the previous period of employment and economic growth, but now appears doubly challenging given surging jobless numbers. It is clear that welfare-to-work and employability policies as they now exist will face important challenges in the light of public spending reductions, a slackening of labour demand, and continued (and heightened) compulsion through the imposition of greater benefits conditionality. The pain of these developments will be borne directly by many benefit claimants but indirectly by the rest of society, which will have to cope with the consequences of a sizeable marginalised group of people.

Given these circumstances it is important to understand more about the factors that influence individual benefit claimants in their attitudes towards the labour market, the part played by external labour market factors such as the demand for labour, and the extent to which IB claimants, as a group, are heterogeneous, with some perhaps having a realistic chance of gaining work relatively soon, and others being much further down the labour queue with no immediate prospects of gaining work – and indeed perhaps never doing so. This latter group poses questions for policy especially in light of prevailing economic conditions; one major issue is whether it is worthwhile for government, and indeed individual claimants, to pursue activation policy with full rigour for those far from employment.

The chapter examines these themes mainly with reference to a survey of IB claimants undertaken in Northern Ireland (NI) during 2006–7. At the end of 'the good years' of economic growth it summarises the position towards the end of the IB regime and just before the introduction of the Employment Support Allowance (ESA). It therefore describes a situation that could be summarised as 'as good as it gets'. The difficulties and problems that are described, therefore, are a conservative estimate of the challenges that might be faced in the severer climate of today (and perhaps the near future). The analysis also neatly 'bookends' one policy and economic period – the pre-recessionary one of expansion and the final years of IB before the introduction of ESA – and therefore provides a historical coda from which future perspectives can be drawn.

The remainder of the chapter is structured as follows. First, the historical evolution since 1997 of welfare and labour market policy in NI and the rest of the UK is reviewed. Then a survey of IB claimants in NI is introduced and the characteristics of claimants are outlined. Next results of exploratory analyses on the factors that shape claimants' perceptions and orientation towards the labour market are presented. Finally, the chapter comments on the extent to which IB claimants as a group were homogeneous and suggests some possible policy implications.

## Employability, employment policy and individualism

The policy context for UK IB claimants since 1997 has been set, in broad terms, by the two concepts of employability and active labour market policy. These, in turn, are framed by a wider suite of labour market and policy ideas that are part of a broader international consensus about the feasibility, extent and nature of state intervention in the labour market. These have driven changes in other nations with welfare states as well as in the UK. Dominant concepts that have informed recent policy include individualisation, localisation, and flexibility, all of which can be interpreted as elements of neo-liberalism and the retreat of the welfare state – including the expectation to guarantee full employment – from its high-water mark in the three decades immediately after the Second World War.

Employability, as theorised and as actually practised, is crucial since it lies at the centre of these concepts and broader ideas. It has been the watchword of successive UK governments in directing labour market and welfare policy. Its origins lie in the assumption that nation states can no longer cope with the turbulent, complex, and risky environment caused by globalisation to provide full and stable employment. Assuming this interpretation is correct, it follows that one plausible response is to provide workers with the personal capacity to manage risk by moving from job to job as needed and to help those not in work to gain employment. In the latter aspect, employability also became an important component in the efforts of previous UK Labour governments to promote social inclusion since employment was viewed as the most effective route out of poverty (DWP, 2006) and also as an efficient means to promote stable communities and responsible individuals.

Given this background it is perhaps not surprising that employability in theory and practical implementation has tended to emphasise the modification and development of personal attributes (in other words, to intervene mainly on the supply side) at the expense of demand-side considerations (for a critique see Peck and Theodore, 2000, and for a full review of the concept of employability see McQuaid and Lindsay, 2005). Personal attributes not only include 'harder' characteristics such as skills, qualification, and training but also 'softer' dimensions like self-presentation, confidence, and appearance. More sophisticated conceptualisations of employability refer to the wider context–including the scale of labour demand and the requirements of employers, but these appear to have had less impact on government understanding of employability than those that are more closely tied to the supply side of the labour market. Critics of UK government policy also draw attention to the futility of not placing labour demand more centrally both in understanding the causes of joblessness and doing something about it (for example, Beatty and Fothergill, 2005). They point out the way that individuals 'churn' in and out of government programmes in places with weak labour markets, and identify the importance of weak labour demand in creating high regional and local levels of benefit receipt.

These understandings of the causes of joblessness (and by implication its cures) have therefore tended to concentrate on individuals and their training, skills, and motivation. As Houston and Lindsay (2010) comment, public debates about joblessness and benefits often focus on the rights and responsibilities of claimants, allied to public fears that benefits can be too easily accessed and are in some cases preferable to working. In practice, this has created an atmosphere where greater compulsion is socially and politically acceptable, and is perceived as being necessary, with a further hardening of policy suggested by the Conservative Party (Houston and Lindsay, 2010). This increase in compulsion has accompanied a greater policy concentration on individuals with increased medical assessment and more personal interviews to boost job search and remotivate – as seen, for example, in the Work-Focused interviews in the Pathways to Work programme. The individualisation of policy (see also Freud, 2007) is also motivated by an official desire to tailor support to individuals' specific circumstances and to deal with their problems by holistically working across domains, although it is noted by Green and Shuttleworth (2010) that this is demanding for

Personal Advisers (PAs) who may sometimes lack knowledge of the full range of facilities. Green and Shuttleworth (2010) also observe that the influence of motivational and behavioural factors is pervasive and reaches throughout government and its agencies with PAs, for instance, tending to treat ill-health as something that could be 'worked around', citing examples of clients with sometimes serious health problems who found work in contrast to others with relatively minor problems who had not. However, although the 'benefits culture' was recognised by PAs as a problem, they were sometimes reluctant to apply to the full extent the powers of compulsion they held because of the risk to the wellbeing of some clients in certain vulnerable groups such as those with mental health problems. Flexibility, local discretion, and a focus on the individual authorises freedom to relax centrally imposed policies.

There is some recognition that IB claimants are heterogeneous in terms of their characteristics and chances of re-engaging with employment – exit rates vary by region, duration of claim, and type of illness (Beatty et al., 2009). Indeed, when announcing welfare reforms in 2006, Work and Pensions Secretary John Hutton claimed that:

> Nine out of 10 people who came on to incapacity benefit expect to get back into work, yet if you have been on incapacity benefit for more than two years, you are more likely to retire or die than ever get another job. That cannot be right.

Nevertheless, the dominant official individualised focus on motivation, behaviour, and attitudes tends towards a sledgehammer approach to IB claimants, with the problem for all reducible ultimately to their willingness to work. But this 'work willingness' is not psychologically given, nor can it be assumed to apply equally to all claimants. There may be merits in 'motivating' some – especially new and younger claimants – but for others there could be significant costs both for the individual claimant and for those administering the policy as well as wider social disadvantages. The latter case might apply particularly to long duration and older claimants, and, in particular in the UK context, to the large cohort of manual workers who were moved onto IB in the 1980s and early 1990s following large-scale redundancies in parts of the manufacturing and mining sector.

Because of the dominance of official discourses about IB claimants' attitudes towards the labour market, and the dangers inherent in assuming that all claimants are the same in this respect, the chapter concentrates on orientations towards employment as the central analytical focus. The chapter's contribution is to examine how these attitudes exist not simply as something as 'given', but instead as dimensions that are shaped by other individual and family factors and also by external labour market conditions, which mean that the appropriateness of labour market activation policies vary between people and places. It therefore considers how views of the labour market vary according to factors such as geography, age, duration of claim, type of illness, and education. More generally, it seeks to highlight the proportion of IB claimants who are isolated from the world of work in that they either do not value work highly or do not expect to work again. This poses the question of how realistic it is to assume that the numbers of IB claimants can be reduced significantly by encouraging moves back into work or whether some are literally 'beyond employment'. In turn this raises the question of where limited resources should be concentrated and of 'targeting' of particular sub-groups of claimants. This question is increasingly pertinent at a time of economic fragility and recession, and is likely to become increasingly salient in the near future.

## Data and methods

The evidence base used is primarily a survey of around 800 IB claimants undertaken in Northern Ireland that was completed early in 2007. The survey was geographically clustered so as to capture information on claimants in different types of area (Catholic/Protestant/Mixed, Urban/Rural). Two areas (Shankill and Falls) were selected in Belfast and these were respectively Protestant and Catholic; two in London/Derry (Lisnagelvin and Foyle), which were also respectively Protestant and Catholic and in a large town; and finally Newry and Enniskillen, which were rural and more mixed in community background. The location of these places in the labour market and economic geography of NI is important. A high proportion of NI employee jobs are concentrated in the East and particularly in Belfast, with the city centre remaining a significant employment focus. In the West and the more remote South, on the other hand, outside larger towns such as Derry, employment opportunities are sparser and economic inactivity benefit rates tend to be higher than in the East (with the notable exceptions of inner-city Belfast areas such as Shankill and Falls where there are also high levels of benefit dependency).

At the time the survey was completed, the respondents might have been considered as having many of the same characteristics and facing many of the same problems as others in low-labour demand UK regions. This point still holds, but when considered in the light of subsequent economic and policy events there is added relevance as the survey was undertaken at the end of the long economic boom of the early twenty-first century. The labour market then was relatively strong in demand terms, and attitudes across society then were presumably also relatively optimistic in contrast with the post-2008 position. This leads to the conclusion that if there were problems then, in the 'good times', they were probably far less severe than now, and that the analysis presents a 'rosy picture' in comparison with a possibly far grimmer reality today.

# Results

## Who are the IB claimants?

The survey sought to profile the individual and family characteristics of IB claimants before considering perceptions of the labour market and motivational issues. The respondents were profiled in terms of variables such as health, educational qualifications, gender, access to transport, and housing tenure. These are important because factors like these have been shown across a wide range of literature to determine the probability that an individual is economically active or in employment (see, for example, Smith and Chambers, 1991; Payne, 1987). Increasing age, poor health, other jobless people in the household, and living in non-owner-occupied housing are often correlated with increased chances of joblessness. Others, such as access to transport, are related to better chances of making the transition back to work after unemployment (see, for example, Shuttleworth et al., 2005). These, and similar characteristics, are also components of the 'employability mix' (DEL Employability Taskforce, 2002; McQuaid and Lindsay, 2005). It is therefore useful, as a first step, to describe the survey respondents so as to estimate where they are situated, on average, in the 'employability queue'.

The majority (60%) of survey respondents were male and, of relevance in the NI context given the divided nature of the community and Fair Employment legislation, 60% were Catholic. This means that both Catholics and men are slightly over-represented with regard to their 2001 Census proportions. IB claimants also had a relatively old age structure, with 66% in the 45–64 years group and a third in the 25–44 band. This is older than the population overall, which only has 22% in the 45–64 year age group. This is representative of the age information held in administrative systems but is somewhat older than the labour force or the general population, indicating that IB claimants are older than might be expected if the incidence of claiming was the same pro rata by age across the whole population. The majority of respondents (57%) – as compared with 42% of the population as recorded by the Census in 2001 – also lacked educational qualifications. Many ended their education at the completion of compulsory schooling – 42% completing their education at 15 years old (or less) and 37% at the age of 16. While in part the high proportion of IB claimants in the survey with no formal qualifications is a function of their older than average age profile, importantly from an employability perspective it also reflects the fact that IB claimants are less well qualified than the their peers (see Monaghan, 2005, for some analyses of Labour Force Survey data). Physical mobility and access to employment did not appear to be a barrier for the majority of individual respondents since 64% held a driving licence and 87% had access to a car or van (as either a driver or a passenger) as compared with 74% of households who owned a car in 2001 – although comparisons are difficult in this case as the Census and the survey measured different things.

Unsurprisingly, given the nature of the survey, a large majority of respondents stated that they identified themselves as being ill and/or disabled. This was much higher than the 11% of the population that identified itself as being economically inactive through ill-health in the 2001 Census. Health is a key element of the employability mix – ill-health can act as barrier to work, but poor health can be a consequence of joblessness too. The leading classes of health problems noted by respondents were arthritis and rheumatism (experienced by 37% of respondents), heart conditions and diseases (19%), asthma and severe allergies (14%), and depression (7%). The latter is lower than the proportion identified in other survey evidence. The reason for this is unknown but could reflect methodological differences between the various surveys or a different health profile for NI IB claimants. Health problems were identified as the major reason for being on IB: 75% of respondents had left their last job because of illness as compared with only 10% for redundancy and 9% for 'other reasons'. These health problems were seen as a major barrier to employment; some 98% considered that these problems prevented them from working in *any* occupation, with 94% stating that it restricted the hours they could work. The identification of health problems as a key barrier to employment is in line with survey findings of IB claimants in Britain (Beatty et al., 2008).

The household characteristics of the respondents are also significant, given that the economic position, income and health status of other household members have implications for means-tested benefits and for propensity to make benefit claims. Less than a quarter (23%) of survey respondents lived alone and 55% were married or cohabiting. Of these, over a third (36%) had a partner claiming benefit, with the majority of these (70%) claiming IB themselves. This indicates the household concentration of benefit dependency and ill-health within households, and the need to consider decision-making about job search and any return to work within a broader household context. Nearly two-thirds of respondents (64%) either owned their homes outright or were buying them with a mortgage – less than the 2001 Census benchmark of 70%. Some 27% were in public authority housing, which was higher than the NI benchmark of 18% observed in the 2001 Census.

In combination, these observations suggest that the IB respondents are some way down the 'employability queue'. Their characteristics are typically associated with joblessness in NI as in other areas. These suggest that there are significant individual and household challenges to overcome if work is to be gained, not least the major difficulty of ill-health: 84% of respondents reported that their own health problems were the 'number one obstacle' in getting a job. The combination of ill-health with other characteristics (for example, no formal qualifications) may lead to multiple disadvantage, which is more difficult to overcome than any obstacle in isolation. So even if an IB claimant's health improved, that individual might still face severe difficulties in finding work because of a lack of formal qualifications restricting the types of jobs that they could apply for. In turn, this suggests a need for interventions across policy domains.

## Understanding labour market attitudes and perceptions

As outlined above, much public discourse about claimants has emphasised attitudinal and motivational deficiencies as primary reasons, if not *the* reason, for continuation on benefit. It is therefore important to assess how attitudes, perceptions, and motivation with regard to the labour market fit into the 'employability mix'. Here attitudes and perceptions are explored not as 'givens' – but rooted instead in concrete individual, family, and geographical circumstances – and thereby part of a wider package of labour market and social disadvantage.

First, objective measures of the labour market are presented in the top part of Table 4.1. Statistical measures of employment opportunity indicate

*Table 4.1*  Labour market perceptions: The external environment

| Social security office | Belfast–Falls | Belfast–Shankill | Derry Foyle | Derry Lisnagelvin | Enniskillen | Newry |
|---|---|---|---|---|---|---|
| Labour market indicators | | | | | | |
| Ratio of jobs to working age per ward of residence | 1.22 | 0.49 | 0.49 | 0.54 | 0.60 | 0.58 |
| Employment Index | 1.07 | 1.11 | 0.26 | 0.21 | 0.13 | 0.23 |
| Job surplus/shortfall within 10 km | 0.00 | 0.00 | –1681.56 | –921.64 | –601.95 | –712.73 |
| Perceptual indicators | | | | | | |
| There are a lot of jobs in my area | 1.56 | 1.59 | 2.30 | 2.00 | 2.28 | 2.85 |
| There are more jobs around here for people with my skills or qualifications than there were 2 years ago | 2.38 | 1.76 | 2.38 | 2.25 | 2.34 | 2.85 |
| You really need a car to get around | 3.21 | 3.76 | 3.81 | 3.70 | 4.36 | 3.65 |
| There are a lot of low-paid jobs in the area | 3.42 | 3.84 | 3.88 | 3.66 | 3.78 | 3.58 |
| Public transport is good in my area | 3.56 | 3.75 | 3.50 | 3.18 | 2.38 | 2.86 |
| Many jobs are insecure | 3.30 | 3.64 | 4.02 | 3.88 | 3.99 | 3.51 |

*Note*: Perceptual indicators: means of a five-range scale where 1 = strongly disagree and 5 = strongly agree.

that there are considerable geographical differences; urban respondents, particularly those from the Belfast locales, live in places where there is no shortfall of jobs and where there is a surplus of local employment as measured by the ratio of jobs to working age population per ward. Moreover, the employment index, which takes account of job opportunities over a wider spatial range, also highlights the richer opportunities of Belfast over sparser rural areas. One important qualifier to these simple indicators is that not all the job opportunities counted in the statistics will be open to all respondents (owing to skills mismatch); that some jobs will be taken by commuting incomers; and that some jobs may be unattractive for a variety of reasons. Moreover, some employment opportunities might remain unknown and there could be other perceptual barriers to employment (see, for example, Green et al., 2005).

Some of these perceptual issues are considered in the bottom part of Table 4.1 where respondents' responses to questions about job quality, job quantity, and spatial mobility are presented. The responses are summarised as arithmetic means of a one-to-five scale where one equals 'strong disagreement' and five 'strong agreement'. Thus, means closer to one indicate disagreement with the statement and those closer to five show agreement with the statement. The picture remains the same regardless of the method used to measure the mean (for example, the mode). There are some interesting contrasts between respondents' views and statistical measures of labour market conditions. There are high levels of disagreement with the statement 'there are a lot of jobs in my area' across all places, but this disagreement is higher in Belfast where, paradoxically, the statistics suggest there are more jobs. There is more general disagreement with the statement that there 'are more jobs around here for people with my skills and qualifications than there were two years ago'. On the other hand, there is a common tendency across all places for agreement with the statements 'there are a lot of low-paid jobs in the area' and 'many jobs are insecure'. There are some urban–rural differences associated with views about car ownership and public transport. The availability of public transport is rated highly in every area except Enniskillen and Newry, whereas there is most agreement in highly rural Enniskillen that 'you really need a car to get around'.

Respondents were also asked to consider a variety of external labour market factors as direct barriers that face job seekers in their locales. Respondents tended to be close to the agreement end of the continuum when presented with the statement that 'wages were too low', and this was especially so in the Belfast areas; surprisingly, lack of private transport was not seen as being more important in the rural areas than in Belfast, perhaps because most respondents had driving licences and most had access to a car; there was agreement across areas that many job seekers' employability was compromised because they had been 'out of work too long', particularly in the Falls, and there were similar sentiments expressed about employers' view of older workers as too old to be employed. However, respondents tended to disagree with the statement that 'employers did not want to employ local people' – except in the Falls, which suggests that there is a perception of stigma attached to residents there.

There is a mismatch between the statistical and perceptual indicators of job availability in Belfast, perhaps suggesting a need to tackle perceptions that are at odds with reality. The results also indicate that there were general perceptions of job shortages even towards the end of a historically prolonged period of economic growth – particularly in urban areas – and also some agreement, although not universal, that jobs were of poor quality. There are some variations between the different locations covered and also contrasts in perceptions of public transport provision and the need for access to a car to get around and access jobs. These imply that physical accessibility, as a barrier, might be much more likely to be an issue in rural areas whereas different obstacles apply in urban locations. When asked to consider the external barriers faced by job seekers, low wages, age, and duration out of work were seen as being the main barriers, although there were interesting differences between places with regard to perceptions of employers' desire to employ local people. In combination, this suggests that the labour market obstacles facing IB claimants vary between places and that geographical context might be important in determining the challenges faced by policy makers when putting provision in place to help get IB claimants back to work.

## Factors driving labour market expectations and attitudes

Attitudes and expectations with regard to the labour market were viewed and assessed through two questions in the survey: (1) how important is it to have a job? and (2) when do you expect to get a job? In the latter case, attention was focused on the extremes of those who felt they would never work again and those who believed they would work again within two years. These two questions capture different but related dimensions of attitude and motivation. These might be expected to be kinds of attitudes that motivational programmes might be expected to work upon – to make more claimants say they value work more highly and to expect to work again within two years. Shifting them from more negative categories might be viewed as significant markers of success for policy makers, as individuals move towards employment.

The first point to note is that views about the importance of a job are polarised. Around 30% stated it was 'not important at all', but the proportion saying it was 'quite important' or 'very important' was 55%. This shows that the majority of IB claimants have a strong attachment to the labour market, and this is surely a positive that calls into question discourses that attribute high benefit claimant levels to a lack of motivation and a lack of work culture. However, there is evidence that a substantial minority of claimants are isolated from work in more profound ways in that they do not even value employment – and it should be remembered that this is probably a minimum estimate of this group since this was a response to a government-sponsored survey. The responses to the question concerning 'when you expect to work again' are even less comforting to policy makers – only 11% of respondents expected to work again in the next two years, with around 46% believing their return was conditional on better health and 43% stating they expected never to work again. In this case, policy faces severe challenges in moving claimants in the latter category towards the first.

These are generalisations for the whole population but, as Figures 4.1 to 4.4 show, expectations of employment and views about the importance of work are strongly structured by age and by duration of claim – and these are positively related to each other.

Figure 4.1 shows how the expectations of never working again increase with age. The higher rate for those aged 18–24 compared with those 25–44

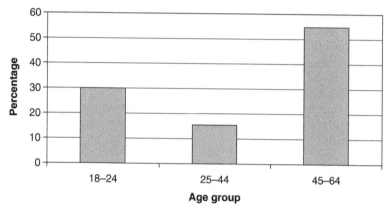

*Figure 4.1*   Percentage expecting never to work again by age group

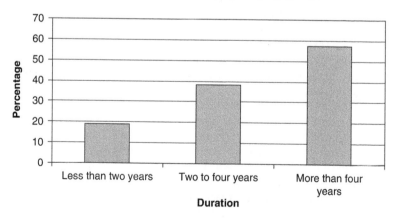

*Figure 4.2*   Percentage expecting never to work again by claim duration

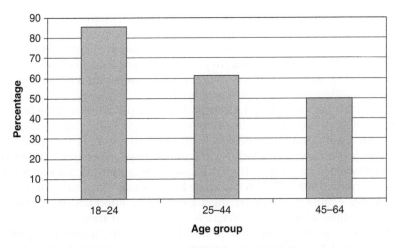

*Figure 4.3* Having a job as important or very important by age

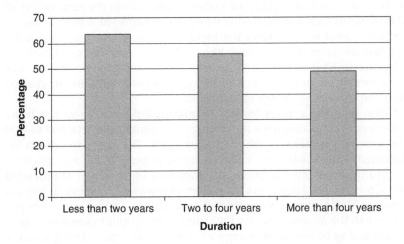

*Figure 4.4* Having a job as important or very important by claim duration

can be discounted as there are very few IB claimants in this category, but there is a very clear pattern in Figure 4.2 by duration of claim. This is good evidence that poor labour market expectations are duration dependent. When ratings of having a job as being 'important or very important' are presented in Figures 4.3 and 4.4, there is clear evidence that positive attitude – as measured by this question – decreases with age and duration of claim.

Given the analysis to date, there is clear evidence that what might be construed as 'attitudinal problems' whether conceived of as pessimism about jobs prospects or the value of work affect a substantial minority of IB claimants, and these problems increase with age and duration of claim. One possible conclusion arising from this would be that motivational measures are desirable and necessary. However, further analysis suggests that while they may be necessary for some they are insufficient for others, and indeed for some claimants could be counterproductive and harmful because of the level of multiple disadvantage experienced.

This task is begun in Table 4.2, which shows the proportions rating having a job 'not at all important', 'important or very important', 'expecting never to work again', and 'expecting to work again in the next two years' by selected background characteristics. It is quite a large and complex table so it is worthwhile noting it presents partial percentages (they do not sum across rows or columns to 100%). What are its key messages? There are differences by gender – more men rate having a job as being important than women (59.3% against 47.4%), and conversely fewer (27.2%) state having a job is not at all important compared to 35.2% for women. However, a greater proportion of men expect never to work again than women. Qualifications stand out as being important in shaping attitudes to work and expectations of never working again, or working again within the next two years. Marital status seems to determine whether claimants value work – married claimants seem to value work less highly than those who are not married, but marital status seems to have little influence on work expectations. Of relevance to NI is religion, and here the results are paradoxical – Catholic claimants appear not to value work as highly as their non-Catholic counterparts but *fewer* expect never to work again.

Claim duration appears to be a significant influence across the board, with shorter claim durations linked to greater significance attached to work and lower expectations of never working again. The ability to drive is also important – those who are mobile are better placed overall, and this is not surprising given other analyses (Shuttleworth et al., 2005; Shuttleworth and Green, 2011). Labour market history as measured by previous pay also seems to shape current attitudes and expectations – those who were paid more than the median wage for the sample appear both to value work more highly and to be less likely to expect never to work again. Having a partner on benefit is also identified as having a negative influence on value attached to work and future expectations. Finally, there are geographical influences at work, with big differences between each of the study areas in all four columns of the table. It is the subjective assessment of job availability, however, that is of most interest here. It does not seem to influence attitudes to work in the expected way – work seems to be valued more highly for respondents who believe there are no jobs in their areas than for those who are more optimistic. But it has a major effect on expectations of working again, with those who believe they live in job-poor areas being more likely to think they will never work again and less likely to believe they will work within the next two years.

*Table 4.2* Percentages rating having a job as 'not at all important', 'important or very important', 'expecting never to work again', and 'expecting to work in the next two years' by selected profile variables

| Variable | Having a job is not at all important | Having a job is important or very important | Expect never to work again | Expect to work in next two years |
|---|---|---|---|---|
| Female | 35.2 | 47.4 | 33.6 | 10.0 |
| Male | 27.2 | 59.3 | 48.8 | 11.5 |
| Some qualifications | 24.4 | 61.6 | 27.0 | 17.1 |
| No qualifications | 35.0 | 49.1 | 54.6 | 6.1 |
| Not married | 26.1 | 58.0 | 43.3 | 13.6 |
| Married | 34.0 | 51.6 | 42.1 | 8.5 |
| Non-Catholic | 28.4 | 58.7 | 46.3 | 10.9 |
| Catholic | 31.7 | 51.7 | 40.2 | 10.9 |
| More than two years on IB | 32.6 | 51.9 | 49.1 | 8.9 |
| Less than two years on IB | 22.8 | 63.6 | 18.9 | 18.3 |
| Unable to drive | 32.2 | 48.6 | 51.2 | 10.2 |
| Able to drive | 30.0 | 57.9 | 37.7 | 11.3 |
| Unhappy | 30.0 | 54.5 | 42.1 | 11.3 |
| Happy | 33.1 | 55.0 | 45.6 | 8.8 |
| Not low pay in previous job | 23.7 | 64.7 | 32.6 | 12.4 |
| Low pay in previous job | 31.0 | 53.2 | 42.1 | 11.5 |
| No arthritis | 26.9 | 52.7 | 38.0 | 14.3 |
| Arthritis and joint problems | 36.4 | 47.3 | 50.5 | 5.2 |
| No heart problems | 30.0 | 54.5 | 37.4 | 12.3 |
| Heart and circulatory problems | 32.0 | 54.9 | 65.3 | 4.8 |
| Partner not on benefits | 29.8 | 54.9 | 39.9 | 11.1 |
| Partner on benefits | 38.1 | 53.2 | 54.6 | 9.9 |
| Non-owner occupier | 27.4 | 58.9 | 48.6 | 14.4 |
| Owner occupier | 32.1 | 52.1 | 39.3 | 8.8 |
| Jobs in area | 33.2 | 50.2 | 38.3 | 12.3 |
| Not a lot of jobs in the area | 24.5 | 63.6 | 51.6 | 7.8 |
| Falls | 9.9 | 80.3 | 73.2 | 5.6 |
| Shankill | 23.6 | 65.4 | 62.9 | 14.5 |
| Foyle | 29.8 | 52.3 | 30.8 | 14.0 |
| Lisnagelvin | 51.3 | 59.3 | 44.9 | 12.6 |
| Enniskillen | 17.1 | 51.0 | 46.4 | 14.0 |
| Newry | 38.7 | 57.8 | 41.6 | 11.4 |

Hence, there is evidence that what some may term 'poor motivation' or 'pessimism', and which can be addressed by compulsion or motivation via active labour market policies, are a product of current household circumstances, past disadvantage in the labour market and in education, and assessments of local job availability. There is a combined package of disadvantage, and individual/psychological factors cannot be abstracted from the underlying geographical and structural factors that have shaped them. A holistic approach is needed. One way to summarise and to explore the patterns in the data to cut through the complexities of Table 4.2 is to use multivariate analysis – see Shuttleworth et al. (2008) for examples of these models. While the methods can be quite complex, the conclusions drawn are simpler to explain, and so a little time will be spent on examining the patterns of meaning that can be extracted from the data.

The first of the attitudinal outcome variables explored is the value attached to work. The factors that are identified as having a positive influence on stating 'a job is important or very important' have a negative effect on stating that 'a job is not important at all'. The reverse applies also, so negative factors for stating 'a job is important or very important' generally have a positive influence on stating that 'a job is unimportant'. Being male has a big positive effect on stating 'a job is important or very important' and a negative effect on viewing work as unimportant. For those with an arthritic condition employment is viewed as important over very important. Other factors that decrease the chances of viewing employment as important include having low pay in a previous job, age, being Catholic, being an owner occupier, and being single. Conversely, possession of a driving licence and being on IB for less than two years increase the chances of viewing work as important.

The second attitudinal variable considered is 'expecting never to work again'. Being male, having a heart condition, low pay in previous job, increasing age, and a shortfall in jobs within a 10km radius of place of residence all increase the chances of expecting to never work again. Decreasing the chances of falling into this category are being Catholic, being less than two years on IB, and being on IB for less than two years.

The final outcome variable to explore is 'expecting to work in the next two years', with being male, being less than two years on IB, and being in an area with a lot of jobs increasing the belief that work can be found within two years, and no qualifications, increasing age, and the perception that there are few jobs decreasing the probability of believing that a job can be found within two years.

## Discussion

The evidence above indicates that there are important differences in the expectations and labour market orientation of IB claimants according to their personal characteristics and their geographical contexts. Some claimants in some locations may well be easier to reintegrate in the labour market than others. The findings also show that attitudes, motivations, and expectations are concretely derived from places and labour market expectations. As such, they are probably not easily modified by motivational programmes and 'carrot and stick' policies that focus on behaviour alone. Instead, holistic policies are needed. In fairness, this is what is aspired to in some policies, with consideration given to themes like childcare, transport, help with health and retraining. However, in practice, these aspirations sometimes founder on the complexity of the institutional environment, which means that it is often difficult to mobilise the resources that ideally would be required (Green and Shuttleworth, 2010). Moreover, the geographical context of labour markets with low-labour demand imposes extra constraints that make it difficult to activate benefit claimants in some places. In a difficult labour market perhaps few would quibble with the belief of many claimants that there are no jobs – or at least suitable ones – in their area. Their pessimism may be realistic and born of long experience, and suggests that an uphill struggle was being faced in some places even before the recession.

The survey evidence also suggests that IB claimants are heterogeneous, albeit that they tend to share some characteristics in common, such as no or low qualifications. This supports the claim made by Little (2007) that it would be mistaken to see all claimants as being equally 'hidden unemployed'; some are much further removed from the labour market than others and have to face greater problems on the road to work. The barriers to work that many claimants face are likely to be complex and deep-rooted, and are unlikely to be fully understood without a wider focus on the broader context (Ritchie et al., 2005). For policy makers the heterogeneity of claimants supports the greater tailoring of interventions to individuals. Given resource constraints it also raises the questions of targeting particular individuals on the basis of their characteristics and of where efforts should be concentrated – for example, on those who appear to be nearer employment? In particular, given the significance of shorter duration claims (that is, less than two years) in each of the models a case can be made for concentrating foremost attention on new and recent claimants, rather than on the larger stock of longer-term claimants – many of whom expect never to work again. On the other hand, focusing attention away from this latter group means consigning some individuals to what might be a lifetime on benefits, and encouraging movement towards employment at some time in the future may have positive spin-offs for the individuals concerned and their families. One possible approach might focus mandatory engagement on those with better employability while support measures could be open to all other claimants on a voluntary basis. There are questions, however, about how feasible this voluntarism would be given the current policy environment, which has emphasised mandatory measures for all.

But further challenges are also posed to policy makers given the importance of labour demand that was highlighted. The results show how local labour market conditions shape self-assessment of labour market prospects and orientations towards work; labour demand matters. The greater importance of the perceptual labour market measure for those expecting to find work within the next two years than for those never expecting to work again perhaps indicates the greater importance of labour market perceptions for those nearer the labour market; some, perhaps, are so distant that they lose any interest in the labour market and their perceptions become less relevant. Labour market conditions as measured by the statistical indicators also emerge as more significant for those expecting to work in the next two years than for those who are more distant from the labour market. Also, it is interesting to note that low pay, which is often a feature of employment for those with poor qualifications, in previous job appears to have a scarring effect on attitudes to and expectations of future employment even if that job had been held a very long time ago. This raises questions about the problems of low-wage regional and local economies and the problems they may store up for the future much further down the line.

Because of this, the low estimates of job quantity and quality made by survey respondents is disturbing given that the research was undertaken at the end of a long economic boom with jobs growth in NI. This seems to have barely (if at all) had a positive influence on claimants' labour market views. The onset of recession is likely to mean that claimants face a much more difficult time in finding work and that activation policies, even if focused and tailored to personal circumstances, will face an uphill struggle in the absence of local job creation measures. Employability alone is not enough. And on the supply side, health remediation programmes are also required.

## References

Beatty, C. and Fothergill, S. (2005) 'The Diversion from Unemployment to Sickness across British Regions and Districts', *Regional Studies*, 39 (7), 837–854.

Beatty, C., Fothergill, S., Houston, D., Powell, R., and Sissons, P. (2009) *Women on Incapacity Benefits* (Sheffield: Sheffield Hallam University).

DEL Employability Taskforce (2002) *Report of the Taskforce on Employability and Long-Term Unemployment* (DELNI: Belfast).

DWP (2006) *A New Deal for Welfare: Empowering People to Work* (London: DWP).

Freud, D. (2007) *Reducing Dependency, Increasing Opportunity: Options for the Future of Welfare to Work* (Leeds: Corporate Document Services).

Green, A. and Shuttleworth, I. (2010) 'Local Differences, Perceptions and Incapacity Benefit Claimants: Implications for Policy Delivery', *Policy Studies*, 31 (2), 223–243.

Green, A., Shuttleworth, I., and Lavery, S. (2005) 'Young People, Job Search and Labour Markets: The Example of Belfast', *Urban Studies*, 42 (2), 301–324.

Houston, D. and Lindsay, C. (2010) 'Fit for Work? Health, Employability and Challenges for the UK Welfare Reform Agenda', *Policy Studies*, 31 (2), 133–142.

Little, A. (2007) 'Inactivity and Labour Market Attachment in Britain', *Scottish Journal of Political Economy*, 54, 19–52.

McQuaid, R. and Lindsay, C. (2005) 'The Concept of Employability', *Urban Studies*, 42 (2), 197–219.

Monaghan, M. (2005) 'Economic Inactivity: Threat or Opportunity', *Northern Ireland Economic Bulletin*, 1, 142–147.

Payne, J. (1987) 'Does Unemployment Run in Families? Some Findings from the General Household Survey', *Sociology*, 21 (1), 199–214.

Peck, J. and Theodore, N. (2000) 'Beyond "employability"', *Cambridge Journal of Economics*, 24, 729–749.

Ritchie, H., Casebourne, J., and Rick, J. (2005) *Understanding Workless People and Communities: A Literature Review*, *DWP Research Report 255* (Leeds: Corporate Development Services).

Shuttleworth, I. and Green, A. (2011) 'Spatial Mobility Intentions, the Labour Market and Incapacity Benefit Claimants: Evidence from Northern Ireland', *Urban Studies*, 48, 911–927.

Shuttleworth, I., Green, A., and Lloyd, C. (2008) *'Incapacity Benefit Claimants: Geography, Households, Decision Making and Welfare Reform'* (Belfast: Department for Employment and Learning).

Shuttleworth, I., Tyler, P., and McKinstry, D. (2005) 'Job Loss, Training and Employability: What Can We Learn from the 2000 Harland and Wolff Redundancy?', *Environment and Planning A*, 37, 1651–1668.

Smith, D. and Chambers, G. (1991) *Inequality in Northern Ireland* (Oxford: Clarendon Press).

# 5
# Redefining 'Fit For Work': Welfare Reform and the Introduction of Employment Support Allowance

*Helen Barnes and Paul Sissons*

## Introduction

This chapter focuses on the introduction of Employment Support Allowance (ESA) as the primary sickness benefit in Britain. ESA represents a major shift in the sickness benefits system, and was introduced with the aim of lowering the number of claimants. This chapter draws on the findings from a major study of the introduction of the new system undertaken for the Department for Work and Pensions (DWP) by the authors while at the Institute for Employment Studies, Brighton, UK.

The chapter first sets out the policy context within which these changes have taken place, and outlines the practical changes to the system. We then go on to describe the employability challenges faced by claimants of ESA, including important health-related issues. We focus largely on the two groups who are the primary focus of this policy change: the Fit for Work (FFW) group, who are deemed ineligible for ESA and well enough to seek work immediately, and the Work-Related Activity Group (WRAG), for whom work is seen as an achievable but less immediate goal despite an acknowledgement of health barriers.

## Policy context

As has been detailed in previous chapters, there has been a rapid expansion in the number of people claiming sickness benefits in the UK in the last 30 years. This trend began in the 1970s, and accelerated through the 1980s and throughout much of the 1990s (Beatty et al., 2009). Its root is generally identified as being in the job losses resulting from economic restructuring in Britain's industrial communities, particularly during the 1980s (Turok and Edge, 1999; Beatty and Fothergill, 1996; Beatty et al., 1997; Fieldhouse and

---

The views expressed in this chapter are those of the authors and not the Department for Work and Pensions. Pseudonyms have been used when quoting claimants.

Hollywood, 1999). Rates of sickness benefit claims in many of these former industrial areas have remained persistently high over the longer term, and claims are no longer solely concentrated among older (usually male) former industrial workers, but now also include large numbers of women and younger people (Beatty et al., 2009).

In order to address this issue successive governments have sought to reform the system by regulating on-flow (tightening both medical assessment criteria and financial eligibility conditions) and increasing off-flow, through introducing additional activation measures. The Personal Capability Assessment (PCA), introduced in the mid-1990s, and revised in 2007, was intended to create an objective and impartial test to determine eligibility for Incapacity Benefit (IB), with reducing the role of discretion for GPs seen as key to minimising on-flows. The very low rates at which claimants leave long-term sickness benefits once in receipt subsequently led to a renewed focus on increasing benefit off-flows in the mid to late 2000s, via the Pathways to Work policy. This ambitious programme introduced a series of mandatory work-focused interviews (WFIs) for those assessed as most likely to benefit, provided support services for the management of health conditions, and created additional financial incentives to a return to work. However, it had only limited impact. While evaluation in the early pilot areas showed a small but significant impact on rates of leaving benefit (and to a lesser extent on returns to work), this was not sustained in the later expansion areas or at national roll-out (Bewley et al., 2009). A recent review concluded that, overall, it was not possible to assess what proportion of job entries or reductions in the IB caseload were attributable to Pathways to Work (as opposed to other elements of reform such as changing the timing of the medical assessment) and that the programme represented 'poor value for money' (National Audit Office, 2010).

The most recent and most radical phase of these ongoing reforms has seen the introduction of Employment and Support Allowance (ESA). This reform was designed to further restrict on-flows to sickness benefits and, in the medium term, also aimed to increase off-flows. ESA was introduced for new claimants in October 2008, replacing Incapacity Benefit and Income Support received on the grounds of incapacity. This involved a number of important changes to the previous regime, including:

- Fewer claimants being exempt from assessment under the Work Capability Assessment (WCA) than under the PCA. The WCA is also a more stringent test. Its aim is to measure functional capability for work – whether claimants are capable of doing 'some work' – rather than their ability to return to their previous type of work (DWP, 2009). Those who fail to meet the threshold for ESA are deemed fit for work (FFW) and no longer eligible for benefit.
- Most claimants are expected to be able to prepare for a return (or move into) work. The majority of claimants entitled to ESA after the WCA are allocated

to a Work-Related Activity Group (WRAG), and receive a Work-Related Activity component (currently £26.75 a week) in addition to the basic allowance, provided they comply with the requirements for work-related activity. These include attending a series of six WFIs to discuss a return to work with an adviser (either at Jobcentre Plus or a private provider).

- If those in the WRAG do not comply with the regime they may lose 50% of their Work-Related Activity component.
- A smaller number of claimants with the most severe work-limiting health problems are assigned to a Support Group. They are not required to carry out any activity to receive their full benefit entitlement and also receive an additional benefit premium on top of the basic allowance.

The growing interest in activation policies in the UK took place against a backdrop of a buoyant labour market in which the majority of those who remained out of work long term were those who faced some kind of disadvantage (although at a local level, some labour markets remained relatively constrained in terms of job opportunities). The introduction of ESA was intended to help meet an explicit target of reducing the number of people on IBs by one million by 2015, and was a response to the welfare reform Green Paper (DWP, 2006: 4), *A New Deal for Welfare*, which argued that 'almost nothing is expected of [incapacity] claimants – and little support is offered'. By an irony of timing, in the event ESA was launched at the start of the deepest recession in recent memory.

It was originally estimated that 60,000 more people a year would 'fail' the WCA (that is, be found FFW and ineligible for ESA) than previously failed the IBPCA (DWP, 2008); this equates to around 10% of the annual on-flow under the former IB regime. However, the actual rate has consistently exceeded this. The latest figures for completed initial assessments (that is, excluding those still in progress or withdrawn before assessment and before taking into account any appeals) to the end of May 2011 show that:

- 62% were found FFW
- 27% were allocated to the WRAG
- 11% to the Support Group

(Source: DWP, 2011a.)

This rate of disallowance has been controversial. The appeal rate among those found FFW currently stood at 36% in 2011, with 39% of decisions being decided in the claimant's favour.

The benefit changes were initially applied to new and repeat claimants only, but between 2011 and 2014 all existing IB claimants are to be reassessed using the WCA, and will become subject to the ESA regime. Having been trialled in Burnley and Aberdeen, the national reassessment of IB claimants began in April 2011. In the trial areas, 32% of those assessed by the new medical were found to be FFW (source: DWP, 2011b. This figure does not include those appealing.)

Since the introduction of ESA there have been a number of other important changes to the sickness benefits regime. The current Welfare Reform Bill, introduced by the Coalition Government, seeks to time-limit eligibility for contributions-based ESA claims in the WRAG from April 2012. It also proposes to increase the conditionality placed on claimants, requiring them to carry out actions suggested by advisers in WFIs (for example, attending a skills assessment or participating in training). A further change means that sickness benefit claimants no longer have access to Pathways to Work, which has been subsumed into a single universal welfare-to-work programme, the Work Programme. In the future, the introduction of a single Universal Credit will replace both means-tested sickness and unemployment benefits.

## Barriers to work and employability

Employability is a broad concept that seeks to measure a wide range of factors that influence an individual's likelihood of being in employment (for an overview see McQuaid and Lindsay, 2005; also McQuaid and Lindsay, 2002; Hillage and Pollard, 1998; Gazier, 1998). The concept can be broken down into:

- Individual factors–including skills, qualifications, labour market attachment, demographic characteristics, health, jobseeking attitudes and behaviours, adaptability and mobility
- Personal circumstances – which include caring responsibilities, access to resources, household situation, household income, transport availability
- External factors – which include the scale and type of vacancies in the local labour market, recruitment practices of employers, and enabling support factors such as the support received by public (or private) employment services, and the replacement rates offered by benefits relative to average earnings. (McQuaid and Lindsay, 2005)

For some sickness benefit claimants, poor health is the sole barrier to employment. Many sickness benefits claimants have a consistent work history and retain the desire to move back into employment if, and when, their condition improves sufficiently. For another group of claimants, however, the interaction between health barriers, social and broader economic circumstances and an individual's employability is less clear-cut.

While health is usually the central barrier to work for sickness benefit claimants, claimants can also experience additional barriers that reduce their overall employability. Often claimants can be affected by multiple barriers to work; having such multiple barriers to work is known to increase the cumulative risk of non-employment (Berthoud, 2003).

Many ESA claimants (and many of the IB claimants who are being migrated to ESA) also live in areas with the poorest job opportunities; this means that in the absence of strong employment creation, supply-side measures are likely to be relatively ineffective in moving people into work (Fothergill and Wilson, 2007). Furthermore, the former industrial areas with highest rates of sickness benefit claims have also tended to experience the largest increases in unemployment as a result of the 2008–9 recession (Sissons, 2009). Weak labour market conditions, increased competition for jobs from the claimant unemployed, and the often multiple barriers to work experienced by sickness benefits claimants suggest that many are likely to find themselves at the 'back of the jobs queue' for those opportunities that do exist (Beatty and Fothergill, 2011; Sissons, 2009).

## Methodology

This chapter draws on the responses to a large survey of ESA claimants, as well as several rounds of qualitative research with claimants, to provide evidence on the employability and health of the ESA group, and to identify the key barriers to work that they face (Barnes et al., 2010). The survey involved two waves of fieldwork. Between December 2009 and February 2010, 3,650 ESA claimants participated in a face-to-face survey (survey work was conducted by IpsosMORI). The respondents had all made a claim for ESA between April and June 2009. The survey disproportionately sampled claimants in the WRAG and Support Groups to ensure sufficient numbers of cases for robust analysis.[1] A second wave of the survey followed up with 1,842 of these respondents by telephone. The survey questionnaire asked a range of questions relating to:

- health condition[2]
- employment and benefit history
- initial claim experiences
- the medical assessment process
- attendance at WFIs
- appeals against decisions
- destinations of those leaving the benefit
- future employment aspirations and barriers to work.

Survey responses were also linked to administrative data on claim outcomes, appeals and benefits held by the DWP.[3] This was important for two reasons. First, there was a good deal of confusion among claimants about their claim group and the status of appeals. Secondly, this allowed us to look at both previous and subsequent benefit claims among survey respondents.

The ESA evaluation also included several rounds of qualitative research with claimants, as well as various stakeholders involved in administering the sickness benefits system. These sought to capture further information about claimants' experiences of making a claim for ESA, their thoughts and feelings about their condition, their views about their claim outcome, and their future employment aspirations and barriers to work. In total more than 100 claimant interviews were completed.

We focus largely on the two groups who are the primary focus of this policy change: the FFW group, who are deemed ineligible for ESA and well enough to seek work immediately, and the WRAG, for whom work is seen as a medium-term goal despite an acknowledgement of health barriers. A smaller number of claimants enter the Support Group. These claimants have the most severe work-limiting health conditions and only a minority are likely to be able to consider a return to work in the foreseeable future. Support group claimants are not required to participate in work-related activities or attend WFIs (although they can attend voluntarily) and so are not explicit targets for back-to-work support.

## The health status of the ESA population

Mental health problems and musculoskeletal conditions were the main health conditions reported by survey respondents (representing 32% and 37% of cases respectively). The type of health condition was influenced by gender, age, and socio-economic group. The prevalence of mental health conditions was higher among women, younger people and those who were previously long-term unemployed or had never worked, while musculoskeletal conditions were more common among men and older people. Around one in five of all conditions reported by ESA claimants (19%) were viewed as directly work-related, rising to around a third (32%) of musculoskeletal conditions; in general there was relatively little difference in the main health conditions cited by WRAG and FFW groups.

Overall, two-thirds of all those who had claimed ESA and who still had a health problem at the time of the survey reported having multiple health problems, with no significant differences between those who had been allocated to the WRAG and those found FFW. Of those who reported a physical health condition as their main health problem, a third (34%) also had a mental health condition, while a slightly smaller proportion (29%) of those who had a mental health condition also had a physical health condition. Over half (51%) of ESA claimants reported a health condition that fluctuated; this was particularly prevalent among those with mental health problems. The great majority of those interviewed (81%) were receiving some form of treatment for their condition at the time they were surveyed, and a substantial minority (38%) were waiting for treatment.

Almost half (49%) of the FFW group identified themselves as unable to work because of their health problem or disability; 27% reported that they were temporarily sick (this group was more or less evenly split between those who had a job to return to and those who did not); while 22% viewed themselves as permanently incapable of work owing to ill-health. Consistent with this, well over half (57%) of those found FFW continued to see their health status as a barrier to finding work, and 46% identified ill-health as their *main* barrier to employment.[4] These figures were higher, as one would expect, for those in the WRAG; close to two-thirds (64%) of this group identified ill-health as their main barrier to employment.

The majority (55%) of claimants who had been employed immediately before their ESA claim identified their health condition as the main reason for having left work; a further 25% had been made redundant. Women and those with a physical health problem were more likely than other claimants to have left their most recent job because of ill-health.

Table 5.1 provides details about the health conditions of ESA claimants. Comparable data are also presented for new claimants of the former IB who were surveyed in 2007, as well as for the wider working age population.

Comparing ESA claimants to new IB claimants, we can see that the differences in condition type are relatively small, although mental health problems were somewhat more widely reported among ESA claimants.

In comparison to the wider working age population, those claiming ESA were more likely to cite a mental health problem as their main health condition. This represents a major barrier to employability; previous research has shown that those with mental health problems are twice as likely as those with any other health problem not to be in work, and employers generally lack awareness of how to manage such conditions in the workplace (Sainsbury et al., 2008). ESA claimants also had a significantly higher incidence of musculoskeletal conditions. By contrast the wider working age population were more likely to report long-term/systemic conditions. These differences

*Table 5.1*  Health characteristics of ESA claimants, IB claimants and the general population

| Characteristic (%) | ESA claimants (WRAG/FFW) | | | IB claimants | General population (16–64) |
|---|---|---|---|---|---|
| Type of main health condition* | | | | | |
| Mental health | 32 | 30 | 33 | 26 | 9 |
| Musculoskeletal | 37 | 37 | 40 | 38 | 28 |
| Long-term/systemic | 16 | 13 | 14 | 20 | 40 |
| Other | 13 | 17 | 10 | 15 | 21 |

*Percentages of those with a limiting health condition. See McManus et al., 2009 for a full discussion.
*Source*: IB comparison from Kemp and Davidson, 2007; General Population from Labour Force Survey, Quarter 3 2010.

in long-term conditions are largely accounted for by the prevalence of conditions like chest/breathing problems and high blood pressure in the general population (see McManus et al. 2009 for a full discussion).

## Employability characteristics of the ESA population

Table 5.2 looks at some key characteristics of the ESA population that may affect their employability. The analysis focuses on the WRAG and FFW groups, as they are the two groups that are the main focus of the changed sickness benefit regime. As discussed above, the Support Group, those with the most severe health conditions, is exempt from activation requirements. The table compares ESA claimants with new IB claimants (who were surveyed in 2007) and with the UK population as a whole. The former enables us to examine whether benefit changes have affected the characteristics of those making a claim for sickness benefits, and therefore the employability of this group, while the latter enables compares the employability

*Table 5.2* Selected employability characteristics of ESA claimants, IB claimants and the general population

| Characteristic (%) | ESA claimants (WRAG/FFW) | | | IB claimants | General population (16–64) |
|---|---|---|---|---|---|
| | **All claimants** | **WRAG** | **FFW** | | |
| Age, gender, and ethnicity | | | | | |
| Male | 63 | 65 | 66 | 59 | 50 |
| Aged over 55 | 18 | 18 | 18 | 23 | 18 |
| White | 90 | 91 | 88 | 91 | 89 |
| Tenure | | | | | |
| Owner-occupiers | 35 | 36 | 33 | 42 | 68 |
| Social renters | 34 | 36 | 34 | 40 | 16 |
| Private renters | 16 | 18 | 17 | 14 | 15 |
| Qualifications | | | | | |
| Degree-level qualification | 8 | 6 | 8 | 11 | 22 |
| No qualifications | 35 | 39 | 36 | 28 | 11 |
| Other labour market disadvantage | | | | | |
| Literacy problems | 22 | 27 | 21 | 16 | * |
| Problems speaking English (ESOL) | 5 | 7 | 4 | 4 | * |
| Numeracy problems | 11 | 11 | 9 | 12 | * |
| Ex-offender | 10 | 10 | 10 | Not asked | * |

*Direct comparisons not possible.
*Source*: IB comparison from Kemp and Davidson, 2007; General Population from Labour Force Survey, Quarter 3 2010.

of ESA claimants with that of the general population, with whom they will potentially be in competition for employment.

Compared with those who claimed IB in the past, ESA claimants are slightly younger; under a fifth (18%) are aged 55 or more, compared with almost a quarter (23%) of those making a new claim for IB. Despite the increasing proportion of women claiming sickness benefits, the ESA population remains largely male; two-thirds (63%) of those claiming are men. The ethnic breakdown of those claiming ESA and IB is similar to that for the UK population as a whole.

In terms of housing tenure, those claiming ESA are much less likely to own or be buying their own home (35%, compared to 68% of the population as a whole), and much more likely to be renting accommodation from a social landlord (34%, compared to 16% of the general population), reflecting a disadvantaged socio-economic position. Housing tenure is potentially important in explaining employment outcomes, for two reasons. One is that it reflects patterns of disadvantage in the labour market, with lower-paid and insecurely employed people more concentrated in the social rented sector. The other is that there are differential work incentive structures according to tenure, with those renting accommodation tending to face more marginal gains from entering low-paid work. Housing tenure can also be important because it can constrain geographical mobility; in particular job-related mobility in the social rented sector has been shown to be 'strikingly low' (Hills, 2007).

Looking at qualifications, compared with the UK population as a whole, those claiming ESA are much less likely to have a degree, and much more likely to have no qualifications; the proportion with no qualifications is also higher than that recorded for IB claimants.

In addition to their generally low rates of qualification, many ESA claimants face further barriers to employment: 22% have literacy problems, 11% have numeracy problems, and one in ten has a criminal record. The proportion with literacy problems is higher among those claiming ESA, compared with those who claimed IB in the past.

There is very little difference observed across the range of employability characteristics between the WRAG and the FFW groups.

In the survey claimants were also asked to reflect on their own barriers to entering employment. Some 31% of the Fit for Work group identified a perceived lack of suitable job opportunities locally for them as being a barrier to work, while 21% felt they lacked the right skills or experience to access work (Table 5.3). Among the WRAG almost one-quarter (24%) similarly felt there were no suitable job opportunities available for them locally, and a fifth reported not having the right skills or experience. Other barriers cited by claimants in the WRAG included low confidence (37%), potential difficulties around their journey to work (19%), and perception of age discrimination among employers (13%).

In many cases ESA claimants face not just a single (health) barrier to work but combinations of multiple barriers. Some of these combinations severely reduce the employability of ESA claimants. For example, 12% of the WRAG and 14% of the FFW group had both no qualifications as well as little or no work experience.

## Employability and barriers to work: Findings from qualitative interviews with claimants

As Kemp and Davidson (2008) have demonstrated previously, both health and closeness to the labour market are important determinants of employability and the likelihood of moving into work for IB claimants. The nature and duration of a person's health condition, their labour market history and barriers, as well as individual motivation and goals all play a part in influencing individuals' views of their own employability. In this section we provide evidence from the qualitative interviews about ESA claimants' own perceptions of their barriers to work.

### The Fit for Workgroup

For those allocated to the FFW, reactions varied; while some people were appealing, others appeared to have a grudging acceptance of the decision; while some felt powerless to appeal, others accepted that their health problem did not prevent them from working (see Barnes et al., 2011 for further discussion). For some in the FFW, health was clearly their primary or sole barrier to work, while at the other end of the spectrum for others it was obviously not a substantive barrier. A middle group had health problems, but it was the combination of these with other circumstances that constituted the main barrier. We will now look at each of these groups in turn providing examples from the research.

*Barriers to work – health only*

Those in the FFW group whose health was their only or main barrier to employment often had long work histories and recent labour market

*Table 5.3* Non-health barriers citied by ESA claimants*, percentage of claim group citing barrier

| Barrier | WRAG (%) | FFW (%) |
|---|---|---|
| Low confidence | 37 | 32 |
| Few suitable jobs in local area | 24 | 31 |
| Doesn't have right skills/experience | 20 | 21 |
| Difficulties with journey to work | 19 | 15 |
| Employers unlikely to offer a job because of age | 13 | 17 |

*Note*: *Table shows the most widely cited barriers by claimants.

experience, but were temporarily or permanently unable to do their usual job because of a health problem.

Yasmin was in her 50s, and had severe arthritis, which caused her considerable pain. She had left her last job, as a healthcare assistant, as it was too physically demanding. Although technically still under consideration for redeployment, she no longer felt that her employers were actively doing anything about this. Yasmin described herself as 'desperate to go back into the workforce', mainly because of financial pressures, as her husband was on a fairly low wage; indeed she felt that her desire to work had not been taken seriously by Jobcentre Plus staff:

> *I think they all just assume you don't want to work and you'd rather be on benefits and that's not the case.*

Jill had a serious long-term mental health problem but had always worked. She had been in her current job as a university porter until the onset of physical health problems, which had made this impossible. Her job remained open to her, but she claimed ESA when her entitlement to SSP expired. Jill was unhappy at being found fit for work, and was appealing this decision, but was nevertheless keen to return to work at the earliest opportunity, saying:

> *I've always wanted to work, schizophrenic or not. So I've not let the mental health issue stop me. I drive, I lead a normal life and I want to lead a normal life. I don't want to be on the scrap heap as a mental health patient and claim benefits. And this is what's annoying me. All I'm trying to do is get a few pounds to pay my bills.*

Jill was awaiting surgery to resolve her condition, but was anxious that in the meantime she would be pressurised to take an alternative job, which would be less well paid, and which might be less suitable.

### Barriers to work – health and other problems

A more complex group of FFW claimants comprises those who have substantive health problems, which might not in themselves preclude a return to paid work, but in combination, or taken together with other difficult personal or domestic circumstances place limits on their current employability. Some claimants were still coming to terms with a recent condition, or had unresolved health issues that were likely to improve over time, but were ill-placed to consider employment when interviewed. Others faced ongoing barriers to employment, such as not being able to speak or write English, a criminal record or not having any qualifications. Although the existence of multiple barriers did not necessarily imply a lack of motivation and a desire to work, it does indicate a need for skilled and long-term support.

Hanif was an example of someone with long experience of the 'low-pay, no-pay cycle'. Now in his 40s, he had worked in the restaurant trade since coming to the UK about twenty years ago. He vividly described the way in which he had repeatedly moved between benefits and work over this period, saying:

> *Sometimes work and sometimes signing on and looking for a job. I get a job for six weeks, six months, one year, two years, and this place may be closed or closing down, which is no good. But I've been coming here to the [Job]centre and signing on. And six months, one year, six months, and then after I start anybody gives me the job and start job again.*

He had started one such job a week before having a heart attack, but had lost it as a result of his illness. At the time of his interview, several months later, Hanif was still feeling quite unwell, and under considerable stress. He had a premature baby, who was in hospital, and was running the household and caring for the couple's other dependant children, while his wife cared for the baby. Hanif was appealing the FFW decision, with the help of a local advice agency. While he said he was actively looking for work, it did not seem a realistic option at the time he was interviewed.

Paula was in her early 40s and being treated for depression following bereavement, and gynaecological problems that had remained unresolved by repeated surgery; at the time of her interview she was on the waiting list for a further operation. Under the previous PCA system, which combined scores for physical and mental health conditions, she appeared likely to have qualified for benefit, but she did not meet the threshold for ESA, which scores these separately. She was unhappy with the FFW decision, and was appealing. Paula faced multiple barriers to work, in addition to her health; she had a criminal record, and had no previous work experience, having been a lone parent for many years. She was keen to find entry-level work once her condition improved, but felt that this was likely to be challenging.

### Barriers to work – non-health

For a minority of those in the FFW group, health was clearly not the main barrier to employment, as their condition was well managed and caused few problems on a day-to-day basis, and they had been working until recently. Inderjit was an example of someone in this group. In his mid-40s, he had diabetes and high cholesterol, and was waiting for a minor operation, but had been in paid work prior to his ESA claim, which he made on the advice of a friend, and said that he generally feels well enough to work. Because he has no qualifications and limited ability in written English, having migrated to the UK in his late teens, Inderjit had always worked in entry-level jobs in the Indian restaurant trade, but the recession had led to a downturn in local demand. Longer term, he also wished to retrain to improve his skills and earnings potential. The FFW decision appears uncontroversial in this sort of case, and Inderjit had accepted this, and simply gone on to claim Jobseekers' Allowance (JSA).

## The WRAG

This section outlines what WRAG interviewees suggested about the future employment aspirations, barriers to work, and engagement with the return to work process of this group of claimants. The interviews suggested that there are several distinct groups within the WRAG, which are located along a spectrum in terms of the level of their attachment to the labour market, as measured by their future employment aspirations.

### *The actively engaged*

There was a group of WRAG claimants who were considerably closer to the labour market. In some cases they were recovering from short-term injuries. In others these were claimants who did not envisage an immediate return to work, but did see it as likely in the foreseeable future. They tended to be somewhat younger and were often much more likely to engage in the support offered through the WFIs. They mostly had short-term conditions and/or less severe limitations. In some cases they were looking at changing their type of work.

Evan, who was in his 40s and had been a self-employed roofer for 13 years, is an example of this. He had been troubled with back pain for some time, but a lifting accident had left him unable to work. Evan said that while his back is recovering he is using the time to explore other options in case he is not been able to return to his previous work. During this time he has completed a computing course and is starting a plumbing qualification.

### *Those who hope to return to work in the future*

There was a group of claimants who felt that while they would like to return to work in future, they had given the possibility little consideration because at the time they found it impossible to see beyond their condition. Claimants who reported feeling like this included:

- those with conditions that were unstable, for example those with substance misuse problems
- those who had suffered from a condition with an immediate onset that had fundamentally altered their capabilities and to which they were adjusting, for example those who had suffered a stroke.

Some of the claimants in this position had found their WFIs a useful way of thinking about future work even if it was not possible currently. Others, for example those undergoing intensive treatment or awaiting operations, felt there was little value in the WFIs until their health issue had been addressed.

Mark, for example, a man in his 40s, suffers from depression and is heavily dependent on drink. Formerly a manual worker, he began suffering depression as a result of his discontent at work. After leaving his job he signed on for JSA for several months before being told to claim for ESA. At present he struggles to see beyond his reliance on drink, and addressing this problem is his primary concern. It is a similar story for Alison, in her late 40s, who has some longstanding health complaints and had recently been made redundant. Alison has recently had back surgery and is waiting for a second operation. At present her mobility is seriously impaired, and although she is keen to return to work she says that is unlikely to be soon.

*The permanently sick*

There were two broad categories of claimants who identified themselves as being permanently off work owing to sickness:

- Those who felt they were too ill to work again. Typically these were individuals that had progressive or deteriorating conditions. These claimants felt they were simply too ill to consider a return to employment. They had often already worked with their health condition for a long period and felt they had stayed in their jobs for as long as was possible.
- Those who felt that their health limitation, in combination with other barriers to work, meant they would not work again. The key additional barrier was often age, but in other cases lack of skill and/or local jobs reinforced this position.

These groups of claimants had no real employment aspirations, even when they retained a latent desire to work. In some cases these individuals actively resented having to attend WFIs, in others they simply viewed them as being an unproductive use of their own, and the advisors', time. In such cases they reported relatively perfunctory appointments.

Sarah, who is in her late 40s, illustrates this position. She had been in her previous job working in an office for 16 years before having to leave when her MS became too severe to continue and is resigned to not working again. It is a similar story for Jean, a woman in her late 50s. Previously a social worker, she has long-term problems with her sight and her back, which have necessitated periods off work over the years. Jean similarly feels that she stayed in work until this became unmanageable, and that she is unable to benefit from being placed in the WRAG:

> *I feel it's a waste of time for me. ... I was in a really well-paid job, a job that I loved and if I had been able to continue in my employment I wouldn't have retired on medical grounds.*

The extent of health barriers in the WRAG was also borne out in interviews with Jobcentre Plus advisory staff, who noted that the claimants in this group were, on the whole, more unwell than those new claimants to IB they had previously dealt with. This made it very difficult for advisors to offer support or services when they felt that claimants were too unwell to undertake them.

## Moving into work and future prospects

The overall return to work rate among the WRAG was very low. By the follow-up survey, which would be between 11 and 14 months after the initial claim, just 9% of those in the WRAG at Wave 1 were in employment. For those in the FFW at Wave 1 the figure was 25%. A large part of these differential employment outcomes is due to differences in health status between the two groups. Looking at longer-term prospects, at the initial survey some 31% of the WRAG felt it likely they would never work again.

Given the wide range and number of barriers that the ESA group face in returning to work it is instructive to assess which have the strongest influence on return to work.

Turning first to the FFW, logistic regression is used to examine the factors that increased the likelihood of being back in employment by the time of the survey (Table 5.4). Logistic regression allows us to show the individual effect of a range of independent variables on an outcome variable. The key statistic is the odds ratio coefficient [Exp(B)], which expresses the direction and strength of an individual factor's association with the dependent variable, with odds ratios less than one indicating a negative effect and those greater than one indicating a positive effect. For the FFW group the dependent variable is whether an individual reports being back in employment, unemployed, or economically inactive. The reference category is economically inactive.

Looking first at the upper half of the table, those who had returned to work by the time of the first wave survey, there are a number of key explanatory variables. Those who were back in work were much less likely to report having a health problem at the time of survey, and this was the strongest predictor. This strongly suggests that the greatest determinant of a return to work is simply recovery. (The regression results show an association but cannot assign causality, for example in some cases it may be that 'recovery' follows a return to work rather than vice versa. It does seem most likely however that in the majority of cases the direction of causality will be 'recovery' followed by entry into employment – this position is supported by the findings from the WRAG, which are subsequently described, which assess the relationship between health trajectory and employment aspirations.) This is important, but also troubling, because the FFW group have not had access to the type of condition management support that is

*Table 5.4*  Factors associated with the employment status of the Fit for Work group

|  | Odds ratio | Significance |
|---|---|---|
| **Employed** | | |
| Whether has health problem which affects daily activities or work activities | | |
| Has health problem, disability or illness which limits daily activities or the work can do | 0.080 | .000 |
| (No health problem, disability or illness which limits daily activities or the work can do) | 1.000 | |
| Situation immediately before claim | | |
|   Other | 0.189 | .004 |
|   Unemployed | 0.514 | .023 |
|   Temporarily sick with no job | 0.348 | .015 |
|   Permanently sick | 0.097 | .001 |
|   (Working or with job but off sick) | 1.000 | |
| Gender | | |
|   Male | 0.849 | .465 |
|   (Female) | 1.000 | |
| Household situation | | |
|   Not living with partner | 0.736 | .171 |
|   (Living with partner) | 1.000 | |
| Work history | | |
|   Mostly in work | 2.616 | .009 |
|   (Mostly out of work) | 1.000 | |
| Disadvantaged group | | |
|   In one or more disadvantaged groups | 0.414 | .026 |
|   (Not in a disadvantaged group) | 1.000 | |
| Age | | |
|   55+ | 1.675 | .329 |
|   50–54 | 1.854 | .273 |
|   35–49 | 2.841 | .032 |
|   25–34 | 3.109 | .028 |
|   (18–24) | 1.000 | |
| **Unemployed** | | |
| Whether has health problem which affects daily activities | | |
| Has a health problem, disability or illness which limits daily activities or the work can do | 0.110 | .000 |
| (No health problem, disability or illness which limits daily activities or the work can do) | 1.000 | |
| Situation immediately before claim | | |
|   Other | 0.669 | .265 |
|   Unemployed | 4.250 | .000 |
|   Temporarily sick with no job | 1.298 | .584 |
|   Permanently sick | 0.665 | .331 |
|   (Working or with job but off sick) | 1.000 | . |

*(continued)*

*Table 5.4*   Continued

|  | Odds ratio | Significance |
|---|---|---|
| Gender |  |  |
| Male | 1.596 | .042 |
| (Female) | 1.000 |  |
| Household situation |  |  |
| Not living with partner | 1.888 | .002 |
| (Living with partner) | 1.000 |  |
| Work history |  |  |
| Mostly in work | 0.777 | .309 |
| (Mostly out of work) | 1.000 |  |
| Disadvantaged group |  |  |
| In one or more disadvantaged groups | 0.647 | .087 |
| (Not in a disadvantaged group) | 1.000 |  |
| Age |  |  |
| 55+ | 0.884 | .734 |
| 50–54 | 1.002 | .995 |
| 35–49 | 1.498 | .192 |
| 25–34 | 1.473 | .305 |
| (18–24) | 1.000 | . |

*Note*: $n = 1,171$. $F = 11.82$, $P < .001$. $R^2 = .33$ (Cox and Snell), .39 (Nagelkerke).

made available to WRAG claimants, even though this might be an effective way of supporting a return to work among the FFW. However, there were also a number of other important employability factors that influenced the propensity to be in employment. Being in employment immediately prior to their claim increased the likelihood of being in work at the time of the survey, as did having a consistent longer-term work history. A return to work was also more likely among those aged between 25 and 49. Being in a disadvantaged group (this includes those who had recently left care, had a criminal conviction, were in contact with secondary mental health services or had moderate to severe learning difficulties) reduced the likelihood of being in employment. Qualifications, when included in the analysis, did not have a statistically significant influence on being in work.

The group that was unemployed at the time of survey was also more likely to report not having a health condition. Being unemployed prior to claiming influenced the likelihood of being unemployed after the claim, and being male and living alone also raised the likelihood of being unemployed.

Overall the FFW data suggest two central explanations of moving into employment among those who claimed ESA but failed the WCA. Recovery from illness was the strongest predictor but labour market attachment over both the short and longer term was also important.

The prospects for the WRAG were assessed in relation to a binary dependent variable–whether respondents reported that they did not expect to work again, as opposed to those who were either looking for work or hoped to work in the future (Table 5.5). Again health was of central importance – those who reported that their condition was improving were very much more likely to expect to work again, while those whose condition was deteriorating were more likely to report themselves as being permanently unable to work. Age was also a factor; being aged over 50 increased the chance of claimants viewing themselves as permanently off work. Employment situation prior to the claim was also significant, with those who were economically inactive before their claim (either permanently sick or 'other', including those with caring responsibilities and those in education and training) less likely to view themselves as being able to move into employment in the future. Other variables considered but which did not have a statistically significant impact included qualifications, type of health condition, number of conditions, longer-term work history, and household employment situation.[5]

The findings from both FFW and WRAG groups show clearly that health trajectory is the central influence on subsequent employment experiences

*Table 5.5* Factors associated with not expecting to work again among WRAG claimants

|  | Odds ratio | Significance |
| --- | --- | --- |
| How condition is currently |  |  |
| Getting better | 0.088 | .000 |
| Fluctuating | 0.595 | .125 |
| Getting worse | 2.515 | .002 |
| (Staying the same) | 1.000 | . |
| Age |  |  |
| 55+ | 6.359 | .000 |
| 50–54 | 3.340 | .014 |
| 35–49 | 1.921 | .118 |
| 25–34 | 1.145 | .819 |
| (18–24) | 1.000 | . |
| Situation immediately before claim |  |  |
| Other | 2.459 | .037 |
| Unemployed | 0.528 | .054 |
| Temporarily sick with no job | 0.270 | .029 |
| Permanently sick | 3.747 | .005 |
| (Working or with job but off sick) | 1.000 | . |
| Gender |  |  |
| Male | 0.677 | .124 |
| (Female) | 1.000 | . |
| Qualifications |  |  |
| No qualifications | 1.526 | .103 |
| (Some qualifications) | 1.000 | . |

*Note:* $n = 1,003$. $F = 7.38$, $P < .001$. $R^2 = .25$ (Cox and Snell), .35 (Nagelkerke).

and aspirations. This again highlights the importance of health support and condition management in preparing claimants for a return to work. Aside from health it is work experience (particularly recent experience) and contact with the labour market that are most important in influencing subsequent outcomes and attitudes. Age was also salient, with older claimants in the WRAG less likely to believe they will work again.

## Conclusions

Those who do not have access to income protection in the event of long-term illness (whether in the form of private income protection policies or occupational sickness pay or retirement schemes) now face increasing financial vulnerability if they develop a health condition that prevents them from working or reduces their attractiveness to employers. While attention has focused on the growth in numbers claiming IBs, and their relative generosity compared to Jobseeker's Allowance, in reality these benefits offer a very low standard of living as a long-term income. Access to IBs is now being dramatically curtailed, both by the imposition of a much stricter medical threshold for entitlement to benefit, and by the proposed withdrawal of contributory benefit after one year for those in the WRAG. There is little evidence to date that policies aimed at activating those on sickness benefits in the UK have had any beneficial effect on increasing the employment prospects of those who are workless as a result of ill-health.

Looking at those in the WRAG, the evidence appears to indicate that some people feel either that their health limitations are too severe, or they are too detached from the labour market for employment to be a realistic prospect in the short or medium term. Nor does the ESA process appear to be having its intended impact in changing claimant views about their health or prospects of a return to work. Similarly, when the circumstances of those found FFW have been considered in detail, it is clear that many of them are ill-suited to the requirements of JSA, owing to the nature of the barriers faced and the extent of additional support required to achieve employment outcomes, including around health condition management. As with the WRAG, there is little evidence that the ESA process is affecting attitudes; being found FFW appears to have little effect on how the individual views their prospects.

These findings chime with Gregg's recent argument that the high failure rate of the WCA has the potential to undermine the purpose of ESA. The argument is twofold; first, that those awarded benefit will be less likely to take work because they fear that if it goes wrong they will be unable to reclaim; secondly, a significant number of people with health problems will be moved onto Jobseeker's Allowance, a benefit 'which is designed for those who are job-ready and offers no help with condition management' (Gregg, 2010). It remains to be seen whether the introduction of a single welfare-to-work programme (the Work Programme) will benefit or hinder this group.

On one hand the 'black-box' approach may allow providers to tailor the individual support needed (including with health), on the other the payments model may not always accurately reflect the complex needs of some among the FFW group, making them less cost-effective to help and potentially more vulnerable to being 'parked' on benefit.

Claimants are not generally regarded as good judges of their own employability, but improved health is associated with employment outcomes. The single most important predictor of a return to work among new IB claimants was an improvement in health (Kemp and Davidson, 2010). Among ESA claimants in the WRAG, health was also the central influence on claimants' views about whether they were likely to ever work again. Measures to facilitate access to treatment, and prevent deterioration in health are therefore likely to be beneficial in increasing benefit off-flows. It may also be possible to improve employment outcomes by delivering targeted help to those most in need of it. Those in older age groups or with no recent work experience are likely to require additional and possibly specialist assistance to return to work. Claimants previously employed in manual occupations may also benefit from opportunities to retrain for alternative occupations.

It is clear from the analysis that health barriers to work are highly significant for both the WRAG and the FFW groups, and that recovery or improvement of a condition appears the best predictor of moving into work. This finding highlights a crucial role for support with health improvement and condition management in influencing moves into employment from both claim groups. Within both groups, however, there are sub-sections where health barriers intersect with social and broader economic circumstances. As such a number of wider employability needs have been observed among ESA claimants. They are more likely to have no qualifications, and significant numbers also have literacy, numeracy or English-language problems. This research has also highlighted the particularly important role that recent (and longer-term) attachment to the labour market plays in influencing the subsequent trajectories of ESA claimants. In many cases claimants experience a combination of barriers, as well as holding a perception that employment opportunities are limited locally. In these cases the central challenge for policy to assist claimants in entering and sustaining employment is to provide holistic support to encourage both health and employability improvements.

## Notes

1. A full technical report of the survey is available at http://research.dwp.gov.uk/asd/asd5/rports2011–2012/ESAtechnicalreport.pdf.
2. It should be noted that throughout the chapter the discussion of health limitations relates to claimants' self-reported information on health rather than the results of their WCA assessment.

3. Respondents were asked during the survey whether they would consent to data-linking: 3,075 out of 3,650 individuals did consent to data-linking.
4. At the first wave of the survey 20% of those in the FFW group were appealing against their WCA result. However by the follow-up survey, excluding those who had successfully appealed, some 30% of the FFW group still viewed themselves as being sick.
5. Analysis undertaken on all ESA claimants suggest that for men, qualifications and longer-term work history are more important in explaining subsequent work outcomes than they are for women. See Sissons, Barnes, and Stevens (2011).

## Bibliography

Barnes, H., Oakley, J., Stevens, H., and Sissons, P. (2011) *Ended Claims for Employment and Support Allowance, DWP Research Report 762* (Leeds: Corporate Document Services).

Barnes, H., Sissons, P., and Stevens, H. (2010) *Employment and Support Allowance: Findings from a Face-to-Face Survey of Customers, DWP Research Report 707* (Leeds: Corporate Document Services).

Beatty, C. and Fothergill, S. (1996) 'Labour Market Adjustment in Areas of Chronic Industrial Decline: The Case of the UK Coalfields', *Regional Studies*, 30 (7), 637–650.

Beatty, C. and Fothergill, S. (2011) *Incapacity Benefit Reform: The Local, Regional and National Impact* (Sheffield: Centre for Regional Economic and Social Research).

Beatty, C., Fothergill, S., Houston, D., Powell, R., and Sissons, P. (2009) 'A Gendered Theory of Employment, Unemployment, and Sickness', *Environment and Planning C: Government and Policy*, 27 (6), 958–974.

Beatty, C., Fothergill, S., and Lawless, P. (1997) 'Geographical Variation in the Labour-Market Adjustment Process: The UK Coalfields 1981–91', *Environment and Planning A*, 29 (11), 2041–2060.

Berthoud, R. (2003) *Multiple Disadvantage in Employment* (Bristol: Joseph Rowntree Foundation).

Bewley, H., Dorsett, R., and Salis, S. (2009) *The Impact of Pathways to Work on Work, Earnings and Self-Reported Health in the April 2006 Expansion Areas, DWP Research Report 601* (Leeds: Corporate Document Services).

DWP (2006) *A New Deal for Welfare: Empowering People to Work* (London: DWP).

DWP (2008) *Impact Assessment of the Employment and Support Allowance Regulations*, http://dwp.gov.uk/resourcecentre/ImpactAssessment180308.pdf, date accessed 6 October 2009.

DWP (2009) *Work Capability Assessment: Internal Review*, http://www.dwp.gov.uk/docs/work-capability-assessment-review.pdf, date accessed 20 December 2011.

DWP (2011a) *Employment and Support Allowance: Work Capability Assessment – Official Statistics, October 2011* (London: DWP).

DWP (2011b) *Employment and Support Allowance: Work Capability Assessment by health Condition and Functional Impairment – Official Statistics, April 2011* (London: DWP).

Fieldhouse, E. and Hollywood, E. (1999) 'Life After Mining: Hidden Unemployment and Changing Patterns of Economic Activity amongst Miners in England and Wales, 1981–1991', *Work, Employment and Society*, 13 (3), 483–502.

Fothergill, S. and Wilson, I. (2007) 'A Million Off Incapacity Benefit: How Achievable Is Labour's Target?', *Cambridge Journal of Economics*, 31 (6), 1007–1023.

Gazier, B. (1998) *Employability – Concepts and Policies* (Berlin: European Employment Observatory).

Gregg, P. (2010) 'Osborne's Haste Will Undermine Incapacity Benefit Reform', *The Guardian*, http://www.guardian.co.uk/commentisfree/2010/jul/06/osborne-haste-undermine-incapacity-benefit-reform, date accessed 6 August 2010.

Hillage, J. and Pollard, E. (1998) *Employability: Developing a Framework for Policy Analysis* (London: Department for Education and Employment).

Hills, J. (2007) *Ends and Means: The Future Roles of Social Housing in England* (London: Centre for Analysis of Social Exclusion, London School of Economics and Political Science).

Kemp, P. and Davidson, J. (2007) *Routes onto Incapacity Benefit: Findings from a Survey of Recent Claimants*, DWP Research Report 469 (Leeds: Corporate Document Services).

Kemp, P. and Davidson, J. (2008) *Routes onto Incapacity Benefit: Findings from a Follow-Up Survey of Recent Claimants*, DWP Research Report 516 (Leeds: Corporate Document Services).

Kemp, P. and Davidson, J. (2010) 'Employability Trajectories among New Claimants of Incapacity Benefit', *Policy Studies*, 31 (2), 203–221.

McManus, S., Meltzer, H., Brugha, T., and Bebbington, P. (eds) (2009) *Adult Psychiatric Morbidity in England, 2007 Results of a Household Survey* (Leeds: Health and Social Care Information Centre).

McQuaid, R.W. and Lindsay, C. (2002) 'The 'Employability Gap': Long-Term Unemployment and Barriers to Work in Buoyant Labour Markets', *Environment and Planning C: Government and Policy*, 20 (4), 613–628.

McQuaid, R.W. and Lindsay, C. (2005) 'The Concept of Employability', *Urban Studies*, 42 (2), 197–219.

National Audit Office (2010) *Support to Incapacity Benefit Claimants Through Pathways to Work* (London: National Audit Office).

Sainsbury, R., Irvine, A., Aston, J., Wilson, S., Williams, C., and Sinclair, A. (2008) *Mental Health and Employment*, DWP Research Report 513 (Leeds: Corporate Document Services).

Sissons, P. (2009) 'Welfare Reform and Recession: Past Labour Market Responses to Job Losses and the Potential Impact of Employment Support Allowance', *People, Place and Policy*, 3 (3), 171–182.

Sissons, P., Barnes, H., and Stevens, H. (2011) *Routes onto Employment and Support Allowance*, DWP Research Report 774 (Leeds: Corporate Document Services).

Turok, I. and Edge, N. (1999) *The Jobs Gap in Britain's Cities: Employment Loss and Labour Market Consequences* (Bristol: Policy Press).

# 6
# A Health Problem? Health and Employability in the UK Labour Market

*Jon Warren, Kayleigh Garthwaite, and Clare Bambra*

## Introduction

Headline figures report that around 2.6 million people of working age in the UK claim health-related benefits. In 2008, the Labour government introduced a new out-of-work health-related benefit – Employment and Support Allowance (ESA) – for new claimants. This replaced Incapacity Benefit (IB). The process of transferring all existing IB recipients to ESA began in 2011. A 'fit note' instead of a 'sick note' was also introduced in April 2010 as a way of preventing movement from short-term to long-term sickness absence. Instead of concentrating upon what patients are not capable of the onus is now placed upon what work patients may be able to undertake. This marks a departure from the previous system, which placed a much greater emphasis upon the deficiencies of individuals. Yet these plans were made prior to the widespread economic recession, which saw job cuts and rising unemployment. The current Conservative–Liberal Democrat coalition government has also focused on those receiving health-related benefits. The government is reassessing all IB and ESA recipients with a view to moving many into work, off benefits or onto benefits paying lower rates with greater conditionality. Yet health-related benefit receipt remains a complex policy issue, one that concerns health, labour markets *and* employability.

The first section of this chapter provides an overview of recent policy discourse and activity on health and employability in the UK labour market, with a focus on notions of 'deserving' and 'undeserving' poor. The second section summarises the evidence on the effectiveness of previous interventions that have attempted to increase the employment of people in receipt of health-related welfare benefits. It finds that UK interventions have focused too much on increasing employability, and too little on improving the health of participants. This is partly because health-related benefit receipt has been treated almost exclusively as a matter of employability rather than as a health issue. This is picked up in the final section of the chapter, which provides empirical evidence from an original survey of ill-health among long-term IB recipients. It shows the extent of poor health and the clear need for health improvement interventions to aid the employment of this group of welfare recipients. In conclusion, we suggest that the welfare reform agenda needs to take a 'health first' approach.

## Recent trends in welfare policy

Recent discussions of health-related out-of-work benefits are underpinned by the assumption that many recipients are not sufficiently sick or disabled to 'deserve' welfare benefits. This is particularly evident in the reform of IB and the corresponding introduction of ESA (see Table 6.1). In October 2008, IB was replaced for new but not existing claimants, by the ESA. IB was introduced in 1995 (as a replacement for Invalidity Benefit and Sickness Benefit). It was the main benefit, paid to 2.7 million people in the UK, who were assessed via the Personal Capacity Assessment (PCA) as being incapable of work owing to illness or disability who had made sufficient social insurance contributions. Those who had not made enough contributions received Income Support, a means-tested benefit (meaning receipt is limited to those in low-income households and with limited savings). IB could be received up to pensionable age and was not subject to reassessment. In contrast, ESA has a two-tier system of benefits in which those judged (via a Work Capability Assessment(WCA) carried out by French private health company Atos) as unable to work or with limited work capacity owing to the severity of their physical or mental condition will receive a higher level of benefit (Support Allowance – essentially IB) with no conditionality, than those who are deemed 'sick but able to work' who will only receive the Employment Support component if they participate in work-related activities such as Pathways to Work. This was accompanied by the introduction of the 'fit note' in April 2010, replacing the old 'sick note'. It was an attempt to reduce the flow of people onto long-term health-related benefits, in the first instance by keeping them in employment. General practitioners are now required to state, after recording the condition that justifies it, if they have advised patients that they are 'not fit for work' or 'may be fit for work', and advise whether the patient will benefit from a phased return to work, amended duties, altered hours or workplace adaptations.

Since February 2011, the ESA system has been extended to over 1 million IB recipients with the intention of eventually reassessing and transferring the remainder onto ESA. All existing IB recipients will be subject to the WCA with three possible outcomes: Fit for Work (FFW); ESA–Work-Related Activity Group (WRAG); or ESA–Support Group. If someone is found fit for work, they will be moved onto Jobseeker's Allowance (paid at a lower rate than IB or ESA and which is means-tested after six months) and will have to actively search for work. The Comprehensive Spending Review in 2010 restricted entitlement to non-means-tested ESA for the WRAG to 12 months (see Table 6.1), after which it will be subject to means testing. In April 2011,

*Table 6.1*  Policies and interventions to tackle health-related worklessness in the UK (1994 to 2010)

| | |
|---|---|
| 1994 | Social Security (Incapacity for Work) Act<br>Introduced the All Works Test and Incapacity Benefit.<br>Access to Work Programme<br>Provided financial assistance towards practical aids, workplace adaptation, fares to work, and personal support. |
| 1995 | Disability Discrimination Act<br>Since 1996, it has been unlawful to discriminate in recruitment, promotion, training, working conditions, and dismissal on the grounds of disability or ill-health (restricted to employers with over 20 employees, reduced to 15 in 1998). Abolished the 3% employment quota of 1944. |
| 1998 | New Deal for Disabled People Pilots<br>A package of different interventions including the Personal Adviser service, the Innovative Schemes, and smaller projects such as the Job Finders Grant. |
| 1999 | Tax Credit Act<br>Introduced the Disabled Person's Tax Credit – a wage top-up for people with disabilities in low-paid employment (merged into the Working Tax Credit in 2002).<br><br>Disability Rights Commission<br>Monitored implementation of the Disability Discrimination Act from 2000 onwards.<br><br>Welfare Reform and Pensions Act<br>Incapacity Benefit became means-tested, Severe Disablement Allowance was age-restricted, and the Personal Capacity Test replaced the All Works Test.<br><br>ONE Pilot<br>People applying for benefits were given an adviser to discuss work options. Compulsory after 2000. |
| 2000 | WORKSTEP Programme<br>Assists with transition from segregated supported work into mainstream employment. |
| 2001 | Special Educational Needs and Disability Act<br>Extended the provisions of the Disability Discrimination Act to education providers (provisions in force from 2002).<br><br>New Deal for Disabled People National Extension<br>Introduced Job Brokers (public, PVS vocational advisers).<br><br>Jobcentre Plus<br>Services of the Employment Service and the Benefits Agency were combined. |
| 2002 | Tax Credits Act<br>Disabled Persons Tax Credit merged into the Working Tax Credit for all low-paid workers |

(*continued*)

*Table 6.1*   Continued

| | |
|---|---|
| 2002 | Tax Credits Act<br>Permitted Work Rules<br>Allows benefit claimants to undertake paid work for up to 16 hours per week. |
| 2003 | Disability Discrimination Act 1995 (Amendment) Regulations 2003<br>Incorporates the Disability provisions of recent EU Employment Directives,<br>removes small employer exemption. Came into force in October 2004.<br><br>Pathways to Work Pilots<br>'Return-to-work' credit for new claimants leaving Incapacity Benefit, Condition<br>Management Programmes, and mandatory Work Focused Interviews. |
| 2004 | Pathways to Work Extension 1<br>Job Preparation Premium paid to those on Incapacity Benefit undertaking<br>return-to-work activity, extended to Incapacity Benefit claims started in last<br>two years. |
| 2005 | Disability Discrimination Act 2005<br>Extends service provisions to transportation. Definition of disability<br>broadened to cover more people with HIV, cancer, and multiple sclerosis.<br>New duty placed on public authorities to promote equality of opportunity<br>for disabled people.<br><br>Pathways to Work Extension 2<br>Pilot measures extended to cover around one-third of the UK.<br><br>Job Retention and Rehabilitation pilot<br>Examines retention in work comparing employment-focused support and<br>health-based support. |
| 2007 | Welfare Reform Act<br>Announced the phase-out of Incapacity Benefit and introduced the<br>Employment and Support Allowance from 2008 (see Box 6.1). Established<br>Work Capability Assessment to assess entitlement to ESA. |
| 2010 | Equality Act<br>Merged previous anti-discrimination legislation relating to age, disability,<br>gender, race, religion and belief, sexual orientation, and gender<br>reassignment into one piece of legislation. Set up the Equality and Human<br>Rights Commission (which incorporated the Disability Rights Commission<br>among others).<br><br>Comprehensive Spending Review<br>Entitlement to Employment and Support Allowance (Work-related activity<br>premium) restricted to a maximum of 12 months. Abolished the mobility<br>element of Disability Living Allowance for people in residential care.<br><br>Welfare Reform White Paper<br>Outlined plans for a new Universal Working Age benefit to replace<br>Jobseeker's Allowance, Employment and Support Allowance, Income<br>Support, etc. It will be rolled out by 2015. A new 'claimant contract' applies<br>sanctions of 3, 6, and up to 3 years' benefit removal for those benefit<br>recipients who refuse to take up a job offer. |

the DWP published statistics for all completed WCA assessments (October 2008 to November2010): 64% of people were deemed 'fit for work', while one in four people (26%) were moved into the WRAG and the remaining 10% of people were placed in the Support Group. Interestingly, of people who made a claim for ESA between October 2008 and February 2010 and who were found Fit for Work at assessment, 36% have had an appeal heard by Tribunals Service to date (DWP, 2011). The DWP state that in 61% of appeals the original decision was upheld, or in other words 39% of appeals are successful. An independent review of the WCA system has found that 'there are clear and consistent criticisms of the whole system and much negativity surrounding the process' (Harrington, 2010, p. 9). Further, there is currently little empirical evidence to suggest that such attempts to restrict entitlements to welfare benefits will have a positive impact on the employment of people with disabilities and chronic illness.

The Welfare Reform White Paper (*Universal Credit: Welfare that Works*, 11 November 2010) outlined further plans to create a 'simplified' and 'demystified' benefits system with the introduction of a Universal Credit, an integrated working age credit that will replace a range of benefits including ESA (see Table 6.1). It includes a new 'claimant contract', which applies sanctions of up to three years' benefit removal for those recipients who refuse to take up a job offer. It will be rolled out between 2013 and 2015. When discussing these proposals, the Secretary of State for Work and Pensions, Iain Duncan Smith, claimed that 'most people in Britain are honest, straight, and hardworking'. Therefore, the underlying suggestion is that there are people receiving benefits (including those suffering from ill-health or a disability) who are in fact the opposite – dishonest, dodgy, and work shy. Indeed, Prime Minister David Cameron stated that if people 'really cannot work', then they will be looked after. However, it is the insertion of 'really' that belies scepticism about the truth of whether people really can or cannot work. Yet according to Beatty and Fothergill (2002) there is no consistent evidence of a dependency culture among IB recipients. For example, Beatty et al. (2010) found that although only 5% of their respondents were actively looking for work, an additional 30% expressed a desire to return to work. The rest overwhelmingly cited poor health as a major obstacle to finding a job. There was little or no evidence of a 'dependency culture', as is often suggested in the media.

These policy discussions draw on notions of the 'deserving' and 'undeserving' poor, implying that people labelled workless are 'undeserving' if they do not at least seek paid employment, regardless of the quantity, quality, and calibre of work available. On the other hand, the 'deserving' poor are those who are making an effort to find work and see this as their responsibility to society regardless of how fruitless their search might be. The separation of people receiving ESA into either a 'support' or an 'employment' group reinforces such distinctions, with certain types of illness or disability perceived as less deserving of unconditional public support than others (Bambra, 2008; Bambra and Smith, 2010; Bambra, 2011). For Grover and Piggott (2010), ESA is thus effectively a form of 'social sorting', separating people who are sick and/or who have impairments into sub-groups of claimants dependent upon medicalised perceptions of their health and/or impairment. Indeed, the conditionality underpinning the latest reforms signals a clear break with the voluntary nature of previous participation in employment interventions for this group, and thus represents a radical new phase in UK policy towards the employment of people with a disability or health problem, one that could be considered as a move towards making these recipients subject to a form of 'workfare' (Bambra and Smith, 2010; Bambra, 2011).

## Increasing employability or improving health?

This shift to 'workfare' was pre-dated by a more active approach to health-related welfare that emerged in the mid-1990s, so-called 'welfare to work', although for those on health-related benefits participation in such schemes was at this time entirely voluntary. Numerous activation policies and interventions to increase the employment of people in receipt of benefits owing to ill-health or disability were initiated in this period, the chronology of which is detailed in Table 6.1. These policy strategies were directed at either the supply side – enhancing the ability of individuals with a disability or chronic illness to be employed, or the demand side – increasing the desirability to employers of recruiting and retaining this particular group of workers (Bambra, 2006). Supply-side strategies are concerned with increasing the availability and work readiness of individuals with a disability or chronic illness. They are designed to overcome some of the employment barriers that people with a disability or chronic illness face, particularly in terms of lack of skills or work experience, and financial uncertainty about the transition into paid employment (Gardner, 1997). UK supply-side interventions have included:

- **Education, training, and work placement schemes**, which aim to increase employment rates by providing vocational skills, work experience, and exposure to employers, or recognised qualifications. UK examples include: New Deal Innovative Schemes; Work Preparation; Residential Training; Workstep; Permitted Work Rules.
- **Vocational advice and support services**, which are designed to help movement into employment by enhancing job search skills, matching individuals to jobs, arranging access to training and education schemes, offering information about in-work benefits, and providing other forms of individualised vocational advice and support. UK examples include: New Deal Personal Adviser Service and Job Brokers; Work Focused Interviews; Disability Service Teams.

- **Vocational rehabilitation** is a long established form of return-to-work policy in many developed countries. Rehabilitation (both medical and vocational) is particularly used to help people who develop a disability or chronic illness while they are in work retain their employment (Bloch and Prins, 2001). UK examples include: Pathways to Work – Condition Management Programmes; Job Retention and Rehabilitation Pilots; NHS Plus.
- **In-work benefits** aim to increase employment by overcoming the problems and the financial disincentives related to taking low-paid jobs, the loss of future benefit entitlement if they become out of work again, the additional costs of employment such as transport costs, or the financial difficulties that the initial loss of benefits could create. UK examples include: Working Tax Credit; Travel to Work; Job Grant (Job Finder's Grant); Back to Work Bonus; 52-week linking rule; Extended Payment of Council Tax Benefit; Extended Payment of Housing Benefit; Help with prescription costs; Pathways to Work – Return to Work credit.

Demand-side interventions focus on increasing the demand for disabled workers among employers. They tend to focus on reducing the costs or risks to employers of employing a disabled person or placing requirements on employers in their recruitment and retention of disabled people (Bambra, 2006). They are attempts to combat the other type of employment barriers faced by people with a disability: employer uncertainty and the physical difficulties of workplaces (Gardner, 1997). In the UK there have been three demand-side approaches in recent decades:

- **Financial incentives for employers** aim to encourage recruitment by offering wage subsidies to cover the initial costs of employment or to compensate for any reduced productivity associated with employing someone with a disability or chronic illness. UK examples include: Job Introduction Scheme; Work Trial; Employment on Trial.
- **Employment rights legislation** such as the Disability Discrimination Act (1995) to increase the employment of people with a recognised disability. Since 2006, all EU member states are obliged to have such legislation (OECD, 2009).
- **Accessibility interventions** are designed to facilitate employment by reducing physical workplace barriers, for instance by providing specialist ergonomic equipment, for people with a disability or chronic illness. The main UK example is Access to Work.

Various evaluations have examined the effectiveness of these 'welfare to work' interventions on employment rates in the UK (Bambra et al., 2005; Bambra, 2006; Clayton et al., 2011). With regard to supply-side interventions, the evidence suggests that vocational advice and employment and training interventions have positive impacts on employment rates ranging from 11% to 50% depending on the characteristics of participants, such as 'job-readiness' or type of illness, as well as the local labour market context (Bambra et al., 2005). However, the vast majority of evaluations were uncontrolled, and it was therefore impossible to determine if the improved employment chances were due to the effectiveness of the welfare to work interventions themselves, self-selection of the most employable onto the initiatives, or to external factors such as a general upturn in UK employment rates. There is little evidence that in-work benefits were effective in increasing employment (Bambra, 2006).

In terms of demand-side interventions, the UK evidence base suggests that such interventions have a very limited impact on the employment of people with a disability or chronic illness. For example, financial interventions designed to incentivise employers were ineffective because they did not adequately offset the perceived risks and costs of employing a disabled person (Bambra, 2006). The employment rights approach was similarly found to be ineffective in increasing the employment rates of people with a disability or chronic illness. The UK evidence suggests that the legislation had no effect on employers' recruitment decisions (with the majority of employers unaware of its employment provisions) (Roberts et al., 2004), and that the employment gap between those with and without a health condition or disability actually increased after the introduction of the Disability Discrimination Act (Pope and Bambra, 2005). Of the demand-side interventions, only accessibility interventions appear to have a more positive employment impact (Hillage et al., 1998; Beinart et al., 1996).

A strong factor behind the rather limited success of these active labour market policies for this particular group of workless people is that they focus almost exclusively on employability. There is little attention to the health needs of this population, who, after all, are workless in the first place as a result of ill-health. Recognising the importance of sickness as a barrier to employment would result in more innovative 'health first' approaches. While such medical and psychosocial rehabilitation has been a common feature of interventions in the Nordic countries, more recently it is beginning to be applied in the UK. For example, recent international evidence-based guidance produced by England's National Institute for Health and Clinical Excellence (NICE, 2009) has recommended a 'health first' case management approach to improving the health and employment of people with a chronic illness. NICE guidance on managing long-term sickness absence and incapacity for work recommends that integrated programmes that combine traditional vocational training approaches, financial support, and health management on an ongoing case management basis should be commissioned to help IB recipients enter or return to work. NICE considers these integrated approaches to be the most effective ways of enhancing the employment of people who are workless owing to ill-health (Gabbay et al., 2011).

One example of a service with more of an emphasis on addressing health prior to employment was the Condition Management Programme. This was provided by Primary Health Care Trusts and Jobcentre Plus as part of the Pathways to Work programme before its withdrawal.

## Health and incapacity

Beyond Beatty et al.'s (2000) notion of 'hidden unemployment', research has shown clearly that people receiving IB face very real and considerable health problems. For example, surveys have consistently found that IB claimants tend to have left their previous employment owing to sickness, and see health problems as a key barrier to work (Beatty and Fothergill, 2002, 2005; Beatty et al., 2009, 2010; Green and Shuttleworth, 2010). Similarly, Kemp and Davidson (2010) found that they had twice as many health conditions affecting their everyday activities as other 'work-ready' benefit recipients. In addition, there is clear epidemiological evidence from the Whitehall cohort studies to suggest that medically certified sickness absence reflects actual morbidity and mortality (Marmot et al., 1995; Kivimaki et al., 2003; Vahtera et al., 2004). This is supported by spatial epidemiology, which has found a strong area-level relationship between IB claims, limiting long-term illness and mortality (Bambra and Norman, 2006; Norman and Bambra, 2007). However, until now, there has been no in-depth survey of the health of the IB population.

In 2009, as part of a larger project commissioned by County Durham and Darlington Primary Care Trust, we started a longitudinal survey of the health of a representative sample of long-term IB recipients in North East England. Participants were recruited to the health survey on a face-to-face basis at a series of IB 'Choices' events run by the South of the Tyne Jobcentre Plus (covering South Tyneside, Sunderland, and County Durham). These events were designed to inform long-term IB recipients of employability courses, schemes, and services available to them in the local area. Between September 2009 and June 2010, Jobcentre Plus invited all eligible long-term IB recipients (IB receipt of over three years) in the region to 28 of these events. The events therefore offered a consistent and representative sampling frame for the survey in that all of those eligible within a given postcode area were invited to the event. Of the 8,858 individuals invited to the events 1,429 attended (16.1%). Of these 1,429, a total of 229 (16.0%) participated in the health survey. Below we describe the baseline measures of this cross-section of long-term IB recipients.

Participants provided demographic and socio-economic data about themselves and their household, as well as their social capital and work history. These questions mirrored those used in large-scale continuous surveys such as the General Household Survey (GHS) and British Household Panel Survey (BHPS). Participants were asked to outline their health conditions, health care use, and their health-related behaviours (alcohol and tobacco use). They were also asked to answer four short validated health questionnaires: EuroQol's (EQ-5D); Quality Metric's Short Form 8 (SF-8); Hospital Anxiety and Depression Scale (HADS); and the Nordic Musculoskeletal Questionnaire (see Box 6.1). EQ-5D is a two-part general measure of health and well being. SF-8 is also a general measure of health and wellbeing (a shortened version of the SF-36) with a physical and a mental scale. HADS is a well-validated measure of mental health, and the Nordic Musculoskeletal Questionnaire a well-validated measure of musculoskeletal (MSK) pain. The latter two condition-specific measures were included as they reflect the two largest clinical reasons for IB receipt in the UK. (Further information explaining these validated measures can be found below in Box 6.1.)

## Box 6.1  Detailed description of health measures used in survey of IB recipients

### EuroQol (ED-5D)

Two parts: a questionnaire and a 'Health Thermometer'. The EQ-5D questionnaire asks participants about their mobility, ability to self-care, their ability to carry out their usual activities, pain and discomfort, and anxiety and depression on the day when they are interviewed. The responses are converted to a value between 0 and 1. The higher the value is the better the health state. The second element is the Visual Analogue Scale, often known as a 'Health Thermometer' after the show card that is used. Participants are asked to rate their health on the day they are interviewed on a scale of 0 to100; 0 represents the worst health state the participant can imagine, 100 represents the best health state they can imagine, with 50 representing the midpoint.

### Hospital Anxiety and Depression Scale (HADS)

There are two parts: HADS-A (Anxiety) and HADS-D (Depression). Both ask participants to choose options that best describe how they are feeling. Both generate a score between 0 and 21. A higher score indicates a higher degree of Depression.

### Quality Metric Short Form 8(SF-8)

SF-8 is a measure of health that produces a physical health score (PCS) and a mental health score (MCS). Participants are asked 8 questions about their health during the past four weeks. These generate two scores, both between 0 and 100: the higher the score the better the health state.

---

### Nordic Musculoskeletal Questionnaire

There are three elements: Nordic 1 is a measure of musculoskeletal problems over the preceding 12 months, and Nordic 2 over the preceding 7 days. In both, participants are asked whether they have had problems with different areas of the body. The measures produce a score of between 0 (no problem) areas and 9 (nine problem areas). Nordic 3 asks whether the musculoskeletal problems have prevented the individual carrying out what they regard as normal activities over the preceding 12 months. Participants are asked whether different areas of the body have prevented them functioning. The measure produces a score between 0 (no problem) areas and 9 (nine problem areas)

---

Demographically, the cohort was 50.2% male and 49.8% female. In February 2010, the comparable national figures were 59% and 41% respectively (DWP, 2010) (2). The group had with a mean age of 48.8 years (range 19 to 63). The median age was 51 and the mode (most commonly occurring figure) was 54. Some 29% of the participants were aged 45 or under; in February 2010 the comparable national figure was 37% (DWP, 2010). In terms of marital status, 46.7 % of the survey population were married, 27.5% divorced and 19.2% single. In terms of socio-economic variables, renting was the most common form of housing tenure (57.6%), with the vast majority (85.3%) living in social housing. In terms of transport, 42.4% had no access to a vehicle (compared to the regional average of 34% and the national average of 25%; ONS (2010). The majority of participants previously worked in semi-skilled (32.43%) or unskilled (33.3%) jobs, with only 3.19% having a professional occupational background.

Nearly two-thirds of participants lived in households in which no one worked (65.1%). The average time spent on IB for the 229 participants was 107.51 months – approximately nine years. If we look at the distribution more closely, the median time on IB is 96 months, around eight years, and the mode is 120 months, or ten years. This confirms the long-term nature of benefit receipt among the survey population. If we look at February 2010 national figures for the duration of IB claims, we find that 89.4% of those receiving the benefit had been doing so for more than two years and 64% had been doing so for more than five years (DWP, 2010).

Musculoskeletal problems were the largest category of self-reported health problems, with almost half (49.55%) of participants identifying this as their primary health problem (in February 2010, the comparable national figure was 22.48% (DWP, 2010) (2)). Mental health was the primary health issue for around a quarter (23.87%) (national figure 49.58%). Other primary problems reported included: digestive/gastric issues (10.36%) (national figure

7.68%), cardiovascular problems (9.46%) (national figure 5.23%), and respiratory problems (2.25%) (national figure 2.07%). The comparison with the national figures for February 2010 (DWP, 2010) (2) would suggest that those with mental health issues are underrepresented in our sample, and those with musculoskeletal conditions are overrepresented. This could be a result of the sampling frame, suggesting that people with mental health issues were less likely to attend the non-compulsory IB Choices event and this led to them being underrepresented in the survey.

Over half, 58.6%, of participants identified themselves as having multiple health problems (three or more); 36.2% of those surveyed were smokers (compared to the England and Wales average of 21%); 47.6% of people reported that they consumed alcohol, with a mean consumption of 18.6 units per week (this is comparable to the regional average of 14.4 units per week and the national average of 11.9 units); 79.9% of the participants had seen a health professional of some kind in the 30 days prior to interview. Table 6.2 provides a detailed summary of all the participants' characteristics.

In terms of the validated health measures, the IB participants surveyed had a consistently lower state of health than the normal population. In terms of the EQ-5D measure, the survey group had a mean score of 0.41 compared to the UK population norm score of 0.86 (Kind, Hardman, and Macran, 1999). The health thermometer (EQ5D–VAS) scores show the group had a mean score of 46.45, compared to the UK population norm score of 82.48 (Kind, Hardman, and Macran, 1999). The mean HADS-A scores of the participants were 10.54 (compared to a UK population norm of 6.14; Crawford et al., 2001). The mean HADS-D score was 8.85 (the UK population norm is 3.68; Crawfordet al., 2001). Those surveyed had a mean SF8 MCS score of 36.9 (compared to a UK population norm score for SF12 MCS from which SF8 MCS is derived of 52.1; Gandeket al., 1998). The mean SF8 PCS score was 33.2 (compared to the UK population norm score for SF12 PCS from which SF8 PCS is derived of 50.9;Gandeket al., 1998). The Nordic Musculoskeletal Questionnaires showed that participants had a mean Nordic 1 score of 5.2, a Nordic 2 score of 4.3, and a Nordic 3 score of 4.0. See Table 6.3 and Box 6.1 for a detailed explanation of these measures.

This cross-sectional health survey reveals in some detail the severity of the ill-health experienced by long-term IB recipients. It shows that return to work for long-term IB and ESA recipients is not simply a matter of forcing the 'undeserving' and 'work shy' off benefits. Recipients will require substantial support and health improvement to make these transitions. This will also require the right sort of jobs to be available for them too. This is often not the case, as the demand for semi-skilled and unskilled workers has dramatically declined in the labour market of the North East of England and other post-industrial areas over the last 30years. Returning to the labour market is only one part of the issue; interventions also need to consider how

*Table 6.2* Characteristics of survey participants (number of participants = 229)

|  |  | Frequency |
| --- | --- | --- |
| Gender |  |  |
| Male | 50.2% | 115 |
| Female | 49.8% | 114 |
| Age |  |  |
| Mean (years) | 48.8 |  |
| Median (years) | 51 |  |
| Mode (years) | 54 |  |
| Range (years) | 19–63 |  |
| 45 years and under | 29% | 65 |
| Over 45 | 71% | 104 |
| Marital status |  |  |
| Married | 47.6% | 107 |
| Divorced | 27.5% | 63 |
| Single | 19.2% | 44 |
| Tenure |  |  |
| Renting | 57.6% | 132 |
| Renting (Social housing) | 85.3% | 116 |
| Transport |  |  |
| No access to a motor vehicle | 42.4% | 97 |
| Last job skill type |  |  |
| Professional | 3.2% | 7 |
| Intermediate | 9.0% | 20 |
| Skilled non-manual | 7.2% | 16 |
| Skilled manual | 14.9% | 33 |
| Semi-skilled | 32.4% | 72 |
| Unskilled | 33.3% | 74 |
| Workless households | 65.1% | 149 |
| Time spent on IB/ESA |  |  |
| Mean (months) | 108 |  |
| Mode (months) | 120 |  |
| Primary health problem |  |  |
| Musculoskeletal | 49.6% | 110 |
| Mental health | 23.9% | 53 |
| Digestive/gastric | 10.4% | 23 |
| Cardiovascular | 9.5% | 21 |
| Respiratory | 2.3% | 5 |
| Other | 4.5% | 10 |
| Multiple (3 or more) health problems | 58.6% | 130 |
| Seen health practitioner in past 30 days | 78.9% | 183 |
| Smoking and drinking |  |  |
| Regular smokers | 36.2% | 83 |
| Drink alcohol | 47.6% | 109 |
| Average units per week consumed | 14.4 units |  |

*Table 6.3* Validated health measures – IB survey versus UK population norms

| Validated measure | IB survey | UK population |
|---|---|---|
| EQ5D | 41 | 86 |
| EQ5D-VAS | 46.45 | 82.48 |
| HADS-A | 10.54 | 6.14 |
| HADS-D | 8.85 | 3.68 |
| SF8-MCS | 36.9 | 52.1 |
| SF8-PCS | 33.2 | 50.9 |

employment can be sustained. The nature of many of the health conditions suffered by those in receipt of IB and ESA means that they have bouts of poor health where they cannot function followed by periods of remission. Consequently finding – or incentivising – employers who will take account of such ongoing health problems and make appropriate allowances is essential. Above all, the survey shows that if return-to-work interventions are to have an impact on the health and employability of this group they must understand that the individuals concerned often face complex and multiple barriers and that ill-health is the major one.

## Conclusion

Recent welfare reforms with their focus on employability are not based on robust evidence of 'what works' but on an ideological view that those in receipt of IB are 'work shy' rather than chronically ill. This is in contrast to the research evidence outlined in this chapter, which shows that people in receipt of IB have multiple and complicated health needs. If welfare reform is actually about getting people into work (rather than just cutting expenditure, shrinking the state, and stigmatising the poor) then improving health is the most important first step in this process. A process that requires an intelligent and integrated approach which will also consider and appropriately address issues such as the local economic conditions and demand for labour, as well as employability initiatives that provide retraining and how return to work can be sustained. Such a process would need to consider how to support not only employees but also employers. However, what is clear is that if health is not prioritised and addressed in a meaningful manner any process aimed at returning those in receipt of IB to the workplace will be fatally flawed.

Currently though, health is not at the top of the agenda. In recent welfare reform discourse, there has been very little mention of illness or of the potential role of health professionals in the process of return-to-work. This is despite the fact that the available research evidence suggests that a 'health first' approach to welfare reform is potentially the most effective (NICE,

2009). Clearly abandoning millions of people in deprived communities in the North East of England and elsewhere to a life on benefits is not desirable, but for welfare reform to be effective it needs to be considered outside the ideological box of expenditure cuts and the presumption of welfare 'dependency', and to be actively based on the available research evidence. This clearly shows that improving the health of IB recipients and involving health professionals (potentially via case management techniques) holds the key to successful social inclusion and a healthy return to work.

## Acknowledgements

The health survey is funded as part of a larger project supported by County Durham and Darlington Primary Care Trust (Principal Investigator C. Bambra, co-investigators, M. Booth and J. Mason). The views expressed in the publication are those of the authors and not necessarily those of the funders. We would also like to acknowledge the data collection work of J. Briggs and K. Ridley, and the ethics support from R. Perrett.

## References

Bambra, C. (2006) 'The Influence of Government Programmes and Pilots on the Employment of Disabled Workers' in K. Needels and B. Schmitz (eds) *Economic and Social Costs and Benefits to Employers for Retaining, Recruiting and Employing Disabled People and/or People with Health Conditions or an Injury: A Review of the Evidence* (London: DWP).

Bambra, C. (2008) 'In Sickness or in Health? Incapacity Benefit Reform and the Politics of Ill Health', *British Medical Journal*, 337, 517.

Bambra, C. (2011) *Work, Worklessness and the Political Economy of Health* (Oxford: Oxford University Press).

Bambra, C. and Smith, K.E. (2010) 'No Longer Deserving? Sickness Benefit Reform and the Politics of (Ill) Health', *Critical Public Health*, 20 (1), 71–83.

Bambra, C. and Norman, P. (2006) 'What is the Association Between Sickness Absence, Mortality and Morbidity?', *Health and Place*, 12 (4), 728–733.

Bambra, C., Whitehead, M., and Hamilton, V. (2005) 'Does "Welfare to Work" Work? A Systematic Review of the Effectiveness of the UK's Welfare to Work Programmes for People with a Chronic Illness or Disability', *Social Science and Medicine*, 60 (9), 1905–1918.

Beatty, C. and Fothergill, S. (2002) 'Hidden Unemployment among Men: A Case Study', *Regional Studies*, 36 (8), 811–823.

Beatty, C. and Fothergill, S. (2005) 'The Diversion from Unemployment to Sickness across British Regions and Districts', *Regional Studies*, 39 (7), 837–854.

Beatty, C., Fothergill, S., and Macmillan, R. (2000) 'A Theory of Employment, Unemployment and Sickness', *Regional Studies*, 34 (7), 617–630.

Beatty, C., Fothergill, S., Houston, D., Powell, R., and Sissons, P. (2009) 'A Gendered Theory of Employment, Unemployment and Sickness', *Environment and Planning C: Government and Policy*, 27 (6), 958–974.

Beatty, C., Fothergill, S., Houston, D., Powell, R., and Sissons, P. (2010) 'Bringing Incapacity Benefit Numbers Down: To What Extent Do Women Need a Different Approach?', *Policy Studies*, 31 (2), 143–162.

Beinart, S., Smith, P., and Sproston, K. (1996) *The Access to Work Programme – A Survey of Recipients, Employers, Employment Service Managers and Staff* (London: Social and Community Planning Research).

Bloch, F. and Prins, R. (2001) *Who Returns to Work and Why?* (London: Transaction).

Clayton, S., Bambra, C., Gosling, R., Povall, S., Misso, K., and Whitehead, M. (2011) 'Assembling the Evidence Jigsaw: Insights from a Systematic Review of UK Studies of Individual-Focused Return to Work Initiatives for Disabled and Long-Term Ill People', *BioMed Central*, 11, 170.

Crawford, J.R., Henry, J.D., Crombie, C., and Taylor, E.P. (2001) 'Normative Data for the HADS from a Large Non-clinical Sample', *British Journal of Clinical Psychology*, 40 (4), 429–434.

DWP (2010) *Universal Credit: Welfare That Works* (London: DWP).

DWP (2011) *Employment and Support Allowance: Work Capability Assessment by Health Condition and Functional Impairment, Official Statistics, April 2011* (London: DWP).

Gabbay, M., Taylor, L., Sheppard, L., Hillage, J., Bambra, C., Ford F. et al. (2011) 'NICE's Guidance on Long-Term Sickness and Incapacity', *British Journal of General Practice*, 61, 118–124.

Gandek, B., Ware, J., Aaronson, N., Apolone, G., Bjorner, J., Brazier, J., Bullinger, M., Kaasa, S., Leplege, A., Prieto, L., and Sullivan, M. (1998) 'Cross-validation of Item Selection and Scoring for the SF-12 Health Survey in Nine Countries: Results from the IQOLA Project', *Journal of Clinical Epidemiology*, 51 (11), 1171–1178.

Gardiner, K. (1997) *Bridges from Benefit to Work* (York: Joseph Rowntree Foundation).

Goldstone, C. and Meager, N. (2002) *Barriers to Employment for Disabled People* (London: DWP).

Green, A. and Shuttleworth, I. (2010) 'Local Differences, Perceptions and Incapacity Benefit Claimants: Implications for Policy Delivery', *Policy Studies*, 31 (2), 223–243.

Grover, C. and Piggott, L. (2010) 'From Incapacity Benefit to Employment and Support Allowance: Social Sorting, Sickness and Impairment, and Social Security', *Policy Studies*, 31 (2), 265–282.

Harrington, M. (2010) *An Independent Review of the Work Capability Assessment* (London: TSO).

Hillage, J., Williams, M., and Pollard, E. (1998) *Evaluation of Access to Work* (Brighton: Institute for Employment Studies).

Kemp, P. and Davidson, J. (2010) 'Employability Trajectories among New Claimants of Incapacity Benefit', *Policy Studies*, 31 (2), 203–221.

Kind, P., Hardman, G., and Macran, S. (1999) *Population Norms for EQ5D*. York University.http://www.york.ac.uk/media/che/documents/papers/discussionpapers/CHE%20Discussion%20Paper%20172.pdf.

Kivimaki, M., Head, J., Ferrie, J., Shipley, M., Vahtera, J., and Marmot, M. (2003) 'Sickness Absence as a Global Measure of Health: Evidence from Mortality in the Whitehall II Prospective Cohort Study', *British Medical Journal*, 327, 364–370.

Marmot, M., Feeney, A., Shipley, M., North, F., and Syme, S.L. (1995) 'Sickness Absence as a Measure of Health Status and Functioning: From the UK Whitehall II Study', *Journal of Epidemiology and Community Health*, 49, 124–130.

NICE (National Institute for Health and Clinical Excellence) (2009) *Public Health Guidance 19: Managing Long-Term Sickness Absence and Incapacity for Work* (London: NICE).

Norman, P. and Bambra, C. (2007) 'Incapacity or Unemployment? The Utility of an Administrative Data Source as an Updatable Indicator of Population Health', *Population, Space and Place*, 13, 333–352.

OECD (Organisation for Economic Cooperation and Development) (2009) *Sickness, Disability and Work: Background Paper* (Paris: OECD).

Office for National Statistics (2010) *Regional Trends Online*, released 8 December 2010, http://www.statistics.gov.uk/downloads/theme_compendia/RegionalSnapshot/directory.pdff (Accessed June 2011).

Pope, D. and Bambra, C. (2005) 'Has the Disability Discrimination Act Closed the Employment Gap?', *Disability and Rehabilitation*, 27, 1261–1266.

Roberts, S., Heaver, C., Hill, K., Rennison, J., Staffors, B., and Howat, N. et al. (2004) *Disability in the Workplace: Employers' and Service Providers' Responses to the Disability Discrimination Act in 2003 and Preparations for the 2004 Changes* (London: DWP).

Vahtera, J., Pentti, J., and Kivimaki, M. (2004) 'Sickness Absence as a Predictor of Mortality among Male and Female Employees', *Journal of Epidemiology and Community Health*, 58, 321–326.

# 7

# The Interaction of Health, Labour Market Conditions, and Long-Term Sickness Benefit Claims in a Post-industrial City: A Glasgow Case Study

*David Webster, Judith Brown, Ewan B. Macdonald, and Ivan Turok*

## Introduction

Glasgow offers a classic example of a local economy of Northern Britain (Rowthorn, 2010), a former industrial city that has lost a huge amount of industrial employment since the 1970s and is still in the process of recovery, with relatively modest service sector expansion and particular reliance on public service jobs. Like other such areas, it has had a very high level of long-term sickness and consequent dependency on sickness-related benefits. In fact it has a higher level of long-term sickness benefit claimants as a proportion of the working age population (12.3%) than any other British big city – even though this level is much lower than it was. With 50,960 such claimants in February 2011, it also has the second largest number of all local authority areas in the UK, after Birmingham (Beatty and Fothergill, 2011). Such a high level of sickness benefit claims is a not only a major fiscal issue but is also generally agreed to reflect an unacceptably low level of well-being in the local population. For these reasons, Glasgow's experience is particularly worth studying.

A series of papers have already provided a foundation for detailed analysis of long-term sickness benefit claims in Glasgow (Brown et al., 2008; Brown et al., 2009; Webster et al., 2010). The most recent of these presented a case study of the rise and fall of Incapacity Benefit (IB) claims in Glasgow. Citing evidence from the Scottish Census, it argued that the city's high rate of claims emerged after the 1970s and was mainly a consequence of its rapid deindustrialisation. Using the detailed data available for the period 1995–2008, it showed that there was no substantial reduction in the level of claims until 2003, when a rapid fall began, which continued for five years. The chapter concluded that this very large reduction in claims was probably due to a strengthening labour market rather than to national policy changes or local programmes. This conclusion has since been supported by another author (McVicar, forthcoming).

However, the chapter was able to consider only very limited evidence on changes in population health that might have contributed to the changes in levels of claims. The main purpose of the present chapter is to consider such evidence, in the form of the Scottish Health Survey (SHeS). The chapter takes advantage of what appears to be an unprecedented opportunity offered by the fact that SHeS has a large enough sample to permit separate analysis for Glasgow. In addition, the earlier paper took the story only to the very beginning of the economic recession that hit the labour market from 2008, and was not able to cover the controversial Employment and Support Allowance (ESA), introduced in October of that year, which has a much stronger focus on claimants' health conditions. This chapter considers the performance of the whole long-term sickness benefit system in Glasgow up to May 2011.

In considering evidence both on population health and on the labour market, this chapter offers the prospect of helping to bridge the gap between what have hitherto been two largely separate literatures (Bambra, 2011, Chapters 5 and 6). One of these has stressed labour market processes, focusing on evidence that a high proportion of people claiming long-term sickness benefits in areas of high unemployment are really 'hidden unemployed'. The other literature has stressed health issues, focusing on evidence that prolonged high levels of unemployment worsen population health, leading to a vicious circle of worklessness, worsened health, and lower 'employability'.

The chapter is laid out as follows. The next section sets out the changes in the level of long-term sickness benefit claims in Glasgow since the late 1990s in the context of the national and local labour markets and examines how they are related to changes in on-flows to and off-flows from benefits. The impact of the 'Work Capability Assessment' (WCA) introduced as part of the new ESA regime is also considered. The third section introduces evidence from the SHeSs of 1995, 1998, 2003, and 2008/2009 and presents time series and cross-section comparisons between Glasgow and the rest of Scotland. The fourth section concludes, with a discussion of the interpretation of the findings.

As time has gone on, more official statistics have become available at local authority level. In this chapter, time series for Glasgow always start as early as possible, and this gives a range of starting dates, from 1992 to 1999. Throughout the chapter, the population considered is people of working age, defined as 16–64 for men and 16–59 for women except where otherwise stated. Women's 'working age' for purposes of social security benefits began to rise from May 2010 onwards to reflect raising of their pension age in steps from 60 to 65, but this change has no significant impact in the period considered here. Wherever possible, the figures presented combine all three long-term sickness benefits that have been in operation during the period considered. These are IB (for which new claims ceased in October 2008), Severe Disablement Allowance (SDA) (for which new claims ceased in April 2001), and ESA (which commenced in October 2008).

## Long-term sickness benefit claims in Glasgow since the 1990s and the labour market context

Figure 7.1 shows the path of the stock of working age long-term sickness benefit claimants (IB plus SDA plus ESA) in Glasgow, the rest of Scotland and Great Britain since 1997, expressed as a percentage of the working age population. Great Britain and Scotland excluding Glasgow have behaved quite similarly. They have had similar levels of claims, both have had plateaus from the mid-1990s up to 2003, and both have seen modest falls of 1–2 percentage points thereafter. Glasgow's experience has been remarkable by comparison. The city has had a much higher level of claims, with an excess over Great Britain of 11.4 percentage points in 1997. However, it then saw a very slight fall from late 2000 followed by a rapid decline from 2003 onwards, so that by 2008 the excess over Great Britain had been reduced to only 6 percentage points. Whereas in the 1990s Glasgow had close to three times the Great Britain level of claims, now it has less than double. But since the middle of 2008, the rate of decline has markedly slowed, and

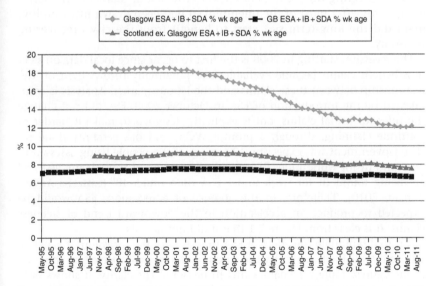

*Figure 7.1* Glasgow, Scotland excl. Glasgow, GB: Total long-term sickness benefit claimants (IB + SDA + ESA) as percentage of working age population
*Source*: DWP Tabtool. ESA from WLPS 100% data; IB and SDA from 5% sample data.

in the latest four quarters there has been no decline at all in Glasgow, although a modest decline has continued in the rest of Scotland and Great Britain.

The labour market indicators in Figures 7.2 and 7.3 broadly mirror the changes in long-term sickness benefit claims. Once again, Great Britain and Scotland excluding Glasgow have performed similarly. In Glasgow, there was a striking long rise in the employment rate of about 13 percentage points, from around 56% in 1998 to about 69% (on the old definition of 'working age') in 2007, bringing the gap compared to Great Britain down from 15 percentage points in 1994 to only 6 percentage points in 2007. Likewise, Glasgow's ILO unemployment rate fell from about 15% in 1994 to 6% in 2007, reducing the gap compared to Great Britain from 6 percentage points to a single percentage point. Those claiming unemployment benefits in Glasgow also showed a big fall, from 12% in 1992 to just over 3% in 2007, with the gap compared to Great Britain narrowing from 4 percentage points to little over 1 percentage point in 2007.

It was primarily this strongly parallel movement in the figures for long-term sickness benefit claimants and for employment and unemployment that led to the conclusion by Webster et al. (2010) that labour market improvement was probably the main explanation for the fall in IB/SDA claims from 2003 to 2008. The fact that the fall in sickness benefit claimants lagged behind the fall in unemployed people could be seen as reflecting the greater closeness to the labour market of the latter group; only after most of the unemployed had been drawn into employment did the long-term sick start to benefit from the city's recovering economy.

The recession starting in 2008 is the first to occur since local data on sickness benefit claims became available, and potentially throws light on the relationship between these claims and the labour market. Analysis is complicated by the introduction of ESA in October 2008. ESA did not change the rules for initial claims, but is explicitly designed to make it harder to continue claiming, through a prompt WCA, and has certainly done so. 'The Government was expecting 12% more of the people being assessed to be found fit for work under ESA. In fact 32% more of those being assessed are being found fit for work under ESA than under IB' (Citizens Advice Bureau, 2010). Therefore, in the absence of a recession, ESA would be expected to produce an acceleration in the downward trend of sickness claims. It is clear from Figure 7.1 that it did not do this.

But to disentangle the effect of ESA from that of the recession, it is necessary to establish when exactly the stricter ESA regime impacted on the total claim figures. Table 7.1 enables this to be done. For clarity, it shows only Glasgow, but the pattern for Great Britain and for the rest of Scotland is similar. In relation to on-flows, ESA had taken over almost completely from IB, and at a similar level, by February 2009. But in relation to exits, ESA did not build up to its current level until November 2009. Therefore the levelling-off

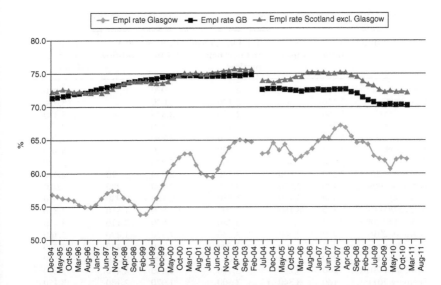

*Figure 7.2* Glasgow, Scotland excl. Glasgow, GB: Employment rate, working age
*Source*: LFS/APS (Nomis), four-quarter averages. Up to 2003, working age is 16–64/59; thereafter 16–64.

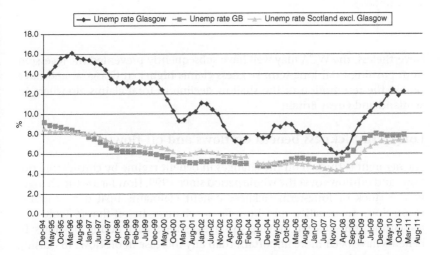

*Figure 7.3* Glasgow, Scotland excl. Glasgow, GB: Unemployment rate, working age
*Source*: LFS/APS (Nomis), four-quarter averages. Up to 2003, working age is 16–64/59; thereafter 16–64.

in the stock of total long-term sickness claimants from August 2008 cannot have been due to the WCA introduced with ESA. Instead, it is likely to have been due to the recession. This pattern is consistent with the view that the labour market is the main influence on the level of sickness benefit claims.

*Table 7.1*   Glasgow: IB/SDA and ESA on-flows and off-flows, 2007–2011

| Quarter ending | IB on-flow | ESA on-flow | Total long-term sickness benefit on-flow | IB/SDA off-flow | ESA off-flow | Total long-term sickness benefit off-flow |
|---|---|---|---|---|---|---|
| February 2007 | 2,730 | – | 2,730 | 3,070 | – | 3,070 |
| May 2007 | 2,770 | – | 2,770 | 3,030 | – | 3,030 |
| August 2007 | 2,980 | – | 2,980 | 3,330 | – | 3,330 |
| November 2007 | 2,780 | – | 2,780 | 3,230 | – | 3,230 |
| February 2008 | 2,780 | – | 2,780 | 3,250 | – | 3,250 |
| May 2008 | 2,850 | – | 2,850 | 3,460 | – | 3,460 |
| August 2008 | 3,100 | – | 3,100 | 2,920 | – | 2,920 |
| November 2008 | 2,260 | 970 | 3,230 | 2,950 | 10 | 2,960 |
| February 2009 | 430 | 2,620 | 3,050 | 2,740 | 280 | 3,020 |
| May 2009 | 360 | 3,170 | 3,530 | 2,100 | 930 | 3,030 |
| August 2009 | 320 | 3,180 | 3,500 | 1,870 | 1,510 | 3,380 |
| November 2009 | 250 | 3,010 | 3,260 | 1,820 | 2,110 | 3,930 |
| February 2010 | 270 | 2,960 | 3,230 | 1,470 | 1,890 | 3,360 |
| May 2010 | 300 | 3,200 | 3,500 | 1,150 | 2,440 | 3,590 |
| August 2010 | 280 | 3,200 | 3,480 | 1,180 | 2,710 | 3,890 |
| November 2010 | 200 | 3,280 | 3,480 | 1,200 | 2,410 | 3,610 |
| February 2011 | 160 | 3,340 | 3,500 | 1,020 | 2,130 | 3,150 |
| May 2011 | 130 | 3,300 | 3,430 | 810 | 2,320 | 3,130 |

*Note*: Rounded numbers of claimants.
*Source*: DWP Tabtool.

Nevertheless, the WCA may well have subsequently prevented the recession from pushing total long-term sickness claims higher in Glasgow, and have caused the resumption of the shallow decline in total claims elsewhere in Scotland and Great Britain.

## Long-term sickness benefit on-flows and off-flows

Further light is thrown on the changes in benefit regime by considering on-flows and off-flows over the whole period since 1999. How far are the changes in the stock of long-term sickness benefit claimants related to changes in on-flows to benefits, and how far to changes in off-flows? Table 7.2, presenting four-quarter moving averages, shows that falling on-flows to benefits have been more important than any increase in off-flows in causing the stock of claimants to fall, especially in Glasgow, where a striking excess of off-flows over on-flows opened up in the years 2003 to 2008. However, rising off-flows did also make a contribution, in the form of an increase in off-flows *as a proportion of existing claimants*. In Glasgow, these off-flows rose from under 5.0% per quarter in 2000 to over 6.0% by 2008 and over 7.0% in 2011. This was a bigger rise than in Great Britain, where off-flows rose from around 5.5% in 2000 to 6.0% by 2008 and just under 7.0% in 2011. As

*Table 7.2* Glasgow and GB: Total long-term sickness benefit on-flows and off-flows (IB + SDA + ESA) 2000–2011

| Quarter ending | GLASGOW | | | GB | | |
|---|---|---|---|---|---|---|
| | On-flow | Off-flow | Net on-flow | On-flow | Off-flow | Net on-flow |
| February 2001 | 1.02 | 0.87 | 0.15 | 0.49 | 0.40 | 0.09 |
| February 2002 | 1.01 | 0.97 | 0.04 | 0.48 | 0.42 | 0.05 |
| February 2003 | 0.97 | 0.94 | 0.03 | 0.47 | 0.42 | 0.06 |
| February 2004 | 0.91 | 0.92 | −0.01 | 0.46 | 0.41 | 0.05 |
| February 2005 | 0.81 | 0.86 | −0.04 | 0.43 | 0.40 | 0.02 |
| February 2006 | 0.76 | 0.90 | −0.14 | 0.39 | 0.39 | 0.01 |
| February 2007 | 0.76 | 0.81 | −0.06 | 0.40 | 0.39 | 0.01 |
| February 2008 | 0.73 | 0.85 | −0.12 | 0.39 | 0.40 | 0.00 |
| May 2008 | 0.74 | 0.82 | −0.09 | 0.39 | 0.40 | −0.01 |
| August 2008 | 0.76 | 0.80 | −0.04 | 0.40 | 0.40 | 0.00 |
| November 2008 | 0.78 | 0.79 | −0.01 | 0.42 | 0.40 | 0.02 |
| February 2009 | 0.82 | 0.76 | 0.06 | 0.44 | 0.40 | 0.04 |
| May 2009 | 0.84 | 0.78 | 0.06 | 0.46 | 0.40 | 0.05 |
| August 2009 | 0.84 | 0.84 | 0.00 | 0.46 | 0.43 | 0.03 |
| November 2009 | 0.85 | 0.86 | −0.01 | 0.46 | 0.43 | 0.03 |
| February 2010 | 0.85 | 0.89 | −0.05 | 0.46 | 0.44 | 0.02 |
| May 2010 | 0.84 | 0.92 | −0.08 | 0.46 | 0.45 | 0.01 |
| August 2010 | 0.85 | 0.90 | −0.05 | 0.46 | 0.45 | 0.00 |
| November 2010 | 0.87 | 0.89 | −0.02 | 0.46 | 0.46 | 0.00 |
| February 2011 | 0.87 | 0.86 | 0.01 | 0.45 | 0.46 | −0.01 |

*Note:* Percentage of working age population; four-quarter moving averages. The table shows the winter quarter for each year up to February 2008. Thereafter each quarter is shown.
*Source:* Claimants – DWP Tabtool; working age population – NOMIS.

a percentage of the working age population, off-flows did not change much over the period 2001 to 2008.

Inspection of Table 7.2 suggests that the onset of the recession in 2008 caused a rise in on-flows, which has since continued in Glasgow but levelled off in the rest of Scotland and even turned into a slight fall in Great Britain. The rise in off-flows as a proportion of existing claimants from 2009 to 2011 in both Glasgow and Great Britain appears most likely to be the result of the WCA.

Table 7.3 gives detail about ESA on-flows and off-flows in Glasgow by main disabling condition. These figures have been published by the Department for Work and Pensions (DWP) only since February 2010. For clarity, the table shows the *net* on-flows to ESA, that is, on-flows minus off-flows, for the six main groups of conditions used by DWP in its statistical summaries. For the largest group, 'mental and behavioural disorders', the table shows a marked fall in net on-flows in the three quarters ending May to November 2010, before a return to the opening position in 2011. A similar but smaller effect is also visible for 'injury, poisoning and external causes'. These effects

*Table 7.3*    Glasgow: ESA net on-flows by category of main disabling condition, 2010–2011

| Quarter ending | Mental and behavioural disorders | Diseases of the nervous system | Diseases of the circulatory or respiratory system | Diseases of the musculoskeletal system and connective tissue | Injury, poisoning and external | Other |
|---|---|---|---|---|---|---|
| February 2010 | 640 | 30 | 90 | 150 | 130 | 20 |
| May 2010 | 370 | 40 | 60 | 80 | 60 | 140 |
| August 2010 | 200 | 30 | 30 | 70 | 20 | 140 |
| November 2010 | 450 | 10 | 70 | 100 | –10 | 250 |
| February 2011 | 650 | 40 | 40 | 160 | 60 | 240 |
| May 2011 | 530 | 40 | 60 | 60 | 70 | 220 |

*Note*: Rounded numbers of claimants.
*Source*: DWP Tabtool.

were due to rises in off-flows rather than falls in on-flows. They were not unique to Glasgow, but they were much greater in the city than in the rest of Scotland or Great Britain.

What this suggests is that the WCA did start by wrongly refusing benefit to substantial numbers of people in the mental and behavioural and injury and external cause categories, particularly in Glasgow, and that subsequently there was either a spate of successful appeals, or a change of policy in response to escalating complaints. Both Professor Malcolm Harrington, in his official review, and the Citizens Advice Bureau concluded that the WCA in its original form did not properly assess some types of condition, including those relating to mental rather than physical issues, and those that are non-continuous (Citizens Advice Bureau, 2010; Harrington, 2010). The WCA has certainly attracted considerable criticism in Glasgow: Wishart (2011) reported that 'The building where most of the Glasgow assessments are carried out is known colloquially as Lourdes ... since the sick go in one door and emerge, miraculously cured of what ails them, from another.' Harrington recommended a number of changes.

## Long-term sickness benefits and health

Webster et al. (2010) looked in detail at the question to what extent the great fall in IB/SDA claims in Glasgow from 2003 to 2008 could be explained by factors other than labour market changes: age structure of the population, changes in benefit rules, or the various national and local programmes to encourage and help claimants to find work. Age structure was quickly ruled out as the older age groups, which are most likely to claim IB/SDA, had actually increased their share of the working age population over the period. Means testing of occupational pensions, introduced in 2001, was considered to have had a possible minor effect on on-flows, and the two-year 'linking period' enabling claimants to return to their previous benefit position if a job did not work out was considered to have had a possible minor effect on off-flows. The various local employment programmes were exhaustively considered and found to have been too small, and too focused on off-flows rather than on-flows, to account for the changes seen. A regression analysis did find a small but statistically significant effect from the government's large-scale Pathways to Work programme of activation and support, which was rolled out earlier in Glasgow than in most places. However, McVicar (forthcoming), using a more sophisticated approach, did not find any effect from Pathways to Work. Moreover, two recent official reviews have concluded that Pathways to Work was not very effective and did not represent value for money (House of Commons Committee of Public Accounts, 2010; National Audit Office, 2010). A new and broader systematic review of studies of individual-focused return to work initiatives for disabled and long-term ill people (Clayton et al., 2011) found quite widespread appreciation of the value to individuals of many of the official interventions, but little hard evidence of effectiveness.

At the time the earlier paper was written, the only available SHeS data were for 1995, 1998, and 2003. However, a large SHeS combined sample for 2008 and 2009 is now available, and the evidence from all four SHeS surveys will be considered here (Joint Health Surveys Unit et al., 1999, 2001, 2011; Scottish Centre for Social Research et al., 2011). The SHeS figures reported here are, unless otherwise stated, for the whole working age population, not for people claiming long-term sickness benefits. The achieved, unweighted sample sizes for the working age population of Glasgow and the rest of Scotland respectively range from 556 and 5,321 in 2003, to 909 and 8,803 in 2008/2009. As a guide to the precision of estimates derived from the survey, the paper *Scottish Health Survey Analysis by Local Authority or Health Board* (28 July 2010), available on the SHeS website, indicates that the 95% confidence interval for the proportion of the Glasgow population of all ages having very good or good health (that is, not fair, bad, or very bad) in 2008/2009 is ±2.6%.

## Health comparisons between Glasgow and the rest of Scotland

Tables 7.4 to 7.7 set out the relevant findings from the SHeS. The most obvious conclusion from the figures is that ill-health is much more prevalent among the working age population in Glasgow than in the rest of Scotland, across almost all indicators. Glasgow's poor level of population health is a reality that has received growing attention in recent years (Landy et al., 2010; Walsh et al., 2010). Out of dozens of available measures, there are only three on which Glasgow scores better than the rest of Scotland; all of these are for 2008/2009. They are doctor-diagnosed cardiovascular disease (Table 7.6), and circulatory and 'other' longstanding illnesses (Table 7.5). It is not easy to assess the significance of Glasgow's comparative score for 'other' longstanding illnesses, because of the large number of conditions this includes (endocrine and metabolic, eyes, ears, skin, blood, digestive and genito-urinary systems, infections and unclassified). The sample sizes do not permit more detailed analysis of these conditions.

*Table 7.4*   Scottish Health Survey: Long-term illness measures available for all years

| | Glasgow | Scotland excl. Glasgow |
|---|---|---|
| Economic status – permanently unable to work | | |
| 1995 | 12.6 | 6.7 |
| 1998 | 14.3 | 6.8 |
| 2003 | 14.2 | 6.3 |
| 2008/2009 | 8.6 | 6.0 |
| Longstanding illness – total | | |
| 1995 | 40.6 | 33.2 |
| 1998 | 40.2 | 35.5 |
| 2003 | 42.2 | 33.6 |
| 2008/2009 | 34.9 | 32.3 |
| Longstanding illness – two or more grouped conditions | | |
| 1995 | 15.6 | 10.2 |
| 1998 | 15.6 | 9.1 |
| 2003 | 16.6 | 11.1 |
| 2008/2009 | 12.3 | 10.5 |
| Limiting longstanding illness | | |
| 1995 | 25.7 | 18.3 |
| 1998 | 28.3 | 19.3 |
| 2003 | 30.9 | 19.5 |
| 2008/2009 | 22.7 | 18.6 |
| Non-limiting longstanding illness | | |
| 1995 | 14.9 | 15.0 |
| 1998 | 11.9 | 16.2 |
| 2003 | 11.2 | 14.0 |
| 2008/2009 | 12.2 | 13.7 |
| Percentage of longstanding illness which is limiting | | |
| 1995 | 63.4 | 55.0 |
| 1998 | 70.4 | 54.3 |
| 2003 | 73.3 | 58.2 |
| 2008/2009 | 65.1 | 57.7 |

*Note*: Percentage of working age population unless otherwise stated.

*Table 7.5*  Scottish Health Survey: Grouped longstanding illnesses

|  |  | Mental and behavioural disorders | Diseases of the nervous system | Circulatory | Respiratory | Digestive | Musculoskeletal | Other |
|---|---|---|---|---|---|---|---|---|
| 1995 | GLASGOW | 4.66 | 4.21 | 8.09 | 9.87 | 5.88 | 17.07 | 8.86 |
|  | SCOTLAND excl. Glasgow | 2.14 | 3.45 | 5.19 | 7.45 | 4.57 | 11.84 | 8.84 |
| 1998 | GLASGOW | 5.02 | 4.57 | 7.13 | 10.14 | 5.35 | 16.28 | 12.15 |
|  | SCOTLAND excl. Glasgow | 2.68 | 3.95 | 5.62 | 7.88 | 3.70 | 12.52 | 10.11 |
| 2003 | GLASGOW | 9.06 | 4.22 | 6.87 | 9.69 | 5.78 | 16.41 | 13.26 |
|  | SCOTLAND excl. Glasgow | 4.19 | 4.04 | 5.86 | 7.23 | 4.13 | 12.61 | 10.14 |
| 2008/2009 | GLASGOW | 10.12 | 3.87 | 4.44 | 8.14 | 3.62 | 10.77 | 10.20 |
|  | SCOTLAND excl. Glasgow | 5.86 | 3.70 | 5.97 | 5.66 | 3.40 | 10.54 | 10.88 |

*Note*: Percentage of working age population; multiple conditions possible for same person.

*Table 7.6*   Scottish Health Survey: Other health measures available for all years

| | GLASGOW | SCOTLAND excl. Glasgow |
|---|---|---|
| GHQ score 4+ (possible mental illness) (higher score is worse) | | |
| 1995 | 23.5 | 15.3 |
| 1998 | 23.9 | 14.6 |
| 2003 | 20.0 | 13.5 |
| 2008/2009 | 19.8 | 13.4 |
| Self-assessed general health Fair, Bad or Very Bad | | |
| 1995 | 31.8 | 21.1 |
| 1998 | 29.7 | 18.6 |
| 2003 | 28.6 | 20.3 |
| 2008/2009 | 24.3 | 18.5 |
| Self-assessed general health Bad or Very Bad | | |
| 1995 | 10.3 | 4.2 |
| 1998 | 9.8 | 4.0 |
| 2003 | 11.1 | 5.3 |
| 2008/2009 | 7.5 | 5.2 |
| Whether talked to doctor in last two weeks | | |
| 1998 | 19.0 | 15.7 |
| 2003 | 19.2 | 16.4 |
| 2008/2009 | 17.4 | 16.8 |
| Mean no. of GP consultations per year | | |
| 1998 | 5.98 | 5.01 |
| 2003 | 6.53 | 5.36 |
| 2008/2009 | 5.80 | 5.47 |
| Doctor-diagnosed cardiovascular disease | | |
| 1995 | 22.3 | 18.3 |
| 1998 | 21.5 | 18.0 |
| 2003 | 20.9 | 20.2 |
| 2008/2009 | 19.2 | 23.0 |

*Note*: Percentage of working age population unless otherwise stated.

Glasgow's scores on GHQ (for all years), PCS-12, MCS-12 (2003) and WEMWBS (2008/2009) are markedly worse than those for the rest of Scotland. These measures are derived from batteries of questions on matters remote from sickness benefit claims. Jones and Latreille (2009) have shown for Wales that the similar PCS-36 and, to a lesser extent, MCS-36 scores are strongly correlated across local authorities with self-reported disability.

The picture is very different for changes over time. For most of the general health measures available for all four surveys (Tables 7.4 and 7.6), Glasgow showed a more or less static picture from 1995 to 2003, but a

*Table 7.7* Scottish Health Survey: Other health measures available for individual years

|  | GLASGOW | SCOTLAND excl. Glasgow |
| --- | --- | --- |
| For 1998: | | |
| Accident in past year 'which caused you to see a doctor, nurse or other health professional, or to take time off work' | 15.6 | 15.1 |
| For 2003: | | |
| Accident in past year 'which caused you to see a doctor, nurse or other health professional, or to take time off work' | 14.2 | 12.1 |
| Self-assessed health (SF12) Fair or Poor | 27.6 | 17.5 |
| Physical PCS-12 (SF12) mean score (higher score is better) | 48.46 | 50.97 |
| Mental MCS-12 (SF12) mean score (higher score is better) | 49.14 | 51.41 |
| Pain interfered with work (inside and outside the home) at least a little bit (SF12) | 21.3 | 14.5 |
| Health limits moderate activities (SF12) | 29.7 | 17.7 |
| Limited in kind of work or other regular daily activities as a result of health (SF12) | 23.1 | 14.7 |
| For 2008/2009: | | |
| WEMWBS (Warwick & Edinburgh Mental Well-Being Scale) score 41 or below (higher score is better) | 17.9 | 14.5 |
| Any depression symptoms (nurse questionnaire, small sample) | 17.9 | 13.1 |
| Any anxiety symptoms (nurse questionnaire, small sample) | 23.9 | 17.1 |
| Ever attempted to take own life (nurse questionnaire, small sample) | 7.0 | 4.6 |

*Note*: Percentage of working age population unless otherwise stated.

marked improvement for 2008/2009. These measures are total longstanding illness, two or more grouped longstanding illnesses, limiting longstanding illness, self-assessed general health, doctor contact in previous two weeks (on the assumption that more contact implies more illness, which may not be correct), and doctor-diagnosed cardiovascular disease. GHQ score 4+ also shows improvement, but from 2003. The pattern for Glasgow contrasts sharply with that for the rest of Scotland, which did not show any similar changes, or indeed any trend at all, except for an increase in cardiovascular conditions and perhaps a small fall in non-limiting longstanding illness.

Glasgow's fall in prevalence of two or more grouped longstanding illnesses from around 16% in 1995–2003 to around 12% in 2008/2009 is likely to be particularly significant for long-term sickness benefit claims, because this indicator is particularly strongly associated with such claims. In the combined sample for 1995 and 1998 for the whole of Scotland, a higher proportion (35.0%) of people with two or more longstanding conditions, whether limiting or not, were receiving IB or SDA than of people with a single *limiting* longstanding condition (31.7%).

Table 7.5 and Figure 7.4 show the figures for Glasgow and the rest of Scotland, for all years, for all the individual grouped conditions that SHeS indicates were numerically important in relation to IB/SDA receipt in 1995 and 1998. Glasgow shows a higher prevalence throughout, except for circulatory and 'other' conditions in 2008/2009. However, there is a clear pattern whereby the differential between Glasgow and the rest of Scotland has fallen markedly for most conditions, particularly between 2003 and 2008/2009. The SHeS data for 1995 and 1998 indicate that different long-standing conditions are associated with widely different probabilities of receiving long-term sickness benefits. Similar differences have been reported by Berthoud (2011) in relation to employment probabilities. Taking individual conditions in order of their apparent impact on long-term sickness benefit claims as shown by the data for 1995 and 1998:

- Mental and behavioural disorders, for which 41.5% of people reported receiving IB/SDA in 1995/1998, have increased in both Glasgow and the rest of Scotland but have been much more prevalent and have increased more in Glasgow.
- Circulatory conditions (32.4% receiving IB/SDA in 1995/1998) were much more common in Glasgow in 1995 but have fallen by almost half in the city while rising a little in the rest of Scotland, and are now less common in Glasgow. In relation to cardiovascular/circulatory conditions, there is previous statistical evidence that Glasgow has improved since 2004 more than the rest of Scotland, at least in relation to heart attacks (Webster et al., 2010, p. 175).
- Musculoskeletal conditions (28.0% receiving IB/SDA in 1995/1998) showed a very striking fall in Glasgow between 2003 and 2008/2009; prevalence was much higher than in the rest of Scotland up to 2003 but is now not significantly higher.
- Nervous system disorders (25.9% receiving IB/SDA in 1995/1998) have been a little more prevalent in Glasgow and have fallen in both Glasgow and the rest of Scotland in 2008/2009 compared with the three previous surveys.

- Digestive system conditions (22.7% receiving IB/SDA in 1995/1998) were substantially more common in Glasgow, but have fallen more in Glasgow than in the rest of Scotland so that by 2008/2009 the prevalence was almost the same.
- Respiratory conditions (14.4% receiving IB/SDA in 1995/1998) have been rather more common in Glasgow but have fallen by similar amounts in both Glasgow and the rest of Scotland in 2008/2009 compared with earlier years.

As a result of these changes, by 2008/2009 Glasgow had a significantly higher incidence of longstanding illnesses than the rest of Scotland only within the 'mental and behavioural', and to a lesser extent, 'respiratory' categories.

Brown et al. (2009) noted Glasgow's large excess of IB/SDA claims in the 'mental and behavioural' category and their rapid growth, and showed that the city's excess was greatest in the sub-category 'other neurotic disorders'. It should not be assumed that this type of disorder is less 'real' than obviously organic conditions. An example of this type of problem was given by the Citizens Advice Bureau (2010): 'A client from a Leicestershire bureau was made redundant and four weeks later his wife died. He became very depressed. His GP felt it was going to take some time before he could focus on looking for work and signed a sick note for four months.' There is good reason to think that multiple economic, social and emotional setbacks are more likely to happen to disadvantaged people in disadvantaged areas, leading to anxiety, depression and loss of normal functions. For instance, poverty, bereavement, and being the victim of a crime are all more likely than in better-off areas. And it should be remembered that there has also been a growth of stress, and of short-term absence due to stress, among people in work (Black and Frost, 2011). The increase in prevalence of longstanding mental and behavioural disorders within the working age population has not led to a corresponding increase in long-term sickness benefit claims. Table 7.8 shows that claims in respect of both mental/behavioural and musculoskeletal conditions fell sharply as a proportion of the working age population in both Glasgow and the rest of Scotland in the mid-2000s, and were then more or less constant from 2005 until the most recent months following the recession when there has been an upturn in both, and especially in musculoskeletal conditions.

What does the pattern of change in longstanding illnesses in the working age population imply for the overall level of long-term sickness benefit claims? In an attempt to answer this question, Figure 7.5 presents, for Glasgow and the rest of Scotland, an index that weights the prevalence of each condition as a percentage of the working age population in each year by the proportion of those with the condition receiving IB/SDA in 1995 and 1998. In effect this is an index of 'long-term sickness benefit claim-generating' illness.

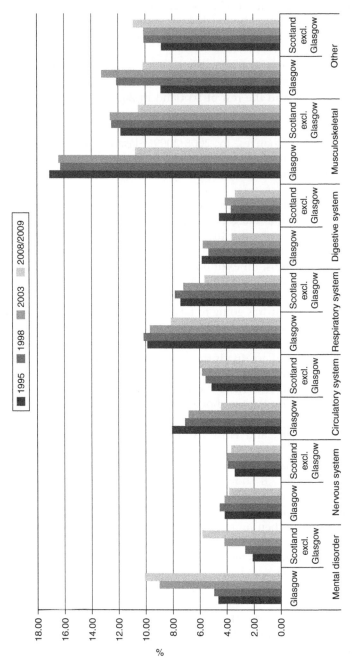

*Figure 7.4* Glasgow and Rest of Scotland: Main groups of longstanding illnesses, SHeS 1995 to 2008/2009 (percentage of working age population)

*Table 7.8* Glasgow and Scotland excluding Glasgow: On-flows to IB/SDA/ESA by category of main disabling condition

| Quarter ending | Mental & behavioural | | Musculoskeletal | | Other | |
|---|---|---|---|---|---|---|
| | GLASGOW | SCOTLAND excl. Glasgow | GLASGOW | SCOTLAND excl. Glasgow | GLASGOW | SCOTLAND excl. Glasgow |
| February 2000 | 0.430 | 0.200 | 0.140 | 0.097 | 0.215 | 0.152 |
| February 2001 | 0.446 | 0.211 | 0.138 | 0.090 | 0.201 | 0.147 |
| February 2002 | 0.454 | 0.226 | 0.140 | 0.087 | 0.209 | 0.144 |
| February 2003 | 0.465 | 0.240 | 0.124 | 0.086 | 0.226 | 0.143 |
| February 2004 | 0.474 | 0.235 | 0.113 | 0.078 | 0.201 | 0.133 |
| February 2005 | 0.375 | 0.207 | 0.091 | 0.067 | 0.185 | 0.122 |
| February 2006 | 0.375 | 0.190 | 0.072 | 0.059 | 0.171 | 0.113 |
| February 2007 | 0.388 | 0.198 | 0.077 | 0.059 | 0.171 | 0.113 |
| February 2008 | 0.386 | 0.195 | 0.074 | 0.052 | 0.201 | 0.115 |
| May 2008 | 0.405 | 0.208 | 0.072 | 0.057 | 0.187 | 0.121 |
| August 2008 | 0.424 | 0.214 | 0.083 | 0.061 | 0.212 | 0.136 |
| November 2008 | n.a. | n.a. | n.a. | n.a. | n.a. | n.a. |
| May 2009 | n.a. | n.a. | n.a. | n.a. | n.a. | n.a. |
| August 2009 | n.a. | n.a. | n.a. | n.a. | n.a. | n.a. |
| November 2009 | n.a. | n.a. | n.a. | n.a. | n.a. | n.a. |
| February 2010 | 0.383 | 0.203 | 0.091 | 0.062 | 0.185 | 0.133 |
| May 2010 | 0.424 | 0.231 | 0.096 | 0.066 | 0.185 | 0.124 |
| August 2010 | 0.424 | 0.220 | 0.096 | 0.064 | 0.193 | 0.123 |
| November 2010 | 0.438 | 0.227 | 0.096 | 0.066 | 0.209 | 0.125 |
| February 2011 | 0.443 | 0.212 | 0.107 | 0.059 | 0.207 | 0.118 |
| May 2011 | 0.449 | 0.225 | 0.091 | 0.060 | 0.198 | 0.123 |

*Note*: Percentage of working age population; n.a. = not available. The table shows the winter quarter for each year up to February 2008. Thereafter each quarter is shown, where available.
*Source*: DWP.

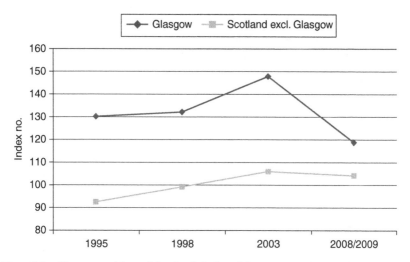

*Figure 7.5*   Glasgow and Rest of Scotland: Index of 'long-term sickness benefit receipt-generating' longstanding illness (Scotland 1995 & 1998 = 100)

The value of the index rose in both Glasgow and the rest of Scotland between 1995 and 2003, and then fell back in 2008/2009. But it fell much more in Glasgow, so that in 2008/2009 its value was only 14% higher in Glasgow than in the rest of Scotland (119 compared to 104), whereas in 1995 it had been 41% higher (130 compared to 92). This is evidence that the change in the pattern of sickness in the Glasgow working age population has been such as to reduce the likely level of long-term sickness benefit claims both absolutely and in relation to the rest of Scotland.

## Interpretation and conclusion

By considering labour market and benefit claimant data covering the current economic downturn, and bringing in data from the Scottish Health Survey, the present chapter has been able to undertake the most comprehensive investigation to date of the changes in levels of claims for long-term sickness benefits in Glasgow and of the potential reasons for them.

The analysis of the trajectory of long-term sickness benefit claims has provided strong evidence of the impact on claims of the onset of recession in 2008 and of the introduction of the WCA. It would be difficult to argue otherwise than that the worsening in the labour market resulting from the recession increased claims, and the WCA reduced them, compared to what they would have been. But what can be concluded about the role of worse health in relation to Glasgow's higher level of claims over the whole period since the mid-1990s, and about the role of the improvements in Glasgow's health between 2003 and 2008/2009 shown by SHeS in relation to the fall in claims from 2003 to 2008?

In attempting an interpretation, some key points need to be borne in mind. First is the fact that there is other evidence to indicate causal processes in both directions. In other words, poor health can reduce employment and increase dependency on sickness benefits; but unemployment and worklessness can also worsen health, and conversely employment would improve it (Waddell and Burton, 2006). In longitudinal studies, Bartley and Plewis (2002) showed that unemployment increased limiting long-term illness, and Korpi (2001) showed that unemployment increased a 'total symptom index' relating to physical symptoms. Unfortunately there does not seem to be research evidence to show whether unemployment increases *non-limiting* long-term illness, or whether, as proposed by Macnicol (present volume), it affects limiting illness by altering the degree of limitation perceived to be imposed by illness. On the whole it seems that within SHeS, reporting of specific longstanding conditions (Table 7.2) is less likely to be influenced by unemployment or worklessness than are more general measures of well-being such as self-assessed general health or GHQ (Table 7.3).

The other point that needs to be borne in mind is that the large fall in claims in Glasgow in 2003–2008 was not unique to the city but was also seen in all other areas with high claims (Webster et al., 2010; McVicar, forthcoming). This fact restricts the range of interpretations that are plausible.

Considering first the overall level of claims, it seems clear that part of the explanation for the higher rate of long-term sickness benefit claims in Glasgow compared to the rest of Scotland and Great Britain must lie in the city's worse state of working age population health. A number of pieces of evidence suggest, however, that worse health is not a full explanation. These include the fact that the relative rate of claims in Glasgow compared to the rest of Scotland has been much greater than the relative prevalence of longstanding illnesses; that a higher proportion of longstanding illness in Glasgow is reported as 'limiting'; and that Glasgow has a lower reported rate of 'non-limiting' longstanding illness. It is also possible that some of the subjective measures of health may themselves be affected by the high levels of worklessness in Glasgow.

While in 1997–1999, the proportion of the working age population in Glasgow claiming IB/SDA was more than twice that in the rest of Scotland (Figure 7.1), the proportion saying they had a limiting longstanding illness in SHeS 1995 and 1998 was only 40–47% higher (Table 7.1). Similarly, Webster et al. (2010: 178) reported that the ratio of IB/SDA claimants at May 2001 to working age people with a Limiting Long-Term Illness in the Census of April 2001 was substantially higher in Glasgow than in the (rest of) Scotland. Also significant is the fact that the proportion of longstanding illness that was said to be limiting was consistently higher in 1995 to 2008/2009 in Glasgow than in the rest of Scotland, while Glasgow consistently had a *lower* proportion of the working age population affected by *non-limiting* longstanding illness (Table 7.1). It would surely be expected that the measures of limiting and non-limiting illness would move up and down together if they reflected health status alone. Moreover, all of the fall in longstanding illness between 2003 and 2008/2009 was in limiting illness. There was no fall in non-limiting longstanding illness. This suggests that given states of health have been more often perceived as limiting in Glasgow than in the rest of Scotland, because they are more often associated with worklessness, and that increased employment between 2003 and 2008 correspondingly reduced the perceived limiting effect of illness. This supports the general observation of Macnicol (present volume) that people are more likely to perceive sickness as work-disabling if they are workless.

Turning to the fall in Glasgow's long-term sickness benefit claims in 2003–2008, there are two strong pieces of evidence that improving health in the Glasgow working age population contributed to the reduction. The first is the fall in the prevalence in Glasgow of two or more grouped longstanding illnesses, which is shown to be strongly related to long-term sickness benefit receipt. The second is the pattern of fall in different types of longstanding illness. This is shown to have been such as to have been likely to reduce long-term sickness benefit receipt in Glasgow (Figure 7.5), and does not seem likely to have been greatly influenced by labour market conditions, especially over such a short period as five years. By contrast, it is more likely that the improvements in self-assessed general health and GHQ, and reduction in doctor contact, were due at least in part to improved employment experience and prospects.

The view that improving health contributed to the fall in claims in Glasgow can be reconciled with the evidence of similar falls in other high-claim areas to the extent that it is postulated that the improvement in health was due to a cohort effect. In other words, ageing of the population could have meant that men aged 60–64 and women aged 55–59, with particularly bad health and high rates of benefit claim, have moved into retirement and have been replaced by younger cohorts of people with better health and lower rates of claim. The evidence of Cattrell et al. (2011) would support this interpretation. They showed that the ratio of mental and behavioural to musculoskeletal conditions among new IB claims had a pronounced and systematic geographical pattern, in which the previously industrial north and west of Britain has uniformly had large increases in the former relative to the latter. It does not seem likely that population turnover through migration could explain the similar changes across otherwise disparate areas. Nor does it seem likely that health would have improved both in Glasgow and in these other high-claiming areas otherwise than through cohort progression without similarly improving elsewhere, unless this was due to the effect of an improved labour market. By contrast, a labour market explanation has no difficulty in explaining the fall in sickness claims across all the high-claiming areas, because it is well established that during a boom there tends to be geographical convergence of unemployment rates, and this is likely to apply to hidden as well as manifest unemployment.

Summing up, the evidence presented in this chapter continues to support the view that worse labour market conditions in Glasgow have been substantially responsible for the higher level of long-term sickness benefit claims in the city, and that improving labour market conditions were substantially responsible for their large fall in 2003–2008. Benefit administration also clearly plays a role. The chapter has demonstrated that Glasgow's higher level of claims is reflected in worse working age population health, and, for the first time, that health improved in 2003–2008 in parallel with the fall in claims. It seems likely that worse health constitutes a partial explanation for the high level of claims in Glasgow, and that improving health, perhaps due at least in part to a cohort effect, partly explains the large fall in 2003–2008. However, there is strong evidence that health cannot be a full explanation for either the level of or the fall in claims.

Whatever view is taken on these issues, the findings presented here underline the importance in any study of long-term sickness benefit claims of examining, wherever possible, data on both health and the labour market. They also show that in relation to sickness benefit claims, 'health' is quite a complex concept. It cannot be easily captured by a single measure such as 'limiting longstanding illness'; behind such a measure lie differing changes in the prevalence of different conditions, and apparently also changes in perceptions of the limitations imposed by illness. It is also hoped that the approach explored in this study may eventually help in the development of improved methods to assess the extent of hidden unemployment.

## Acknowledgement

The Scottish Health Survey is sponsored by the Scottish Office Department of Health and its successors. The SHeS data used in this chapter has been downloaded from the UK Data Archive. The authors would like to thank Julie Ramsay of the Scottish Government SHeS team for providing the Glasgow City identifier for the four SHeSs, which is not available on the public data archive, and for methodological advice. They would also like to thank David Walsh of the Glasgow Centre for Population Health for helpful comments and advice, and Nick Bailey and Julie Clark of Urban Studies, University of Glasgow, for advice. The analysis and interpretation in the present chapter are the responsibility of the authors alone.

## References

Bambra, C. (2011) *Work, Worklessness and the Political Economy of Health* (Oxford: Oxford University Press).

Bartley, M. and Plewis, I. (2002) 'Accumulated Labour Market Disadvantage and Limiting Long-Term Illness: Data from the 1971–1991 Office for National Statistics' Longitudinal Study', *International Journal of Epidemiology*, 31, 336–341.

Beatty, C. and Fothergill, S. (2011) *Incapacity Benefit Reform: The Local, Regional and National Impact*, Centre for Regional Economic and Social Research, Sheffield Hallam University, November.

Berthoud, R. (2011) 'Trends in the Employment of Disabled People in Britain', Institute for Social and Economic Research, University of Essex, Working Paper No. 2011–03, January.

Black, C. and Frost, D. (2011) *Health at Work – An Independent Review of Sickness Absence*, Cm 8205, November, TSO.

Brown, J., Hanlon, P., Turok, I., Webster, D., Arnott, J., and Macdonald, E. (2008) 'Establishing the Potential for Using Routine Data on Incapacity Benefit to Assess the Local Impact of Policy Initiatives', *Journal of Public Health*, 30 (1), March, 54–59.

Brown, J., Hanlon, P., Turok, I., Webster, D., Arnott, J., and Macdonald, E.B. (2009) 'Mental Health as a Reason for Claiming Incapacity Benefit – A Comparison of National and Local Trends', *Journal of Public Health*, 31 (1), March, 74–80.

Cattrell, A., Harris, E., Palmer, K., Kim, M., Aylward, M., and Coggon, D. (2011) 'Regional Trends in Awards of Incapacity Benefit by Cause', *Occupational Medicine*, 61, 148–151.

Citizens Advice Bureau (2010) *Not Working: CAB Evidence on the ESA Work Capability Assessment*, March.

Clayton, S., Bambra, C., Gosling, R., Povall, S., Misso, K., and Whitehead, M. (2011) 'Assembling the Evidence Jigsaw: Insights from a Systematic Review of UK Studies of Individual-Focused Return to Work Initiatives for Disabled and Long-Term Ill People', *BMC Public Health*, 11, 170.

Harrington, M. (2010) *An Independent Review of the Work Capability Assessment* (London, TSO), November.

House of Commons Committee of Public Accounts (2010) *Support to Incapacity Benefits Claimants through Pathways to Work*, First Report Session 2010–11, HC 404, September.

Joint Health Surveys Unit of Social and Community Planning Research and University College London (1999) *Scottish Health Survey, 1995* [computer file]. 3rd edition. Colchester, Essex: UK Data Archive, February. SN: 3807, http://dx.doi.org/10.5255/UKDA-SN-3807-1.

Joint Health Surveys Unit of Social and Community Planning Research and University College London (2001) *Scottish Health Survey, 1998* [computer file]. Colchester, Essex: UK Data Archive, July. SN: 4379, http://dx.doi.org/10.5255/UKDA-SN-4379-1.

Joint Health Surveys Unit, University College London and Medical Research Council, Social and Public Health Sciences Unit (2011) *Scottish Health Survey, 2003* [computer file]. 2nd edition. Colchester, Essex: UK Data Archive, June. SN: 5318, http://dx.doi.org/10.5255/UKDA-SN-5318-1.

Jones, M. and Latreille, P. (2009) 'Disability, Health and the Labour Market: Evidence from the Welsh Health Survey', *Local Economy*, 24 (3), May, 192–201.

Korpi, T. (2001) 'Accumulating Disadvantage: Longitudinal analyses of Unemployment and Physical Health in Representative Samples of the Swedish Population', *European Sociological Review*, 17 (3), September, 255–273.

Landy, R., Walsh, D., and Ramsay, J. (2010) *The Scottish Health Survey: The Glasgow Effect*, Edinburgh, Scottish Government, November.

McVicar, D. (forthcoming) 'Local Level Incapacity Benefits Rolls in Britain: Correlates and Convergence', *Regional Studies*, available online since 28 October 2011 at http://www.tandfonline.com/doi/pdf/10.1080/00343404.2011.607807.

National Audit Office (2010) *Support to Incapacity Benefits Claimants through Pathways to Work*, report by the Comptroller and Auditor General, Session 2010–2011, HC 24, May.

Rowthorn, R. (2010) 'Combined and Uneven Development: Reflections on the North–South Divide', *Spatial Economic Analysis*, 5 (4), December, 363–388.

Scottish Centre for Social Research, University College London. Department of Epidemiology and Public Health and Medical Research Council. Social and Public Health Sciences Unit (2011) *Scottish Health Survey, 2009* [computer file]. 4th edition. Colchester, Essex: UK Data Archive [distributor], November. SN: 6713, http://dx.doi.org/10.5255/UKDA-SN-6713-2.

Waddell, G. and Burton, A.K. (2006) *Is Work Good for Your Health and Well-Being?* (London, TSO).

Walsh, D., Bendel, N., Jones, R., and Hanlon, P. (2010) 'It's Not "Just Deprivation": Why Do Equally Deprived UK Cities Experience Different Health Outcomes?', *Public Health*, 124, 487–495.

Webster, D., Arnott, J., Brown, J., Turok, I., Mitchell, R., and Macdonald, E.B. (2010) 'Falling Incapacity Benefit Claims in a Former Industrial City: Policy Impacts or Labour Market Improvement?', *Policy Studies*, 31 (2), March, 163–185.

Wishart, R. (2011) 'First and Last Hope: The UK's Oldest Citizens' Advice Bureau Faces a Raft of New Problems', *The Herald*, Glasgow, 15 October.

# 8

# The Impact of the UK's Disability Benefit Reforms

*Christina Beatty, Steve Fothergill, and Donald Houston*

## Introduction

Between 2006 and 2010 the UK government initiated major reforms to disability benefits. By 2011 the impacts were only beginning to be felt, but from 2012 onwards the reforms are scheduled to hit hard and in rapid succession.

The reforms matter because they affect so many people. In total across Britain, nearly 2.6 million men and women of working age were out-of-work on disability benefits in 2011, far more than the 1.5 million out-of-work on Jobseeker's Allowance (JSA) even in the wake of recession.

Furthermore, disability benefit claimants are far from evenly spread around the country. In Britain's older industrial areas, in particular, the share of adults of working age claiming disability benefits often exceeds 10%. By contrast, in large parts of Southern England the claimant rate is far lower, typically 2–4%. What this means is that the disability benefit reforms can be expected to have a far greater impact in some areas than others, and it is Britain's most disadvantaged communities that will often be hit hardest.

Over the last 20 years or so the very large numbers on disability benefits in the UK have hidden the true scale of unemployment (see, for example, Beatty and Fothergill, 2005). That does not mean fraudulent claims were widespread. Rather, the medical threshold for access to disability benefits was set at a level that allowed substantial numbers of men and women with health problems or disabilities to claim disability benefits instead of unemployment benefits. Also, at various times Jobcentre Plus and its predecessors encouraged claimants to move across to disability benefits. The effect was to hide the scale of labour market distress in Britain's weaker local economies.

Until at least the mid-2000s the key players were often happy to collude in the diversion onto disability benefits. Governments were happy that it reduced the numbers on unemployment benefits and made their economic policies appear more successful. Companies were happy because it absolved them of the responsibility to employ men and women with health problems or disabilities. And it benefited claimants because, if they were going to be out-of-work for long periods, being on disability benefits was often the best way to maximise their household income.

Welfare reform has shattered this consensus. In effect, the diversion onto disability benefits is now being put into reverse. Unemployment that was once 'hidden' will increasingly become 'visible' once more. Financial hardship that was eased by access to disability benefits will become more acute as claimants are diverted to means-tested JSA, to other means-tested benefits, or denied access to benefits altogether.

These changes will hit some individuals much harder than others, but because disability benefit claimants are highly unevenly spread around the country they will also hit some places much more than others.

But just how many men and women will lose their entitlement to disability benefits? How many will be pushed onto JSA instead? And how many will be pushed out of the benefits system altogether?

The purpose of this chapter is to present estimates of the likely scale of the diversion of people off disability benefits, and its geographically uneven impact. The chapter concludes with an assessment of the likely success or otherwise of the recent and forthcoming reforms to disability benefits in the UK.

The themes of this book – labour markets, employability, and health – are all pertinent here. Labour markets matter because disability claimants are concentrated in Britain's weakest local economies, with the fewest job opportunities and the greatest competition from other job seekers. Employability matters because disability claimants often have few qualifications, tend to be advancing in years, and have mostly not worked for several years. And health matters because ill-health or disability usually constrains the work they can do. Together, these factors pose immense challenges in finding work.

## The reform of disability benefits

The key reforms to disability benefits in the UK are:

- a tougher medical test
- the re-testing of existing claimants
- new requirements to engage in work-related activity
- time-limiting the entitlement to non-means-tested benefit.

The **tougher medical test**, known as the Work Capability Assessment (WCA), was introduced by Labour and has applied to all new disability claimants since October 2008. Prior to October 2008, new claimants were first signed off by their own GP and then, after six months, had to go through a Personal Capability Assessment (PCA) run by doctors working for Jobcentre Plus. The pre-2008 claimants received Incapacity Benefit (IB) or, in the case of claimants with a poor National Insurance (NI) contributions record, Income Support (IS) on the grounds of incapacity (though the government still counted these as 'IB claimants'). Smaller numbers of pre-2001 claimants with a high level of disability and a poor NI record received Severe Disablement Allowance (SDA) instead.

The WCA takes place three rather than six months into the claim. It uses a points-based system and examines what activities the claimant is capable of undertaking. If the claimant scores sufficiently highly they then qualify for Employment and Support Allowance (ESA), the replacement for IB. The initial expectation, based on a pilot study, was that around 12% of the claimants who qualified for IB under the old medical test would not qualify for ESA under WCA (DWP, 2007). In practice the failure rate has proved much higher.

The effect of the tougher medical test is that the 'gateway' to disability benefits – these days ESA – has narrowed.

The second key reform, **the re-testing of existing claimants**, was also introduced by Labour, though it was not part of their initial plans for ESA. The intention is that by March 2014 all existing disability claimants – that is, all the pre-2008 IB and SDA claimants – will be called in for the new medical test. They will then be routed onto ESA or, if they fail to qualify, onto other benefits such as JSA or (if they fail to qualify again, for example because of means-testing thresholds) out of the benefits system altogether. The re-testing of existing IB and SDA claimants was piloted in Aberdeen and Burnley in late 2010 and early 2011. From April 2011 re-testing was rolled out nationally, with the number of tests carried out each week gradually ramping up.

With the re-testing spread over three years, comparatively few IB or SDA claimants had been called in by late 2011, but the process will eventually draw in all but those who will reach state pension age before March 2014.

The third key reform, the introduction of a **new requirement to engage in work-related activity**, is another Labour measure. All those who qualify for ESA are allocated to one of two groups – a Support Group, who are deemed to have sufficiently serious health problems or disabilities to receive unconditional support, and a Work-Related Activity Group (WRAG), for whom ESA comes with strings attached. All claimants in this second group are required to attend work-focused interviews, initially at monthly intervals, at which they are advised on steps to find suitable work including training, voluntary work or job placement for a few hours a week, or physical or mental rehabilitation. Advisers then draw up an 'action plan' to which claimants are expected to adhere. Failure to engage in the work-related interviews runs the risk of benefit sanctions.

The underpinning assumption is that, for WRAG, ESA should only be a temporary benefit, pending the claimant's return to work.

The fourth key reform, **the time-limiting of entitlement to non-means-tested benefit**, is an addition by the Coalition Government that came to power in May 2010. Incapacity Benefit itself has never been means-tested except for a small number of post-2002 claimants with significant income from a personal or company pension. This means that other sources of household income – a partner's earnings, for example – are not docked off a claimant's IB entitlement. Only the IB claimants who receive IS (for example, because their NI contributions record fails to qualify them for IB itself) have previously faced means-testing. Likewise, ESA claimants with sufficient NI contributions have so far not faced means-testing.

However, from April 2012 onwards there will be a 12-month limit on the duration of non-means-tested ESA for those in the WRAG. After the expiry of the 12-month period these claimants will only be eligible for the means-tested version. This has profound implications for those with other sources of household income or with significant savings. Many will find that they no longer qualify for ESA except on a 'NI credits only' basis that involves no financial payment. Others will find that the value of their benefits is reduced because other household income is docked from their means-tested entitlement. Claimants who are denied access to means-tested ESA will find that the same means-testing rules will also deny them access to JSA or indeed IS. The vast majority will therefore be pushed out of the benefits system altogether.

Taken as a whole, these reforms represent a fundamental shift in the nature and scale of income protection for those with health problems or disabilities. In particular, they represent a shift from the principles of social insurance towards a much more 'active' system with greater conditionality. Under the previous system, if an individual had made sufficient recent NI contributions and met the medical requirements, they were entitled to IB paid at a flat rate unrelated to other household income. Subject to periodic medical assessment, the benefit was then payable until they returned to work, reached state pension age, or (in a few cases) died. This principle of social insurance is now being eroded by the introduction of conditionality and the time-limiting of eligibility.

The new conditionality and the time-limit on eligibility – both applying to the WRAG within ESA – reflect a 'Work First' strategy intended to prevent poverty and increase the responsibilities and expectations placed on citizens (Lindsay and Houston, 2011). The assumption – almost certainly correct – is that in the vast majority of cases work pays more than benefits, so that people are better off in work. Significantly, however, the reforms to disability benefits apply to many men and women who are unlikely to find it easy to move back into employment.

The welfare-to-work agenda is nevertheless based on questionable assumptions about behaviour and the operation of the labour market (Peck, 2001). First, it assumes that people are strongly motivated by (and aware of) financial incentives, in particular the differences in income available on benefits and in work. Cutting benefits will encourage claimants to move into work, the logic goes (Williams, 1999). In fact, the evidence on disability claimants is that they mostly stay on benefits because of few job openings, low skills, and poor health (Beatty et al., 2009).

The second assumption behind the welfare-to-work agenda is that dependency on benefits has developed, reducing claimants' work ethic and motivation to find work (Fraser and Gordon, 1994). Mandatory activation and conditionality are therefore thought to be required in order to get claimants back to work (Taylor-Gooby, 2008). Again, however, the evidence on incapacity claimants is that measures of work commitment are unrelated to the likelihood of returning to work (Kemp and Davidson, 2010), and although only a minority of longer-term claimants express a desire to return to work this often reflects a realistic assessment of their chances of finding suitable employment. Claimants generally see their ill-health or disability, rather than financial considerations, as the primary obstacle to taking a job (Beatty et al., 2009).

The third assumption behind welfare-to-work is that increasing labour supply will restrain wages and thereby boost the demand for labour (Martin and Morrison, 2003). However, even leaving aside the question of whether benefit claimants looking for work will restrain wages, particularly in local labour markets that already have high levels of unemployment, the demand for labour is clearly influenced by a wide range of other factors such as public and private expenditure, the supply of capital, and international competitiveness (Sunley and Martin, 2000).

## Estimating the impact

The estimates of the impact of the disability benefit reforms, presented here, cover the period through to 2014 and are taken from a report by two of the present authors (Beatty and Fothergill, 2011). The full details of methods and the resulting estimates for every local authority in Britain are presented in this earlier document.

In practice, of course, there are influences on claimant numbers two or three years into the future that have nothing to do with the reforms. These include the growth of the national economy, the effectiveness of back-to-work initiatives such as the Work Programme, and the impact of changes elsewhere in the benefits system. In the figures presented here *all other factors have been held constant*. The estimates therefore make no assumptions about the trajectory of economic growth but only reflect the anticipated impact of reforms themselves.

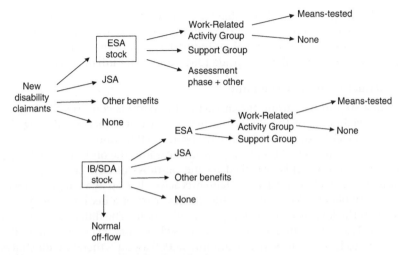

*Figure 8.1*   Trajectory of disability benefit claimants

Coalition ministers argue that welfare reform will raise employment by making work financially worthwhile and that the disability reforms, in particular, should mean that more people will look for work and find work. The estimates presented here do not start from this assumption, though the final part of the chapter does comment on the extent to which increases in employment are likely to be a result of the reforms. Instead the estimates focus on the diversions within the benefits system that the government itself acknowledges the reforms are set to trigger. The calculations are also rooted as far as possible in the government's own data and forecasts. In a sense, therefore, the figures are close to the ones the government itself would generate if it chose to work through the full consequences of the reforms that have been set in motion.

To assist in understanding the calculations necessary to measure the impact of the reforms, Figure 8.1 presents a flow diagram showing the trajectory of disability claimants through the system.

### Existing claimants

The starting point in estimating the impact of the reforms is the existing stock of claimants. Across Great Britain as a whole in February 2011, 1,940,000 men and women claimed IB or SDA and a further 630,000 claimed ESA – a grand total of 2,570,000 incapacity claimants. Except for a very small number undertaking 'permitted work' as a form of rehabilitation, none of these claimants were in work, and they are a group that is entirely separate from the unemployed on JSA.

As the maps presented in Chapter 2 showed, disability claimants are highly unevenly spread across the country. Broadly, the places with the highest claimant rates are the older industrial areas of the North, Scotland, and Wales, plus a number of seaside towns and inner urban areas.

## The reduction in new claimants

The first step in measuring the impact of the reforms concerns the impact on new claimants of the WCA, the new medical test that is reducing the flow onto ESA below what would have been the flow onto IB.

Prior to the introduction of the new medical test, the off-flows of existing claimants were roughly balanced by the on-flows of new claimants. This resulted in a stock of incapacity claimants across Britain as a whole that was broadly stable at 2.5–2.7 million for the best part of a decade, falling only gently in the last years of the long economic boom. The difference between the off-flows from IB/SDA, which is closed to new claimants, and the on-flows to ESA – a difference of around 45,000 a year – therefore illustrates how the new medical test is squeezing incapacity numbers by restricting access to new claimants.

The figures presented build in this reduced on-flow. They also use the government's own figures (DWP, 2011a) on what happens to those who fail to qualify for ESA:

- 50% go on to claim JSA instead
- 20% move onto another benefit (for example, IS or Carers Allowance)
- 30% move off benefit.

## The reassessment of existing claimants

The best evidence on the likely impact of re-testing existing IB/SDA claimants comes from the pilots in Aberdeen and Burnley. These are two contrasting labour markets – Aberdeen is relatively prosperous whereas Burnley is one of Britain's weaker local economies – so together they probably offer a useful guide to what will happen across Britain as a whole.

The government's initial assessment of re-testing in Aberdeen and Burnley (DWP, 2011b) shows that:

- 30% were placed in the Support Group
- 40% were placed in the WRAG
- 30% were found fit for work (in other words, were denied access to ESA).

However, there are good reasons to suppose that the local geography will vary. In particular, in so far as the stock of IB/SDA claimants in some places includes a higher proportion of 'hidden unemployed' – those who would have been in work in a fully employed economy – it is reasonable to expect that re-testing will deny ESA to a higher proportion of claimants in some places than others. The estimates presented here therefore allocate the 30% denied access to ESA in the following way:

- One-third in proportion to the stock of IB/SDA claimants in each district. This assumes that the tougher medical test impacts on some claimants in all areas.
- Two-thirds in proportion to the estimates of hidden unemployment among IB/SDA claimants in each district (Beatty, Fothergill, Gore, and Powell, 2007).

As noted earlier, the government's assessment is that of those found fit for work:

- 50% will move onto JSA
- 20% will move onto another benefit
- 30% will move off benefit.

### The time-limiting of non-means tested benefit

The time-limiting of non-means tested benefit affects claimants in the Work-Related Activity Group of ESA.

The government's assessment (DWP, 2011c), based on detailed modelling of household income, is that when entitlement to non-means-tested benefit comes to an end after 12 months, 40% of claimants in the WRAG will fail to qualify for means-tested ESA. The estimates presented here incorporate this assumption.

However, a distinctive geography can again be expected. In London the proportion in the WRAG who receive only contributions-based (that is, non-means-tested) ESA is lower than elsewhere. The estimates presented here therefore assume that fewer ESA claimants in the WRAG in London will lose their entitlement because of time-limiting.

### The impact on national totals

Table 8.1 shows the estimated impact of the disability benefit reforms on national totals. The figures cover the period from 2011 to 2014, by which time the migration of claimants from IB/SDA to ESA is expected to have been completed. The table presents four separate sets of figures.

The first and most striking set of figures deals with the reduction in the headline total of disability claimants. These figures show an overall fall of just less than 1 million (970,000). Of these, 830,000 are existing claimants who will lose their entitlement, either at the point of reassessment or as a result of the introduction of means-testing. Another way of looking at the same figures is that around a third of the existing stock of disability claimants will lose entitlement to disability benefits.

*Table 8.1*  Estimated national (GB) impact of disability benefit reforms, 2011–2014

| | |
|---|---:|
| Reduction in disability claimants | |
| Reduction in new claimants | 140,000 |
| IB/SDA claimants denied ESA | 410,000 |
| Due to time-limiting of non-means-tested ESA | 420,000 |
| Total reduction | 970,000 |
| Removed from benefits entirely | |
| New claimants denied | 40,000 |
| IB/SDA claimants denied at reassessment | 120,000 |
| Denied due to time-limiting | 420,000 |
| Total removed | 580,000 |
| Increase in JSA | |
| New claimants diverted to JSA | 70,000 |
| IB/SDA claimants diverted to JSA | 210,000 |
| Total increase | 280,000 |
| Additional compulsory labour market engagement | |
| Increase in JSA | 280,000 |
| Work-Related Activity Group (2014) | 630,000 |
| Total engagement | 910,000 |

*Note*: Sheffield Hallam estimates based on DWP.

By any standards this is a huge reduction over a very short space of time. In 2006 the previous Labour Government set a target of a 1 million reduction in disability benefit numbers by 2016 – a ten-year period. The Coalition Government now looks set to achieve the same objective in a third of the time. A reduction of 1 million in disability numbers is equivalent in scale to cutting the number of unemployed on JSA (c. 1.5 million in late 2011) by two-thirds in just three years.

The second part of Table 8.1 shows that nearly 600,000 claimants will be removed entirely from the benefits system. All bar around 40,000 (who are new claimants denied access to ESA) will be existing disability claimants who will lose their entitlement. Or to put this another way, more than a fifth of the existing stock of disability claimants will not only be denied access to disability benefits but be pushed right off benefits altogether.

Some of this will occur at the point existing IB/SDA claimants are reassessed for ESA, but the main impact, accounting for an estimated 420,000, will arise from the time-limiting of entitlement to non-means-tested benefit. Removing 600,000 disability claimants from the benefits system is equivalent in scale to withdrawing benefit from all the 600,000 lone parents who currently receive Income Support.

The third part of the table shows that the numbers on JSA can be expected to increase by some 280,000 as claimants are diverted from disability benefits.

The majority of the increase will occur as existing IB/SDA claimants are called in for reassessment. As noted earlier, DWP anticipates that half of those who are found fit for work (and thereby denied ESA) will then claim JSA instead.

The final part of the table deals with the increase in compulsory labour market engagement. Hitherto, the vast majority of disability claimants have not looked for work, in part because the benefits system has not required them to do so but also because they take a dim view of their chances of finding work. This is set to change. Those who find themselves diverted to JSA will be required to look for work as a condition of benefit receipt, but in addition the ESA claimants placed in the WRAG will be required to engage in activity to prepare for work. These two groups add up to 900,000 – a huge increase in compulsory labour market engagement without adding in any of those who are denied access to benefit and subsequently look for work.

The disability benefit reforms are therefore set to increase recorded unemployment. An increase in JSA numbers of 280,000 arising from the reforms represents nearly a 20% increase on JSA levels in 2011. Not all of the ESA claimants in the WRAG can be expected to meet the unemployment criteria in the Labour Force Survey – 'looking for work' and 'available to start work' – but if half were to do so then along with the extra JSA claimants this would raise unemployment on the Labour Force Survey measure by around 600,000 (from a 2011 level of 2.5 million).

## The impact by region

Table 8.2 shows the estimated impact by region. In this table the regions are ranked by the anticipated reduction in disability claimant numbers expressed as a share of the working age population.

The table shows that Wales, the North West, the North East, and Scotland (in that order) are the regions where the disability benefit reforms will have the greatest impact. For example the anticipated reduction in Wales, as a share of the working age population, is more than two-and-a-half time greater than in the South East of England.

There are three reasons why disability benefit reform will impact much more on some parts of the country than others:

- First and most importantly, some places simply have a great many more disability claimants. It should come as no surprise therefore that the North, Scotland, and Wales will feel the impact most acutely.
- Second, insofar as disability benefits have hidden unemployment in parts of the North, Scotland, and Wales to a greater extent than elsewhere, it is reasonable to expect that the new tougher medical test will deny ESA to a higher proportion of claimants in these areas. In the more prosperous parts of the South, where job opportunities are less often a problem, only those with formidable physical or mental obstacles to working have

needed to claim disability benefits, and many of these men and women might be expected to qualify for ESA.
* Third, the share of disability claimants receiving only non-means-tested benefit is lower in London than elsewhere, so the time-limiting of non-means-tested entitlement will impact less in London.

## The impact by district

Figures 8.2 and 8.3 show the estimated reduction in disability numbers by district, expressed as a share of the working age population.

These maps underline the point that the reforms will impact very unevenly across Britain. It is the older industrial areas of the North, Scotland, and Wales that shine through as most acutely affected. By contrast, in large parts of Southern England the disability benefit reforms look set to have little more than a marginal impact.

To underline this point, Table 8.3 shows the top 20 and bottom 10 districts ranked according to the anticipated reduction in disability numbers. The list of the top 20 is dominated by the older industrial areas of the

*Table 8.2*   Estimated regional impact of disability benefit reforms, 2011–2014

| | Reduction in disability claimants | | Removed from benefits entirely | | Increase in JSA claims | | Additional compulsory labour market engagement | |
|---|---|---|---|---|---|---|---|---|
| | No | As % working age | No | As % working age | No | As % working age | No | As % working age |
| Wales | 75,000 | 3.9 | 45,000 | 2.3 | 23,000 | 1.2 | 65,000 | 3.4 |
| North West | 160,000 | 3.6 | 90,000 | 2.0 | 49,000 | 1.1 | 135,000 | 3.0 |
| North East | 60,000 | 3.5 | 35,000 | 2.0 | 19,000 | 1.1 | 50,000 | 3.0 |
| Scotland | 115,000 | 3.4 | 65,000 | 1.9 | 36,000 | 1.1 | 100,000 | 2.9 |
| West Midlands | 90,000 | 2.6 | 55,000 | 1.6 | 26,000 | 0.7 | 80,000 | 2.3 |
| Yorkshire & the Humber | 90,000 | 2.5 | 55,000 | 1.6 | 25,000 | 0.7 | 80,000 | 2.3 |
| East Midlands | 70,000 | 2.4 | 40,000 | 1.4 | 20,000 | 0.7 | 60,000 | 2.1 |
| South West | 70,000 | 2.1 | 45,000 | 1.4 | 18,000 | 0.6 | 65,000 | 2.0 |
| London | 100,000 | 1.8 | 55,000 | 1.1 | 29,000 | 0.5 | 120,000 | 2.3 |
| East of England | 65,000 | 1.7 | 40,000 | 1.1 | 15,000 | 0.4 | 60,000 | 1.7 |
| South East | 80,000 | 1.5 | 55,000 | 1.0 | 16,000 | 0.3 | 80,000 | 1.5 |
| GB | 970,000 | 2.5 | 580,000 | 1.5 | 280,000 | 0.7 | 910,000 | 2.3 |

*Note*: Sheffield Hallam estimates based on DWP.

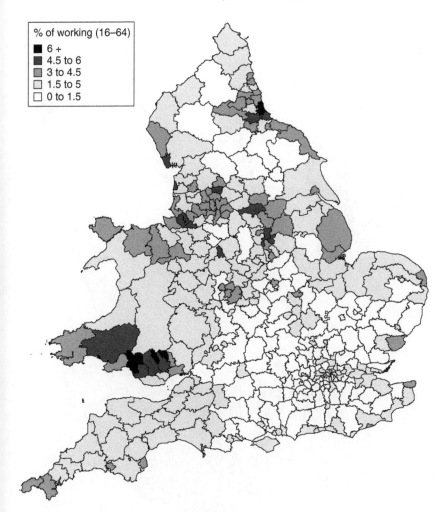

*Figure 8.2* Estimated reduction in disability claimants, 2011–2014, England and Wales
*Note*: Sheffield Hallam estimates based on DWP.

North, Scotland, and Wales. The Welsh Valleys are heavily represented, but major cities such as Glasgow and Liverpool also figure on the list. By contrast, all the bottom 10 are districts in the South. Only a single London borough (Islington) and only two districts in the South East (Hastings and Thanet) come within the top 100 in terms of the anticipated impact of the reforms.

In Merthyr Tydfil it is estimated that the reduction in disability claimant numbers will be equivalent to 7% of the entire working age population.

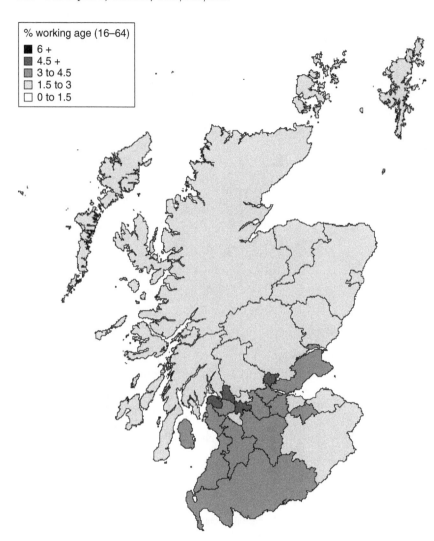

*Figure 8.3*   Estimated reduction in disability claimants, 2011–2014, Scotland
*Note*: Sheffield Hallam estimates based on DWP.

Merthyr is a relatively small place so the numbers are small – just 2,500 – but in Glasgow, where a 5% reduction is anticipated, disability numbers look set to be cut by more than 22,000, of whom more than 12,000 will be denied benefit entirely.

In the top 20 districts affected by the IB reforms, the estimated reduction in the number of claimants is between 40 and 50%. Most of these – accounting for around 85% of the reduction – will be existing claimants who will lose their entitlement to disability benefits. Around a quarter of

*Table 8.3* Estimated impact of disability benefit reforms by district, 2011–2014

| | Reduction in disability claimants | | Of which: Removed from benefits entirely |
|---|---|---|---|
| | As % of working age | No | |
| Top 20 districts | | | |
| Merthyr Tydfil | 7.0 | 2,500 | 1,300 |
| Easington | 6.9 | 4,200 | 2,000 |
| Blaenau Gwent | 6.5 | 2,800 | 1,500 |
| Neath Port Talbot | 6.3 | 5,500 | 2,900 |
| Knowsley | 5.7 | 5,500 | 2,900 |
| Caerphilly | 5.7 | 6,300 | 3,200 |
| Rhondda Cynon Taf | 5.5 | 8,300 | 4,600 |
| Glasgow | 5.4 | 22,500 | 12,200 |
| Inverclyde | 5.2 | 2,700 | 1,500 |
| Liverpool | 5.2 | 16,100 | 8,800 |
| Barrow-in-Furness | 5.2 | 2,300 | 1,200 |
| Blackpool | 5.1 | 4,400 | 2,600 |
| Hartlepool | 5.0 | 2,900 | 1,500 |
| Burnley | 5.0 | 2,700 | 1,400 |
| Stoke on Trent | 5.0 | 7,700 | 4,200 |
| Barnsley | 4.8 | 7,100 | 3,700 |
| Mansfield | 4.8 | 3,100 | 1,600 |
| West Dunbartonshire | 4.7 | 2,800 | 1,500 |
| Carmarthenshire | 4.7 | 5,200 | 2,800 |
| Halton | 4.7 | 3,700 | 2,000 |
| Bottom 10 districts | | | |
| Uttlesford | 0.8 | 400 | 300 |
| South Northamptonshire | 0.7 | 400 | 300 |
| Richmond-upon-Thames | 0.7 | 900 | 700 |
| Runnymede | 0.7 | 400 | 400 |
| Elmbridge | 0.7 | 600 | 500 |
| South Buckinghamshire | 0.7 | 300 | 300 |
| Kingston-upon-Thames | 0.7 | 800 | 600 |
| Surrey Heath | 0.7 | 400 | 300 |
| Wokingham | 0.6 | 700 | 500 |
| Hart | 0.6 | 300 | 300 |

*Note*: Sheffield Hallam estimates based on DWP.

the claimants in the top 20 districts can expect to lose their entitlement to benefit entirely.

Two key aspects of the district-by-district geography of the impact of the disability reforms should not escape comment:

• The reforms will hit the weakest local economies in Britain hardest. It is the older industrial areas of the North, Scotland, and Wales, still struggling to recover from years of job loss, that face the biggest upheaval.

- The Coalition Government is presiding over a national welfare reform
  that will impact principally on individuals and communities outside its
  own political heartlands.

What should also not escape comment is that the individuals who lose
entitlement to disability benefits or find that their payments are reduced
by means-testing will often be the same individuals who are also losing out
as a result of other welfare reforms. Disability Living Allowance (DLA), for
example, which is currently received by just under half of all IB claimants, is
to be replaced by a new benefit – Personal Independence Payment – targeted
at a smaller group with more acute needs. Many of those who are denied
ESA by the new, tougher medical test might expect to find that they will also
be denied DLA's replacement. And the reforms to Housing Benefit, currently
claimed by more than 40% of those on IB, will often reduce household
income as well.

## Jobs to the rescue?

Let us now consider Coalition ministers' argument that the reduction in
disability claimant numbers is actually a good thing – quite apart from the
money it saves the Treasury – because married to the assistance provided by
the Work Programme it will lead to more people in employment. Ministers
also argue that the disability reforms are best understood alongside the
planned introduction of Universal Credit, which will eventually replace the
means-tested element of ESA and is intended to ensure that in all circumstances claimants are financially better off in work.

Coalition ministers (and their Labour predecessors) are correct to flag up
the extent to which men and women have hitherto been 'parked' on disability benefits. Few expectations have previously been placed on IB claimants
and, in practice, whatever their initial aspirations or residual thoughts on
working again, most long-term claimants gave up the idea of ever working
again. Even fewer actually looked for work. If men and women don't look
for work they are most unlikely to find work, and it was one of the tragedies
of the long economic boom to 2008 that so few disability claimants took
advantage of the opportunities to return to work.

But *looking* for work and actually *finding* work are two different things.
Also, if a former benefit claimant finds work that does not necessarily mean
that the overall level of employment is any higher or that the numbers on
benefits any lower. One jobseeker can displace another in the competition
to find work.

One of the ways in which extra labour supply can lead to extra employment is by addressing a shortage of labour. At various times, in various
places and in particular sectors and occupations, labour shortages do
unquestionably arise, but it is hard to characterise the UK in the wake of

the 2008–9 recession as an economy that is constrained by a shortfall in labour supply.

The other way in which extra labour supply can lead to extra employment is if demand and supply are brought into balance through wage adjustments – if extra labour supply forces down wages so that businesses are more competitive and employers take on more workers. Taking the very long view, market economies such as the UK do work in this way. The weakening of trade unions' power over wages has probably accelerated the speed of wage adjustments though the national minimum wage – a key measure in combating in-work poverty – sets a lower limit on how far the process can go. However, the process of wage adjustment operates effectively only over the *very long run* – a timescale of decades rather than years.

The point here is that exceptionally large numbers of disability claimants are set to be pushed back into the labour market over a very short space of time – by 2014. There seems little hope that normal labour market adjustments will be able to absorb such a large influx of potential new workers over such a short period. Moreover, the additional labour supply arising from disability benefit reform is occurring not only in the wake of a recession but also at a time when the increase in the state pension age and reforms to benefits for lone parents will also add to labour supply.

Two further factors work against the expansion of employment in response to the reduction in disability benefit numbers. The first is the characteristics of the claimants themselves. All too often employers prefer healthy, young, well-qualified, and well-motivated workers with recent work experience. Disability claimants tend to fail on just about all these counts. Even if they are deemed 'fit for work' under the new medical test, former IB claimants will normally still be affected by health problems or disabilities that limit the work they are able to undertake. They tend to be an older group, often over 50, who previously worked mainly in low-grade manual jobs, and a high proportion have no formal qualifications at all. They have often been out-of-work for many years and their motivation has often been sapped. They are extremely unlikely to be employers' first choice.

The other factor that works against an expansion of employment is the location of so many of the disability claimants who will be thrust onto the labour market. As the evidence presented here shows, they are disproportionately concentrated in Britain's weakest local economies. Indeed, it is the very weakest local economies of all – places such as the Welsh Valleys – that have the very highest disability claimant rates and can expect the very largest numbers to be thrown off benefit. In these places, former disability claimants face little chance of finding work.

Of course, there will be some success stories, and these will no doubt be trumpeted. Some former disability claimants will find work, even perhaps in the Welsh Valleys. All the individuals who have their benefits withdrawn will not remain permanently outside the labour market. But to focus on individual success stories would be to miss the point. In a difficult labour market there are not enough jobs for everyone, and if one person finds a job it is most likely to be at the expense of someone else.

## Is there an alternative?

If there is to be a long-term solution to the large numbers on disability benefits, without simply diverting people from one part of the benefits system to another or denying them benefits altogether, four things are really necessary:

- **A sustained national economic revival.** New jobs need to be generated in large numbers. This requires an improvement in the trading performance of the UK economy, so that spending is rooted in incomes rather than public or private borrowing. It requires a shift from consumption to exports, and a new emphasis on manufacturing in particular. Job growth brings down benefit claimant numbers: in the long economic boom to 2008 it cut the numbers on JSA and even began to bring down the numbers on disability benefits from around 2003 onwards.
- **Renewed priority for regional and local economic development.** Economic growth and jobs need to be nurtured most in the places where disability claimants are concentrated, above all in Britain's older industrial areas. Local and regional economic development works: the employment and population levels in Britain's weakest local economies are higher now than they would have been in the absence of regeneration efforts. And the biggest reductions in disability numbers after 2003 were mostly in these places.
- **Practical support to raise the employability of disability claimants.** Jobs need to be available, and in the right places, but that still leaves problems of poor skills, low motivation, and demoralisation to be addressed. These need to be tackled through intensive support tailored to the needs of the individual. The UK government was slow to address these issues and missed an important opportunity to assist claimants during the years of strong job growth. There is a growing body of experience and good practice on which to draw, but it needs to become central to policy interventions.
- **Measures to address claimants' ill-health and disabilities.** The health problems and disabilities that so many see as an obstacle to working are real enough, even if not necessarily an insurmountable barrier. In this respect, UK policy remains poorly developed, with the 'employment' and 'health' services still largely operating in separate silos. Health services focused on rehabilitation and occupational health policies all have roles to play, including in the workplace.

Action is needed on all these fronts. By themselves, the supply-side interventions favoured by the UK's Coalition government, such as the Work Programme, designed mainly to promote labour market engagement among benefit claimants, stand little chance of success. The barriers posed by ill-health and disability also need to be addressed, and there needs to be an adequate supply of jobs for former claimants to fill. But even if action on a broad front were to be forthcoming and highly successful, it would still take the labour market many years to absorb the enormous accumulated stock of disability claimants. In the short-run, the way forward is to go easy on the pace of benefit reform.

The Labour Government's original reforms, announced in 2006, seemed to recognise that there were limits to how fast disability numbers might be brought down without causing unnecessary hardship. These reforms set in motion the introduction of ESA, the new medical test and the new requirement for all but the most severely ill or disabled ESA claimants to engage in work-related activity. Crucially, at this stage ESA applied only to *new* claimants. Since most new claimants have recent work experience and many express a desire to return to work, it seemed reasonable to target back-to-work efforts at this group.

The effect of the 2006 reforms would have been to gradually reduce the stock of IB claimants and replace them with a smaller number of ESA claimants who in most cases had always had to engage in work-related activity. No new requirements were being placed on the existing IB claimants. In this respect these reforms followed the model used in 1995, when Incapacity Benefit replaced Invalidity Benefit and existing claimants were allowed to retain their previous terms and conditions.

In important respects the Labour Government's second round of reform, announced in 2008, was already a step too far. The extension of compulsory work-focused interviews was perhaps a reasonable move, providing the opportunity to draw attention to the assistance available to return to work. However, the re-testing of existing IB claimants and the requirement (for those transferred into the ESA Work-Related Activity Group) to draw up plans to move closer to employment were always going to be contentious.

The problem is that existing IB claimants, a high proportion of whom have been on disability benefits for many years, often stand little realistic chance of finding work. Their long period on benefits frequently disqualifies them in the eyes of employers, let alone their often advancing years, poor qualifications, low-grade work experience, and poor health. That so many IB claimants live in the weakest local economies up and down the country adds a still further twist. Labour's second round of reforms was always set to trigger much distress for very little reward.

The Coalition's time-limiting of entitlement to non-means-tested benefit will merely crank up the levels of distress. Not only will claimants have to jump through new medical hoops and prepare themselves for jobs they are most unlikely to find, but large numbers will also discover, from 2012 onwards, that their benefit is cut or withdrawn altogether. The only winner is the Treasury.

In terms of the numbers affected and the scale and severity of the impact, the reforms to disability benefits that are now underway are probably the most far-reaching changes to the benefits system for at least a generation. They will impoverish vast numbers of households, and cause untold distress in countless more. The disability benefit numbers need to be brought down, but this is not the way.

## References

Beatty, C. and Fothergill, S. (2005) 'The Diversion from Unemployment to Sickness across British Regions and Districts', *Regional Studies*, 39 (7), 837–854.
Beatty, C. and Fothergill, S. (2011) *Incapacity Benefit Reform: The Local, Regional and National Impact* (Sheffield: Centre for Regional Economic and Social Research).
Beatty, C., Fothergill, S., Houston, D., Powell, R., and Sissons, P. (2009) *Women on Incapacity Benefits* (Sheffield: Sheffield Hallam University).
DWP (Department for Work and Pensions) (2007) *Transformation of the Personal Capability Assessment: Technical Working Group Phase 2 Evaluation Report* (London: DWP).
DWP (2011a) *Employment and Support Allowance: Impact Assessment* (London: DWP).
DWP (2011b) *Press release*, 10 February.
DWP (2011c) *Time Limit Contributory Employment and Support Allowance to One Year for Those in the Work-Related Activity Group: Impact Assessment* (London: DWP).
Fraser, N. and Gordon, L. (1994) 'A Genealogy of Dependency: Tracing a Keyword of the US Welfare State', *Signs: Journal of Women in Culture and Society*, 19 (2), 309–336.
Kemp, P. and Davidson, J. (2010) 'Employability Trajectories among New Claimants of Incapacity Benefit', *Policy Studies*, 31 (2), 203–221.
Lindsay, C. and Houston, D. (2011) 'Fit for Purpose? Welfare Reform and Challenges for Health and Labour Market Policy in the UK', *Environment and Planning A*, 43 (3), 703–721.
Martin, R. and Morrison, P. (2003) 'Thinking about the Geographies of Labour', in R. Martin and P. Morrison (eds) *Geographies of Labour Market Inequality* (London: Routledge).
Peck, J. (2001) *Workfare States* (New York: Guilford).
Sunley, P. and Martin, R. (2000) 'The Geographies of the National Minimum Wage', *Environment and Planning A*, 32 (10): 1735–1758.
Taylor-Gooby, P. (2008) 'Choice and Values: Individualised Rational Action and Social Goals', *Journal of Social Policy*, 37 (2): 167–185.
Williams F. (1999) 'Good-Enough Principles for Welfare', *Journal of Social Policy*, 28 (4): 667–687.

# 9

# Germany: Attempting to Activate the Long-Term Unemployed with Reduced Working Capacity

*Martin Brussig and Matthias Knuth*

## Introduction

Unlike in the United Kingdom, there is nothing in Germany that could be aptly called a 'disability crisis', and there is no equivalent discourse. Although it has often been hinted that restrictions on early retirement, which have become effective gradually in Germany since 1997, would result in an increased influx into disability pensions, there is no empirical sign of this. Strict gatekeeping and financial unattractiveness of disability pensions have led to a decline in take-up, arguably aided by improvements in public health in general.

If there is anything related to disability that could aptly be named a crisis, it is the poverty risk. Payments of disability pensions have fallen, gatekeeping has been tightened, and increasing numbers of people with a health condition find themselves not eligible for a disability pension and thus in receipt of the 'Minimum Income Benefit for Jobseekers'. This is an activating and 'Work First' regime, equivalent to Jobseeker's Allowance in the UK, but in practice and on average, people with restricted working ability are activated less. It can be demonstrated, however, that activation works for them as well, though a higher dosage is needed in order to produce any effect.

Combining employment assistance with support for health improvements appears a logical consequence, but such measures are still in their pilot stage, and 'hard' evidence for their effectiveness is lacking. It must be admitted, however, that work will not be a viable solution for some of these people. Therefore, against the backdrop of comparatively low disability figures, a voluntary option out of the activation regime seems justified.

## The institutional framework of disability pensions

### Relevant features of the German pension system in general

Germany's mainstream provision for disabled workers is an integral part of the pension system. Basically speaking, there are three types of pensions: (1) old-age pensions, (2) pensions paid because of reduced earning capacity (*Renten wegen verminderter Erwerbsfähigkeit*), referred to as 'disability pensions' throughout the remainder of this chapter, and (3) surviving dependants' pensions, which will be of no further concern here. Among the old-age pensions, the mainstream type is the pension at statutory retirement age of currently 65, already legislated to rise gradually to 67 between 2012 and 2029. In addition, there are several types of old-age pensions that are prematurely available under certain conditions. Among these, the old-age pension for severely handicapped persons (*Altersrente für schwerbehinderte Menschen*) is of some concern in the context of this chapter because, at the earliest from the age of 60, it may serve as an alternative to a disability pension.

In the German pension system, 'Bismarckian' principles of social insurance are still more purely preserved than in most of the other four pillars of social insurance.[1] Of these principles, which explain why Germany has seen a decline rather than an expansion of disability pensions, the following seem relevant to be highlighted in the context of disability:

- **entitlements are contribution-based**: there is no entitlement without a sufficient contribution record (with sufficiency defined differently for different types of benefits);
- **employee-centredness**: with few exceptions, social insurance contributions are tied to wages and salaries of dependant employees in the two-fold sense that these contributions are compulsory and that voluntary contributions are not accepted;[2]
- **equivalence**: contributions (which are equally shared between employers and employees in most branches of social insurance[3]) are proportional to earnings, and pensions, in particular, are proportional to lifetime contribution records;
- **redistribution-adverseness**: as far as pensions are to reflect considerations other than lifetime contributions (such as career interruptions for the raising of small children), the resulting costs have to be funnelled into the pension fund from national tax revenue;
- **risk principle borrowed from private insurance**: benefit entitlements are linked to clearly and legally defined risks and, in some cases, to causal chains (like pensions arising from work accidents and recognised occupational diseases).

With regard to the risk principle, old-age pensions are construed as covering the risk of surviving beyond statutory retirement age, whereas disability pensions are to cover the risk of becoming unable to work before reaching statutory pension age. Consequently, disability pensions may be taken up at any workable age but are automatically transposed into old-age pensions at statutory pension age.[4] The payment level of the pension is not affected by this redefinition, which means that low disability pensions lead to low old-age pensions (see discussion below on payment levels). It is only in the age span between 60 and 65 that a disability pension and a premature old-age pension for the handicapped can be an alternative if both requirements are met.[5]

## Access to disability pensions

Owing to the contribution principle, the risk of disability is only covered for those who have been in employment subject to social insurance contributions for at least three years during five years preceding the inception of their disability.[6] Contributions are also paid for unemployed persons while they are receiving benefits from the unemployment insurance fund (maximum duration of 12 months; up to 24 months for older workers). Furthermore, until the end of 2010, contributions were also paid for jobseekers without (or after exhaustion of) insurance entitlements but receiving means-tested benefits. Being very small, these contributions did not contribute substantially to augmenting pension entitlements; in the case of disability pensions, however, they could serve to fulfil the 'three in five years' rule. Thus, the recent abolishment of pension fund contributions for jobseekers on minimum income benefits will further restrict the access to disability pensions.

Persons affected by disability while not attached to the labour market at all are excluded from disability pensions; they will receive means-tested social assistance if they are in need. Disabilities resulting from work accidents or recognised occupational diseases are insured in a separate pillar of social insurance.[7] Contrasting the latter, the cause or origin of a disability is of no concern when applying for a disability pension. However, entitlement for disability pensions requires a strict medical examination by a doctor commissioned by the pension fund. The degree of disablement will be assessed in terms of the reduced number of working hours the person in question would still be able to perform per day 'under the customary conditions of the general labour market'.[8] Only slightly more than half of the applications for disability pensions result in approval, with a declining tendency (Brussig, 2010).

Since a reform in 2001, occupations have become disregarded;[9] inability to perform the kind of work a person used to be engaged in does not qualify for a disability pension if the person is considered able to perform some other kind of work. Two degrees of disability are now distinguished: A person unable to sustain at least three hours of daily work will be regarded as 'fully disabled', whereas the attested ability to work more than three but less than six hours will only entitle a person to a pension because of 'partial disablement'. The latter pays half the amount of a pension because of full disability;[10] the idea is to combine such a partial disability pension with a part-time job. Only if the person in question is unemployed at the time of the decision and if part-time jobs are unavailable in the respective region and sector may a person only partially disabled receive a full disability pension.[11] In the years 2002 to 2009, after the new system introduced in 2001 had bedded in, around two-thirds of annual new entries into disability pensions were based on full disability, and percentages of additional full pensions awarded because of labour market considerations ran between 14% and 16%, with only modest reactivity to unemployment rates (see Figure 9.1).

According to the law, new disability pensions should be awarded for periods of three years at the most, after which working ability will be reassessed; only after nine years should such pensions become open-ended until the recipient, upon reaching statutory retirement age, is transferred to an old-age pension. Thus, there is a strong 'back-to-work' or even 'Work First' principle inherent in the scheme, at least in theory.[12] According to expert interviews at the German Pension Insurance Fund, however, around half of the new disability pensions are actually awarded open-ended from the beginning, legally based on the assumed improbability of the person's recovery.

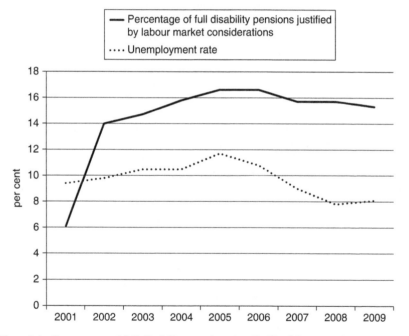

*Figure 9.1*  Percentages of full disability pensions justified by labour market considerations in total take-ups of disability pensions, 2001–2009
*Source*: German pension insurance fund, http://forschung.deutsche-rentenversicherung.de/ForschPortalWeb/contentAction.do?statzrID=6F7C2D590833F2A6C1256F2A0033EDE8&chstatzr_Rente=WebPagesIIOP119&open&viewName=statzr_Rente#WebPagesIIOP119.

In conjunction with the division of social insurance into several separate pillars whose representatives carefully monitor whether their funds are being 'misused' for outside purposes, the risk principle works as a barrier against disability pensions being utilised for buffering regional labour market problems as an intentional policy. This does not preclude, however, that regionally elevated unemployment may instigate more applications for disability pensions or that widespread experience of long-term unemployment may aggravate health problems in the region affected. Furthermore, where regional labour market problems have resulted from the decline of 'old' industries they may coincide with a concentration of displaced workers who once were subjected to physically demanding and damaging working conditions. However, to our knowledge, the regional variation in disability pension claims has not yet been investigated in Germany beyond the customary differentiation between East and West Germany. Except for the above-mentioned small window through which the vagaries of the labour market may transform a partial into a full disability pension, the gatekeeping at the entrance to disability pensions is not supposed to react to labour market conditions. Besides, disability pensions are not financially attractive.

## Unattractiveness of disability pensions

Following from the equivalence principle, the foremost parameter determining the level of individual pensions of any category is the relative position of contributable lifetime earnings. A person earning average wages during a given calendar year will acquire one credit point; above or below average earners will receive a multiple or fraction of a credit point, depending on their relative earnings position.[13] Where disability pensions rather than old-age pensions are concerned, contribution careers are incomplete by definition. This is only compensated in part by allotting credit points for fictitious earnings during the period between pension take-up and the 60th birthday. Career promotions recipients might have received if they had been able to continue working are not taken into account, and the extrapolation of their contribution record stops short of statutory (65 years) as well as statistical average pension age (63.9 years for men and 63.6 years for women in 2010).[14] In analogy to the rules applying to old-age pensions, deductions of 0.3% of the payable amount were introduced for each month of entering a disability pension before the 63rd birthday (counting only from the 60th birthday, thus the maximum deduction is 10.8%).[15] As a consequence of these rules, disability pensions tend to be low, and the payable amounts have actually decreased in nominal terms, so even more in real terms (see Figure 9.2). This applies to pensions because of full disability but even more to those because of partial disability.

The low financial attractiveness of disability pensions can be demonstrated by a comparison between their monthly payable amounts and those of

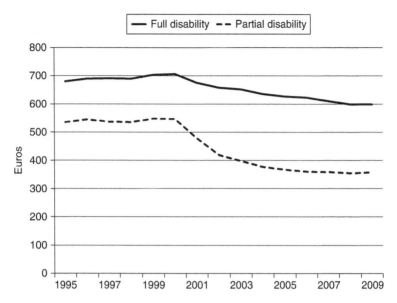

*Figure 9.2*  Average monthly payments at take-up of pensions because of full or partial disability (Euros)

Source: German pension insurance fund, http://forschung.deutsche-rentenversicherung.de/ ForschPortalWeb/contentAction.do?statzrID=6F7C2D590833F2A6C1256F2A0033EDE8&chstatzr_ Rente=WebPagesIIOP119&open&viewName=statzr_Rente#WebPagesIIOP119.

*Table 9.1*  Average monthly payments of disability pensions and old-age pensions at take-up; minimum income benefits, 2009 (Euros)

|  |  | Disability | Old age | | Disability/ all old age | Minimum income benefits for jobseekers |
|---|---|---|---|---|---|---|
|  |  |  | All old-age pensions | Statutory age only |  |  |
| West | Men | 643 | 860 | 665 | 0.75 | 634 |
|  | Women | 562 | 463 | 298 | 1.21 |  |
| East | Men | 570 | 891 | 951 | 0.64 | 602 |
|  | Women | 602 | 671 | 624 | 0.9 |  |

*Source*: German pension insurance fund, http://forschung.deutsche-rentenversicherung.de/ ForschPortalWeb/contentAction.do?statzrID=6F7C2D590833F2A6C1256F2A0033EDE8&chstatzr_ Rente=WebPagesIIOP119&open&viewName=statzr_Rente#WebPagesIIOP119.

old-age pensions in 2009. It turns out that disability pensions are generally lower for men and higher only for West German women (see Table 9.1). The latter paradox is brought about by female employment patterns in the West: After childbirth, many women have not been in employment at all (or only in atypical forms of employment not covered by social insurance). Therefore, their pensions are low and only become available at statutory pension age. In other words, employment careers of West German women with contribution records that qualify them for a disability pension are not comparable to the average of women taking up a pension at statutory pension age.

A second reference for comparison may be minimum income benefits. A single adult in need and thus entitled to minimum income benefits (see section on 'Access to disability pensions' above for details) will receive a monthly allowance of 364Euros plus the costs for 'adequate' housing and heating, the average amount paid to single-person households being 259 Euros in December 2009 (270 Euros in the West, 238 Euros in the East). In other words, average payments of disability pensions are close to or even below minimum income benefits. Where pensions because of partial disability are concerned, they tend to be lower than subsistence level. Unless this is compensated by other sources of income within the household, possibly including a complementary part-time job taken up by the pensioner, disability pensioners will have to rely on supplementary means-tested benefits.

## Preliminary conclusion

Taking all this together, gatekeeping for German disability pensions appears to be strict, these pensions do not appear to exert a strong pull effect, and their modest reaction to the labour market situation is confined to switches from partial to full disability pensions once disability as such has been recognised. Thus, these pensions seem to be a solution of last resort for persons who really cannot work any longer but are too young to qualify for an old-age pension.[16] Average age at take-up of a disability pension has declined from 58 (cohort of 1904) to 52 (cohort of 1944). Analysed by birth cohorts, the percentage of persons taking up a disability pension has drastically declined, which applies even more strongly to women than to men (see Figure 9.3). Such an analysis by cohorts is of necessity restricted to cohorts that have attained statutory retirement age. Therefore, the main declining effect must be attributed to improvements in working and health conditions of the population in general.

As a result of declining take-ups, the proportion of pensioners in the disability category is currently only 9% of all pensioners (excluding survivors' pensions), or 3.2% of the population 20 to under 65, or 4% of the active population of that age (unemployed considered 'active'– see Table 9.2).

So if one were to speak of a German disability crisis at all, it certainly does not consist of growing caseloads in disability pensions. Rather, the crisis seems to lie in the potential poverty related to disability, which is reflected in rising numbers of recipients of minimum income benefits because of full disability (Figure 9.4).

*Figure 9.3* Take-up of disability pensions as percentages of all pension take-ups by birth cohort (West Germany)

*Source*: German pension insurance fund, http://forschung.deutsche-rentenversicherung.de/ ForschPortalWeb/contentAction.do?statzrID=6F7C2D590833F2A6C1256F2A0033EDE8&chstatzr_ Rente=WebPagesIIOP119&open&viewName=statzr_Rente#WebPagesIIOP119.
Long time series allowing cohort analysis are not available for East Germany.

*Table 9.2* Stock of pensioners by pension type and gender, 31 December 2010

|  | Men | Women | Total | Percentage of women |
|---|---|---|---|---|
| Disability | 827,494 | 761,835 | 1,590,329 | 47.9 |
| Old-age | 7,782,010 | 9,836,778 | 17,618,788 | 55.8 |
| Of these: premature old-age pensions for severely handicapped persons (60 to 64 only) | 242,989 | 181,659 | 424,648 | 42.8 |
| Percentage of disability pensions in all pensions | 10.6 | 7.7 | 9.0 | |
| Disability pensioners + premature pensioners because of handicap as percentages of... | Population 20 to under 65 | | 4.1 | |
| | Active population 20 to under 65 (unemployed included) | | 5.0 | |

*Source*: German Pension Insurance Fund; Federal Bureau of Statistics.

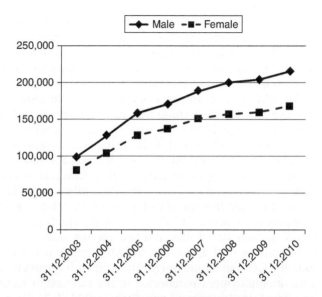

*Figure 9.4* Recipients of minimum income benefits because of full disability
*Source*: Federal Statistcal Bureau, downloaded from database on 05.11.2011.

These social assistance-type, means-tested benefits are paid either as a complement to pensions because of full disability if recipients of low pension payments are in need, or they are paid to persons whose full disability has been recognised but who lack a sufficient contribution record to qualify for a pension. It is therefore unclear how many of the almost 400,000 recipients of this benefit should be added to the number of almost 1.6 million disabled.

Furthermore, it has been demonstrated that German unemployment, high in European comparison before the crisis of 2008/2009 raised unemployment levels in other countries, can in part be attributed to restricted access to a disability status as an alternative (Börsch-Supan, 2011; Erlinghagen and Knuth, 2010). Since unemployment caused by restricted working ability tends to be persistent, it will lead to the exhaustion of wage-replacing unemployment benefits and thus into receipt of means-tested minimum income benefits as a last resort. In order to have a balanced view of disability in Germany, one has to identify those with reduced working capacity among the claimants of this benefit.

## Minimum income benefits for jobseekers

Persons unable to find or to sustain work for reasons of poor health but not qualifying for a disability pension (see section on 'Access to disability pensions' above for entitlement rules) have to rely on means-tested income support systems. Taking effect from January 2005, unemployment assistance (a tax-funded and means-tested benefit proportional to previous earnings and paid only after the exhaustion of unemployment benefits) was merged with social assistance as far as claimants were considered able to work.[17] The definition of 'able to work' mirrors the threshold for 'full disability' as explained above: Those not able to work for at least three hours per day but not qualifying for a full disability pension because of an insufficient contribution record or receiving such a pension with an insufficient payment level continued to receive social assistance (renamed 'minimum income benefit for disabled persons').[18] Everybody considered able to work for three hours or more but currently unable to support themselves and their families qualifies for the new work-oriented benefit called 'Unemployment Benefit II' (UB II). UB II, which can be seen as paralleling UK 'income-based' JSA, has become the mainstream benefit for jobless persons as well as for the 'working poor', whereas the currently favourable German employment situation with relatively few fresh entrants into unemployment is reflected in the rareness of recipients of contribution-based unemployment benefits (see Table 9.3). There is great variation in regional recipiency rates of UBII in a range between 2% (surroundings of Munich) and more than 18% (Gelsenkirchen, northern Ruhr district), with a rate of currently 6.8% for Germany as a whole.

Among those receiving UB II are people who would qualify for a pension because of partial disability on medical grounds (working ability between

*Table 9.3*   Allocation of workless people to income support systems by virtue of their ability to work and their pension contribution record

| Daily working ability | Medical category | | Sufficient contribution record? | Primary benefit category | Supplementary benefit category in case of neediness at household level |
|---|---|---|---|---|---|
| <3 hr | Fully disabled | Provisionally | No | Full disability pension | Social... ...assistance |
| | | | Yes | | Minimum |
| | | Permanently | No | | income benefit... |
| | | | | | ...for disabled persons |
| 3 to >6 hr | Partially disabled | | Yes | Partial disability pension | Minimum income benefit ... |
| | | | No | | |
| 6 hr and more | 'Full' working ability | | | | ...for jobseekers (UBII) |

*Source*: Own *calculations*.

## The customer survey

The data used for the analysis in the analysis below originate from a computer-aided telephone 'customer survey' of 25,000 respondents receiving UB II, part of which was organised as a panel. Sampling was restricted to 154 (of roughly 440) regional units in Germany, and was stratified in several dimensions to capture sufficient numbers of individuals in defined target groups, such as lone parents, handicapped persons etc. The analysis presented here is based on the panel, that is, those 11,108 respondents who had been sampled from the caseload as it existed between September 19 and 18 October 2006, and who were actually interviewed twice. The first wave of interviews was conducted between January and April 2007, the second wave between November 2007 and March 2008. As far as possible, individual interviews were sequenced in such a way as to have roughly equal time spans between the first and the second wave. Percentages calculated in this chapter have been adjusted for sample stratification and for differing response rates in different strata of the sample. However, it should be noted that – strictly speaking – these findings are representative only for the 154 regional units and not for the Federal Republic as a whole. The selection of regional units relates to the principal purpose of the research, which was to evaluate two competing organisational models concerning the implementation of the new benefit system (cf. Bundesregierung, 2008; ZEW, IAQ, and TNS Emnid, 2008).

three and six hours per day) but lack a sufficient contribution record, as well as those who do receive a partial disability pension which, however, does not meet their household's needs (a partial disability pension pays only half the amount of a full disability pension), and who do not manage to find the complementary part-time job they are supposed to look for. As Table 9.3 demonstrates, UBII has become the benefit of last resort for several categories of working-age people with reduced working capacity, including those who are considered able to work for six hours per day but not a full working day.

## Health conditions of recipients of minimum income benefits for jobseekers

As a consequence of the institutional setting explained in the previous section, numbers of people with reduced health capacity are quite high in the new benefit system, which is oriented towards activation and towards quitting the benefit through taking up employment. The health condition of recipients can be represented by responses to a large customer telephone survey, which was conducted in the framework of evaluating the implementation of the new benefit regime (see box).

With regard to self-assessed ability to work, almost 4% of the respondents appear to be misplaced in the system because they say they cannot even sustain three hours of daily work (see Table 9.4); 13.8% of respondents place themselves in the still problematic category between three and under six hours of daily working ability, and there are another 19% who say they can work only between six and eight hours. In this category, however, there are considerable percentages of respondents assessing their health as satisfactory or better, which may indicate a misconception of the question in the direction of 'availability for work' rather than 'ability'.

For purposes of multivariate analysis, the two survey items were combined into one ordinal scale where those 47.1% able to work eight hours or more and with at least 'good' health make up health category (1), whereas those with slight impairments (working ability between six and under eight hours or only 'satisfactory' health condition make up category (2). Those 5.7% who can only work between three and under six hours *and* find their health 'not so good' or 'bad' make up category (4), and the 3.1% who say they cannot even work three hours and find their health 'not so good' or 'bad' make up category (5), the hard core of health impairment. Finally, the 'in-betweens' where reported working ability and health condition does not quite seem to match are categorised as (3).

For descriptive purposes, and to be taken up again below, it should be noted that almost 9%, the recipients of 'unemployment benefit II', are clearly disadvantaged in terms of their working capacity. This amounts to around 400,000 persons. According to the official statistics of the German Public Employment Service, 17.6% of the *unemployed* receiving this benefit were suffering from 'restrictions of their health with detrimental effects on the possibility to place them' in 2009 (Bundesagentur für Arbeit, 2011) – again roughly 400,000 persons, although the categories are not the same.

*Table 9.4*   Index of health-related capacity (percentages of responses)

| | | Daily working capability (in hours) | | | | |
|---|---|---|---|---|---|---|
| | | 8 hr or more | 6 to <8 hr | 3 to <6 hr | <3 hr | Total |
| Health condition | Very good | 18.9 **(1) 47.1** | 3.1 **(2) 28.8** | 1.0 | 0.0 **(3) 15.1** | 23.2 |
| | Good | 28.2 | 7.0 | 2.7 | 0.2 | 38.2 |
| | Satisfactory | 12.8 | 5.9 | 4.4 | 0.5 | 23.7 |
| | Not so good | 2.4 | 2.2 | 3.7 **(4) 5.7** | 1.0 **(5) 3.1** | 9.3 |
| | Bad | 0.9 | 0.7 | 2.0 | 2.1 | 5.7 |
| | Total | 63.3 | 19.0 | 13.8 | 3.9 | 100.0 |

*Source*: UB II customer panel (stock sample only), own calculations.

If we adopt a broader definition by considering all those in Table 9.4 who say they cannot work 8 hours *and* do not assess their health at least as 'good', we end up with roughly 1 million claimants of a 'Work First' benefit whose access to employment may be hampered by weakness of their health. Comparing this to the almost 1.6 million claimants of disability pensions (see Table 9.2), the number of health-restricted would-be jobseekers is smaller but nevertheless considerable.

## Activation of people with impaired health: Results from a standardised survey[19]

Both in rhetoric and institutional set-up, a strong Work First approach is implemented in the regime of 'minimum income benefits for jobseekers'. For instance, the very name of the benefit ('unemployment benefit II') labels recipients as 'unemployed', although less than half of them actually count as such, whereas the others are employed but earn too little, are attending school or are exempted from job search because of sickness or caring responsibilities. While work incentives have been broadly discussed in the reform discourse, health has not been explicitly addressed. Medical rehabilitation in cases of officially recognised handicaps has suffered from the institutional split between unemployment insurance and basic income support for jobseekers (Rauch and Dornette, 2010).

At the time of the customer survey, more than two years after their creation, the newly established jobcentres still fell far short of their official mission of comprehensive activation. Only slightly more than two-thirds (69.8%) of the respondents had had at least one interview with their personal advisor during the six months prior to the survey. Only less than half (47.7%) had a currently valid personal action plan (*Eingliederungsvereinbarung*), and only slightly more than one quarter (27.9%) had ever received an offer for a job or for an apprenticeship (in the case of young people) since entering the system or since being referred to it from the two preceding minimum income benefit systems as of 1 January 2005. Even among those recipients officially registered as unemployed and thus considered available for employment, only 70.4% had had a jobcentre interview during the last six months, and only 50.5% had a valid personal action plan. In other words, even among those whose need for activation was beyond doubt, considerable numbers were being neglected.

Against this background, it seems relevant to ask how activation is related to the index of health-related capacity introduced above. Are those with health problems activated more because they need more support? Or are they activated less due to 'creaming' decisions in an environment with still much too high caseloads of personal advisers?

Whereas the incidence of interviews varies little with health, personal action plans as well as job offers are fewer in the groups with weaker health

*Table 9.5*   Activation and health-related capacity

| | Index of health-related capacity | | | | |
|---|---|---|---|---|---|
| | (1) Very good | (2) Good | (3) Fair | (4) Poor | (5) Very poor |
| Interview with personal advisor during the last 6 months | 0,698 | 0,702 | 0,708 | 0,692 | 0,676 |
| Valid personal action plan | 0,506 | 0,492 | 0,446 | 0,354 | 0,398 |
| Offer of job or apprenticeship | 0,306 | 0,285 | 0,244 | 0,221 | 0,245 |
| Average number of activation items (max. 3, min. 0) | 1,473 | 1,454 | 1,365 | 1,263 | 1,262 |

*Source*: UB II customer panel (stock sample only), own calculations.

(see Table 9.5). On the one hand, this seems logical and reflects the emphasis on work in the new regime of basic income support for jobseekers. On the other hand, the fundamental justification for the reform that led to the merger of benefits and services from the two preceding benefit systems was to create more comprehensive services including psychosocial and other concomitant services. Even where work is not an immediate option, a personal action plan might include steps towards improving a person's health status, or there could be job offers adjusted to the individual's health condition. However, low intervention rates were found with regard to social or psychological problems (ZEW, IAQ, and TNSEmnid, 2007). Concepts and measures suited to address the often multi-morbid or unspecific syndromes of psychosomatic problems among long-term unemployed are evolving but slowly and sporadically (see section on 'Health support for jobseekers' below). This explains why the health score is inversely correlated with the activation score.

For minimum income benefit claimants, a positive impact of the above-mentioned forms of activation on employment take-up and quitting the benefit in conjunction with employment take-up[20] can be shown (see Table 9.6). Here, different aspects of activation are integrated into one cumulative index. The higher the index value is (minimum 0, maximum 3), the more comprehensive the activation has been.[21] The probit regressions reveal that activation does work in the expected direction of facilitating the take-up of employment, whereas its effects with regard to simultaneously quitting the benefit are somewhat weaker. Women experience a slight disadvantage on both outcome dimensions, and labour market conditions[22] work in the expected direction, albeit with small coefficients and at a low level of significance. Contrasting both with labour market conditions and activating treatment, health stands out as the single strongest predictor for entering employment and leaving the benefit (see Table 9.6).

*Table 9.6* Effects of activation on employment outcomes

|  | Employment take-up | Quitting the benefit in conjunction with employment take-up |
|---|---|---|
| Number of applicable items of activation (reference category: none) | | |
| 1 | 0.127±(0.040) | 0.076*(0.042) |
| 2 | 0.271±(0.039) | 0.213±(0.041) |
| 3 | 0.377±(0.048) | 0.295±(0.050) |
| Index of health-related capacity (reference category: fair) | | |
| 1 Very good | 0.219±(0.046) | 0.444±(0.053) |
| 2 Good | 0.147±(0.047) | 0.343±(0.054) |
| 4 Poor | −0.181**(0.083) | −0.164(0.102) |
| 5 Very poor | −0.456±(0.119) | −0.436±(0.152) |
| Gender: female (reference category: male) | −0.198±(0.033) | −0.155±(0.034) |
| Regional labour market (reference category: average) | | |
| Below average | −0.115±(0.037) | −0.116±(0.038) |
| Above average | 0.123±(0.036) | 0.065*(0.038) |

*Note*: Also controlled for age and belonging to one or more 'target groups' of labour market policy (parents with small children, lone parents, handicapped persons, and migrant background). Coefficients, in parentheses standard errors.
±, **, *: significant *at* 1%, 5%, and 10% level, respectively.
*Source*: UB II customer panel (stock sample only), own calculations.

However, these analyses do not sufficiently take into consideration that people with a weaker health-related capacity are activated less intensively and perhaps in different ways. How do health and activation interact with regard to employment outcomes? Does activation work differently for groups with different health-related capacity?

To explore this question, four probit models were estimated for two employment outcomes (employment take-up versus quitting the benefit in conjunction with employment take-up), separated for two health categories: superior ('very good' + 'good') and inferior ('fair' + 'poor' + 'very poor'). Again, activation is represented here as a cumulative index consisting of the number of applicable items.

As Table 9.7 shows, activation does work for both subpopulations in the expected direction and in a consistent pattern. However, those with inferior health need more activation (at least two applicable items) to experience a statistically significant improvement of the more demanding employment outcome indicator, that is, quitting the benefit. Only where all three items of activation are applicable do differences between the coefficients for the two subpopulations become negligible. The effects of gender and of regional labour market conditions are significant only for the group with superior

*Table 9.7*   Health-differentiated effects of activation on employment outcomes

| | Employment take-up | | Quitting the benefit in conjunction with employment take-up | |
|---|---|---|---|---|
| | **Health-related capacity** | | | |
| | **Superior** | **Inferior** | **Superior** | **Inferior** |
| Number of applicable items of activation (reference category: none) | | | | |
| 1 | 0.144±(0.046) | 0.043*(0.088) | 0.102**(0.047) | 0.047 (0.110) |
| 2 | 0.259±(0.044) | 0.307±(0.087) | 0.213±(0.045) | 0.308±(0.105) |
| 3 | 0.382±(0.054) | 0.344±(0.116) | 0.300±(0.055) | 0.338**(0.139) |
| Gender: female (reference category: male) | −0.235±(0.037) | −0.087(0.076) | −0.162±(0.037) | −0.189**(0.090) |
| Regional labour market (reference category: average) | | | | |
| Below average | −0.115±(0.041) | −0.099 (0.087) | −0.115±(0.042) | −0.067 (0.105) |
| Above average | 0.134±(0.041) | 0.118 (0.077) | 0.089**(0.042) | 0.084 (0.094) |

*Note*: Also controlled for age and belonging to one or more 'target groups' of labour market policy (parents with small children, lone parents, handicapped persons, and migrant background). Coefficients, in parentheses standard errors.
±, **, *: significant at 1%, 5%, and 10% level, respectively.
*Source*: UB II customer panel (stock sample only), own calculations.

health, which can arguably be taken as an indication that the employment and benefit status of those with inferior health will not improve automatically as a regional labour market recovers; it is only active support that will have some positive effect on this group.

According to these results, activation does work even for people with reduced health-related capacities, but a higher dosage is needed before effects become visible. Given the sufficient dosage, the differential effect of activation as compared with no activation becomes equivalent for the two subgroups with 'superior' and 'inferior' health-related capacity. This does not alter the fact that those of inferior health are less likely to take up employment, be it with or without activation. Because activation of people with impaired health requires higher intensity to be effective at all while still producing lower rates of desired outcomes, it is more costly, but these expenses are not wasted.

## Health support for jobseekers

In recent years, several attempts have been made to deal with health problems of unemployed jobseekers. At a fundamental level, we distinguish two approaches how this can be achieved: institutional cooperation and institutional innovation. *Institutional cooperation* is cooperation between different pillars of social insurance several of which are directly or indirectly concerned with health. This is obvious for health insurance funds, but also the unemployment insurance fund and the pension insurance fund have mandates for rehabilitation and spend resources accordingly in order to help claimants return to work or to avert claims. In 2010, the pension insurance fund has spent almost 5.6 billion Euros (around 2.3% of its total spending) on rehabilitation. The statutory health insurance funds spent 2.4 billion Euros on rehabilitation and more than 5 billion Euros on preventive measures in 2008. There is an overlap of responsibilities and a massive volume of regulations about which pillar of social insurance is to pay for which rehabilitation measures under which conditions. Compared to over-regulation in the field of rehabilitation, it appears that it should be easier to liaise between the only softly regulated responsibilities of health insurance funds for preventive measures and health promotion by jobs. Here, only two of the five pillars of social insurance would be concerned; however, the fragmentation of health insurance into 153 separate funds does not make things as easy as they might appear.

Although, in recent years, some prominent commitments for institutional cooperation have been achieved and some more are under way (GKV-Spitzenverband, 2010), a lively institutional cooperation between different pillars of security is not easily attained. In some cases, interests of pension insurers and labour market policy are contradictory even though both follow a work-oriented approach. For instance, unemployed persons to be rehabilitated by the pension insurance funds may receive a hiring subsidy for their employer by the pension insurance, and at the same time by the Public Employment Service (PES). Both hiring subsidies may constitute an attractive bundle for the employer. However, both pension insurance funds and PES evaluate independently of each other whether such a hiring subsidy would be appropriate. While the PES pursues an uncompromising Work First approach, the pension insurance fund is more concerned with the adequacy of working conditions and whether they might aggravate existing health risks to such an extent that the person in question would eventually qualify for a disability pension (Zwick et al., 2006). Such an outcome would still be cost-saving for the unemployment insurance fund or the minimum income benefit budget, but not for the pension insurance fund. This exemplifies how the separation of social insurance into separate pillars with different responsibilities and rationales is hampering institutional cooperation. Cooperation between the PES and health insurance is equally difficult to attain. The areas of responsibility do not seem to be clearly defined at the interface of the two 'pillars' of social insurance concerned. Negotiations between these actors can be very tedious and only lead to locally or regionally limited agreements.

*Institutional innovation* means that labour market policy enlarges its traditional set of instruments by health-related programmes. Institutional

*Table 9.8*  Programmes to support health and work promotion

|  | Aim | Approach |
|---|---|---|
| JobFit | Develop and test a successful link between health and employment promotion with a special focus on joint financing<br>• Embedding health competence in the PES-setting by means of qualifying the staff<br>• Stress coping and individual health competence consulting with special focus on stress caused by unemployment | • Jobcentres offer individual health competence consulting<br>• Insurance funds finance a prevention course for jobseekers run by a provider of training courses<br>• The JobFit approach can be realised in every region provided that an agreement between health insurance funds and jobcentres or rather providers of educational courses has been concluded |
| AmigA | • Unemployed persons and jobseekers suffering from impaired health<br>• Health and employment promotion are objectives of equal rank | • Health-and employment-oriented case-management in the PES<br>• Case managers are supported by an interdisciplinary team of health professionals and psychological psychotherapists |
| AktivA | • Improving psychological and physical well-being of the unemployed<br>• Empowering the unemployed in planning activities and in constructive thinking as well as enhancing their social skills and contacts | • Education and training of disseminators in educational institutions that work with unemployed persons |
| Perspective 50plus–Employment pacts for older workers in the regions | • Promotes the (re-) entry in the labour market of older long-term unemployed | • Not a health-promoting-project by itself, but enables jobcentres to implement health-related measures (by financial resources)<br>• National programme issued by the German Federal Ministry of Labour and Social Affairs |

*Source*: Brussig, M., N. Dragano, and S. Mümken (2011) 'Poor Health as a Cause and as an Effect of Unemployment: What Can Be Done, What Should Be Done in Activating Labour Market Policy? Experiences from Germany'. Presentation at the 9th ESPAnet conference, September 2011.

innovation depends less than cooperation on the willingness and abilities of other partners, but might be implemented autonomously. So far, practical implementation has taken place only in pilot programmes. Some of the biggest programmes in terms of regional distribution and case numbers are summarised in Table 9.8

These programmes differ in their approach, demonstrating that health problems may take different forms, result from several causes, affect specific groups differently, and allow for various ways to promote health support for jobseekers. In two programmes (JobFit, AmigA), labour market policy and health insurers cooperate in programme financing.

At the current stage, three problems stand out:

First, health promotion for jobseekers stands in contrast to the 'activation'-regime as implemented in Germany. As in Great Britain, but in contrast to, for example, The Netherlands and Ireland, Germany pursues a 'sanctioning activation' in contrast to an 'assisting activation' (Schünemann and Boyle, 2011). In a 'sanctioning activation' regime, which might also be described as a 'Work First' regime with strong punitive elements, the main criterion for success or failure of a labour market programme is reintegration into jobs. Typical goals of health-promoting programmes are, however, not to achieve immediate reintegration, but to restore employability and self-esteem first as a precondition to find a new job later. Within a 'sanctioning activation' regime, the goals of health-supporting programmes are not easy to integrate.

Second, skills and competencies of the staff in jobcentres and training agencies as well as the work organisation seem to be a major problem. For a long time, education and training of staff in PESs focused on administrative procedures. The overwhelming majority of street-level workers in jobcentres are not trained to identify health problems of their clients or to conduct a meaningful interaction on how to improve one's health under conditions of joblessness and poverty. This of course is not only a question of mere skills. Case load and work organisation often do not allow an in-depth profiling of clients (which would reveal health problems), nor does it allow the building up of trust between street-level worker and the client (which would be necessary to report intimate problems, such as alcohol problems). The integration of health support programmes for jobseekers requires resources and routines that hardly exist today, but from which most clients could benefit, not just those with health problems.

Third, evaluation of these programmes is underdeveloped, in particular in comparison with 'traditional' labour market programmes (training programmes, hiring subsidies, work creation schemes), which have been evaluated intensively with state-of-the-art-techniques. This is partly due to practical problems, such as the relative newness of these programmes, their uneven regional distribution, and the lack of standardised data on these new measures in the PES data systems. Furthermore, important conceptual issues are not yet resolved. Criteria for the success or failure of a health promotion programme are more difficult to define, control groups – necessary for a systematic comparison of a treatment effect – are harder to identify, and there is selectivity in the implementation of a programme that might influence the outcomes.

## Does Germany need a more generous provision for disabled people?

The principal disability problem in Germany does not seem to be a surge or high proportion in disability-related benefits (see Figure 9.3 and Table 9.2). Rather, there is a problem in that the mainstream provision for working-age people in need has to sustain a considerable proportion of claimants whose placement in the 'regular' labour market is highly improbable because of their reduced working ability. From the perspectives of countries attempting to reactivate claimants of disability benefits by redefining the benefit and making it conditional on job search, the German situation may be favourable because disability-related benefit provisions have never been designed as an escape from the labour market. From the perspective of the German minimum income benefit system, which is supposed to 'activate' people who cannot reasonably be activated for employment, the search for alternative benefits for the hard core of those concerned seems legitimate.

Building on the existing framework of categorising people according to their assessed daily working capacity, two categories come under consideration: Those not able to work three hours per day, and those only able to work between three and under six hours. The former category is misplaced in the minimum income benefit system for jobseekers even according to existing regulations. Reluctance of the PES to reallocate such cases into the receipt of minimum income benefits for disabled persons can be explained by considerations that in this way they would have shifted financial burdens to their municipal partners in cooperation with whom they run most of the jobcentres. These apprehensions may change gradually since procedures for assessing ability to work have been redefined as from January 2011, and municipalities will increasingly be compensated from the federal budget for these benefits.

However, those not able to work at least six hours per day are severely disadvantaged in the labour market as well. The classical part-time job with fixed hours is disappearing, as employers are increasingly using part-time as a buffer of permanent availability. Actual hours may fluctuate, and the part-time nature of the job bears out only as an average. Under such conditions, employers will be reluctant to hire people with restricted working ability even for jobs that are nominally part-time. Therefore, if a near-to-full working capacity of at least six hours per day cannot be restored by health-supporting measures, this category should be allowed to opt out of the activation system by opening up the 'minimum income benefit for disabled persons' for those in the category of working ability between three and six hours.

## Conclusion

The German experience sharply contrasts with that in the UK in that disability pensions have strongly declined. Contrary to a widespread notion that sees 'Bismarckian' systems of social protection in contradiction to 'activation' and a 'Work First' orientation, it appears that the German system of disability pensions developed strict gatekeeping and a 'back-to-work' orientation out of its own insurance logic long before the 'activating' turn in social policy. However, such a system excludes increasing numbers of people with reduced working ability, especially those who experienced atypical and unstable employment when they were still at work and therefore do not qualify for contribution-based disability benefits. Since the reform of benefits for workless people in 2005, people with reduced working ability tend to concentrate among the recipients of 'Minimum Income Benefit for Jobseekers', whereas fully disabled people who do not qualify for a disability pension or receive only pension payments below subsistence level will receive minimum income benefits for disabled people. Recipients of either of the two minimum income benefits cannot simply be added to recipients of disability pensions because of overlap. Disregarding this overlap, a total recipiency rate of around 5.4% of the working-age population marks a disability level with an order of magnitude comparable to the UK, though still considerably lower.

Insofar as disability pensions are discussed as a problem in Germany, these discussions have focused either on the restricted access to this type of benefit or on the growing share of disability pensions based on diagnoses of mental disorders. Since overall numbers of claimants have been declining, a possible regional concentration of claimants has not been a matter of concern so far. Therefore, research into the regional distribution of claimant rates is still lacking, to our knowledge. It appears quite plausible to assume that such regional variation exists and that it reflects both employment structures of the past and employment opportunities of the present. However, in the German context, it seems that research into regional variations in the process of applying and gatekeeping, including regional variations in the medical assessment of claimants' working abilities, seems more relevant than establishing regional variation in recipiency as such. It is in these assessment processes where the allocation of persons with reduced working capacity to different benefit categories is decided.

Minimum Income Benefit for Jobseekers (or 'UB II'), the default benefit for people not qualifying for a pension because of full disability, is claimed to be a 'Work First' regime. Since activation shows positive employment outcomes even for claimants with reduced working capacity, it may actually be an advantage to have these people within a general work-oriented regime from the beginning rather than having to redefine a benefit regime once constructed 'outside the labour market' as now 'work oriented'. Integrating health promotion into employment assistance may augment the effectiveness of activation, and there is some experimentation as to how this can be done. However, the potential of such programmes seems to be limited, which leads to the question whether people who cannot find work because of their reduced working ability, after a certain period of unsuccessful employment assistance, should be offered a voluntary escape from an activation regime that does not produce any progress for them. The question that inevitably follows is which kind of alternative benefit (or special status within an existing benefit) would be suited to provide such an escape.

## Notes

1. Besides (1) the federal pension fund, there is (2) the unemployment insurance fund, (3) a multiplicity of currently (1 August 2011) 153 statutory health insurance funds, which also manage (4) compulsory long-term care insurance, and then there are (5) sectoral insurance funds covering work accidents and occupational diseases.
2. This excludes civil servants (whose needs are taken care of directly by their public employers), self-employed, and those working 'mini-jobs' with earnings of no more than 400Euros per month as their only job.
3. Work accident and occupational disease insurance is an exception here because it is tied to employers' total payrolls rather than individual earnings, and it is paid by employers alone.
4. Not surprisingly, the OECD (2009, p. 229) finds that Germany has the highest share of disability benefit beneficiaries moving to retirement.
5. 'Handicap' (*Behinderung*) is a concept related to a person's entire ability to function and to participate in society. It is assessed as a percentage of full functionality typical for a person's age, and impairments in this dimension entitle people to all sorts of amenities, such as reduced fares. 'Disability' (actually, reduced earnings capacity – *Erwerbsminderung*) is related only to the ability to participate in gainful employment, and it is assessed in terms of daily working ability. Admittedly, the parallel existence of these two concepts may be confusing.
6. It is no surprise, then, when the OECD finds that 'Benefit recipients in Germany have substantially longer working experiences compared with non-recipients'(OECD, 2009, p. 219), and that mini-jobs dot not reduce the chances of employment in Germany, in contrast with other countries (p. 226). Although German institutional characteristics are reported correctly, they are not taken into consideration in the authors' interpretations.
7. Annual take-up of this type of pensions has declined drastically from around 4 cases per 1,000 full time equivalent jobs in 1960 to 0.5 cases in 2009, whereas take-up of pensions because of recognised occupational diseases has fluctuated at a low level under 10,000 cases annually (BMAS (Bundesministerium für Arbeit und Soziales), 2011, pp. 68, 70).

8. The expression 'general labour market' draws the distinction with sheltered workshops, make-work projects and the like.
9. For persons born 1961 or later, that is, at age 40 or younger.
10. While the statistical average of payments for pensions because of partial disability is higher than half the average payments for pensions because of full disability, this probably reflects the different composition of the two groups: Those earning relatively more enjoy relatively better working conditions, are less fatigued, and therefore qualify only for partial disability.
11. This clause was not found in the legal text since 2001 but was reintroduced by jurisdiction, drawing on principles derived from the previous system before the reform of 2001.
12. Although the OECD ascribes to Germany the highest 'integration index ranking' in the OECD (indicating policy priorities – OECD, 2009, p. 233)), it finds the lowest share of beneficiaries exiting to employment in Germany (p. 229).
13. There is a cap on the level of earnings taken into consideration. Earnings above this annually adjusted cap are not liable to contributions and do not raise the level of an eventual pension.
14. Such cross-sectional averages may be misleading because of uneven cohort sizes, especially in birth cohorts following the end of the Second World War. However, averages by birth cohorts can only be computed for cohorts that have passed statutory retirement age. The most recent value is 63.3 years for men and 63.2 years for women in the birth cohort of 1946. These are the highest values since the birth cohort of 1912, reflecting early retirement policies that affected a whole generation.
15. This is only an analogy insofar as the reference point for deductions from old-age pensions is the statutory pension age of currently 65. Premature pensions are currently being phased out, first by introducing deductions, later by raising the minimum age of take-up until all premature pensions will have disappeared except the one available from 63 under the condition of 35 years of contributions or activities regarded as equivalent to work, such as child rearing.
16. By contrast, the OECD ascribes to Germany an above-OECD-average generosity indicator (OECD, 2009, p. 233) made up of coverage, minimum disability level entitling to a full benefit, maximum earnings replacement rate, permanence of benefits, medical assessment, vocational assessment etc. (p. 232). How Germany could rank high on these dimensions appears rather unclear; namely, assessing financial generosity by 'replacement rate for average earnings with a continuous work record' is based on two unrealistic assumptions.
17. For a general overview of the reform, see Barbier and Knuth (2011).
18. At the end of 2009, there were slightly over 350,000 persons in receipt of this benefit. However, one cannot simply add this figure to that of the recipients of disability pensions because the minimum income benefit may either supplement an insufficient disability pension or replace it where eligibility is denied because of an insufficient contribution record.
19. Parts of this section draw on Brussig and Knuth (2010).
20. Taking up employment and quitting the benefit are only loosely connected since, on the one side, earnings may be too low to become independent of the benefit, whereas neediness of the household can also end because other members find work, take up some other benefits like a pension or leave the household.
21. Alternative models with single items that constitute the activation index (interview, integration plan, job offer) confirm the influence of these services on

employment outcomes, and the outstanding influence of health on these out-comes.

22. The Federal Institute for Employment Research provides a composite indica-tor for regional labour market performance, which is made up of the regional unemployment rate, the seasonal volatility of the labour market, population density, degree of tertiarisation of the job structure, regional job density and the influence of neighbouring regions (Blien, Hirschenauer, and Hong Van, 2010). The typology arrived at through cluster analysis (12 categories) was simplified into three categories for the purpose of our analysis, the middle category being used as the reference category.

# References

Barbier, J-C. and Knuth, M. (2011) 'Activating Social Protection against Unemployment: France and Germany Compared', *Sozialer Fortschritt*, 60 (1–2), 15–24.

Blien, U., Hirschenauer, F., and Hong Van, P.T. (2010) 'Classification Of Regional Labour Markets for Purposes of Labour Market Policy', *Papers in Regional Science*, 89 (4), 859–880.

BMAS (Bundesministerium für Arbeit und Soziales) (2011) *Sicherheit und Gesundheit bei der Arbeit 2009: Unfallverhütungsbericht Arbeit* (Dortmund/Berlin/Dresden: BMAS).

Börsch-Supan, A. (2011) 'Health and Disability Insurance', *Zeitschrift für Arbeitsmarkt Forschung*, 44 (4), 349–362.

Brussig, M. (2010) *Künftig mehr Zugänge in Altersrenten absehbar: Gegenwärtig kein Ausweichen in die Erwerbsminderungsrente zu beobachten* (Duisberg/Essen: IAQ).

Brussig, M. and Knuth, M. (2010) 'Rise Up And Work! Workless People with Impaired Health under Germany's New Activation Regime', *Social Policy and Society*, 9 (3), 311–323.

Bundesagentur für Arbeit (2011) *Arbeitsmarkt 2010 (Amtliche Nachrichten der Bundesagentur für Arbeit No. 58. Jahrgang, Sondernummer 2)* (Nürnberg: Bundesagentur für Arbeit).

Bundesregierung (2008) *Bericht zur Evaluation der Experimentierklausel nach § 6c des Zweiten Buches Sozialgesetzbuch: Unterrichtung durch die Bundesregierung* (Bundestagsdrucksache No. 16/11488) (Berlin: Bundesregierung).

Erlinghagen, M. and Knuth, M. (2010) 'Unemployment as an Institutional Construct? Structural Differences in Non-employment in Europe and the United States', *Journal of Social Policy*, 39 (1), 71–94.

GKV-Spitzenverband (2010) *Leitfaden Prävention: Handlungsfelder und Kriterien des GKV-Spitzenverbandes zur Umsetzung von §§ 20 und 20a SGB V vom 21. Juni 2000 in der Fassung vom 27. August 2010.* Retrieved from http://www.gkv-spitzenverband. de/upload/Leitfaden_Praevention_2010_web_14422.pdf. Date accessed 1 December 2011.

OECD (2009) *Employment Outlook: Tackling the Job crisis* (Paris: OECD).

Rauch, A. and Dornette, J. (2010) 'Equal Rights and Equal Duties? Activating Labour Market Policy and the Participation of Long-Term Unemployed People with Disabilities after the Reform of the German Welfare State', *Journal of Social Policy*, 39, 53–70.

Schünemann, W.J. and Boyle, N. (2011) 'Die vielen Gesichter aktivierender Arbeitsmarktpolitik: Deutschlands Hartz-Reformen im Vergleich zur aktivierenden

Arbeitsmarktreformen in den Niederlanden, Großbritannien und Irland', *Sozialer Fortschritt*, 60 (9), 189–196.

ZEW, IAQ and TNS Emnid (2007) *Evaluation der Experimentierklausel nach § 6c SGB II - Vergleichende Evaluation des arbeitsmarktpolitischen Erfolgs der Modelle der Aufgabenwahrnehmung 'Optierende Kommune' und 'Arbeitsgemeinschaft': Untersuchungsfeld 3: 'Wirkungs- und Effizienzanalyse'* (Mannheim: Erster Bericht durch den Forschungsverbund).

ZEW, IAQ, and TNS Emnid (2008) *Evaluation der Experimentierklausel nach § 6c SGB II - Vergleichende Evaluation des arbeitsmarktpolitischen Erfolgs der Modelle der Aufgabenwahrnehmung 'Optierende Kommune' und 'Arbeitsgemeinschaft':* Untersuchungsfeld 3: 'Wirkungs- und Effizienzanalyse' (Mannheim, Gelsenkirchen, Bielefeld: Abschlussbericht).

Zwick, T., Ammermüller, A., Bernhard, S., Boockmann, B., Brussig, M., Jaenichen, U. (2006) *Evaluation der Maßnahmen zur Umsetzung der Vorschläge der Hartz-Kommission. Arbeitspaket 1: Wirksamkeit der Instrumente*, Modul 1d: Eingliederungszuschüsse und Entgeltsicherung: Endbericht 2006 durch den Forschungsverbund. Retrieved from http://213.241.152.197/externe/2006/k060703f28.pdf. Accessed 1 December 2011.

# 10
## Incapacity Benefits – Change and Continuity in the Swedish Welfare State

*Rickard Ulmestig*

### Introduction

Sweden, as in much of the developed world, has seen a transition to a flexible and post-industrial labour market that excludes those not perceived as fully 'able'. How the Swedish welfare state has responded to these changes is examined in this chapter, both in terms of labour market policy and social insurance policy. The political discourse surrounding the reform of social insurance in general, and of disability benefits in particular, is critically evaluated in light of empirical evidence.

The high expenditure during the first decade of the 2000s put pressure on Swedish politicians to implement considerable reforms with regard to social insurance. Most of these reforms were launched in 2008.

The 'incapacity' debate in Sweden has centred on the perceived need to reduce costs associated with disability benefits. The debate has involved strong political rhetoric as well as reforms to the welfare system itself. This chapter analyses different claims made by policymakers and assesses the impact of reforms on social security systems. An important claim in the debate is that some people are not willing to work or are even cheating the social security system. The Swedish media reproduced and reinforced this discourse at the expense of other, more nuanced, understandings of the 'high costs' debate, such as damaging working environments and higher demands for efficiency and flexibility in the workplace.

The political debate has clearly influenced reforms to the welfare system. Disability benefits and employment policy are interconnected and can to some degree be described as 'commuting vessels', that is, as exerting strong influences on each other. The UK and rest of the Europe, in the wake of the financial crisis, are set to tackle high and rising welfare costs. This is an example of how high costs, together with a changing conception of what 'disability' is and how it should be handled, can precipitate considerable reforms within mature welfare states.

The level of expenditure on disability benefits has been and remains, to some degree, an issue in Sweden, which had the highest incapacity-related expenditure as a proportion of GDP in 2007 of all OECD countries (OECD, 2011). In 2007 Sweden's expenditure on disability benefits represented 5% of GDP compared to an OECD average of 2.1%. Swedish spending was also high in comparison to other countries with universal welfare systems. There is a lack of evidence on the reasons for these high costs, which has left the door open for policymakers and the media to indulge in speculation and design reforms based largely on political rhetoric.

There are difficulties in comparative social policy research. Different systems in different countries can sometimes obscure both differences and similarities. However, in this chapter the focus is on the logic behind social insurance broadly and more specifically the system of disability benefits. The systems for disability and unemployment benefits in Sweden will be described briefly. This will make international comparisons simpler than intricate descriptions of the institutional setting for people claiming disability benefits (for a more detailed description of the Swedish social insurance system in English, see Försäkringskassan, 2011a).

The effects of the reforms to disability benefits have not been fully evaluated since their introduction in 2008 (SOU, 2011:11, p. 158). However, official statistics and public reports on the changes in the systems have been published. The public reports are produced by the Swedish Social Insurance Authority (Försäkringskassan) and are based on official statistics on the social insurance system. The chapter draws some interpretative conclusions on these reports and official statistics, in light of evidence from previous research.

The next section sets out how the high costs of disability benefits and potential solutions have been represented by politicians and the media. The third section outlines the disability benefits system in Sweden. The fourth section describes the backdrop to the reform of disability benefits, including changes within the labour market and wider social insurance reforms. The fifth section describes the key reforms to disability benefits, followed by an assessment of political claims around the need for reform in light of empirical evidence, based on Johnson's (2010) analysis.

## Policy change and reforms in the wake of high costs

In order to analyse the reforms to disability benefits, it is important to understand the political debate within which they took place. In this section, the measures taken in 2008 to combat the perceived high costs of disability benefits are discussed in relation to the political debate and discourse leading up to the reforms. An important component of the political landscape in Sweden is a changing conception of social insurance and its purpose (Junestav, 2010).

In the election of 2006, social insurance, including disability benefits, became a crucial, perhaps the most crucial, political issue. The media and politicians portrayed, on weak empirical evidence, these systems as exploited by people who were well enough to support themselves (Johnson, 2010). It was generally argued that people were not knowingly cheating per se, but had become 'passive' as a result of the benefits system, and that the existence of the sick-leave scheme actually made people more sick, for example depression resulting from a lack of human interaction while not working. The 2006 election in Sweden saw a shift of political power to the right. One of the new government's first goals was to reconstruct the social insurance system.

The policy changes made by the right-wing government were presented as possible and desirable long before the 2006 election, which created the political will to strengthen work incentives in the Swedish welfare state (Bjerstedt, 2009). It is also reasonable to assume, however, that some of the changes in, for example, eligibility criteria and time limits would also have been introduced if the Social Democrats had won the election in 2006. The policy change in 2008 cannot only be understood as a political change made by a new government. The change must also be understood as a wider change in the perception of what the social insurance system is for and how the rise in costs can be explained.

Indeed, the reforms came after significant economic restructuring and welfare reforms in the 1990s aimed at lowering the expenses of 'passive' programmes (Bjerstedt, 2009). According to Bjerstedt,

> In this new vision social security should not primarily provide protection but support. Thus social security is no longer seen as protection from socioeconomic failures, but is rather understood as an aid for individuals to change their own behaviour so as to match the demands arising from a liberalized labour market.
>
> (Bjerstedt, 2009: 227)

Despite reforms in the 1990s aimed at making the Swedish welfare state more 'active', the main explanation for the rising costs of disability benefits lay with the labour market, in particular increased demands of the workplace. This explanation had almost full political consensus, and the solutions on the agenda were to give employers incentives to improve occupational health practices. But in 2002 the leader of KD (a Christian conservative party) suggested that the rise in costs could perhaps be understood as a consequence of changing norms in Swedish society, with an erosion of the 'work ethic'. By this he meant that people were now more willing to use the social insurance system and remain 'passive' at home. The first response from the media and other political parties, including other parties on the political right, was that the KD leader was spectacularly out of step with the consensus view. However, the employers' association and some conservative editorial writers were more supportive of his position (Johnson, 2010).

This broad initial scepticism against abuse of the system as an explanation for high costs for social insurance would soon change (Johnson, 2010). Stories about people not willing to work or cheating made better stories and headlines in the media than bad working environments or higher demands for efficiency and flexibility in the labour market. An example of the type of headlines used from one of the largest newspapers, *DN*, was: 'The social insurance agency will hunt cheaters'.

The employers' organisation was also successful in changing perceptions of social insurance by making a big play of the results of a survey about hypothetical behaviour. The costs kept on rising and the then Social Democratic government faced considerable criticism from the political opposition. The government was under pressure, and a political goal was formulated in 2003 that sick leave, in different forms, should be reduced by half by 2008 (SOU, 2004:127, p. 14). The Social Democrats made various adjustments to the system but were unable to tackle the problem in a way that was perceived as effective.

The 'passiveness' representation of the high costs 'problem' was strengthened by economic research examining work incentives. For example, an official report (*Långtidsutredningen – Bilaga 14*, SOU 2004:2) entitled 'Who will profit from work?' highlighted that there were weak economic incentives for work in both the social insurance and unemployment systems, but that the incentives were stronger in the unemployment system (SOU 2004:2, p. 51).

The rhetoric about people abusing social insurance became a powerful tool in the right-wing argument against excessively generous welfare systems making people passive. From 2005 the abuse explanation was dominant (Johnson, 2010). The right-wing minister of finance was cited in 2006 in one of the major Swedish newspapers, *SVD*, as saying: 'it's obvious that there is systematic overexploitation within the social security system'.

## Sickness and disability benefits in Sweden

### Sick leave

People who end up on disability benefits usually come via the sick-leave system (Palmer, 2005). The system of sickness benefits is therefore crucial for the understanding of disability benefits, even although Sickness pay and Sickness benefits are not directly included in the definition of disability benefits. 'Incapacity benefit' is reserved for those who are deemed unlikely to be able to work full-time again owing to a disability, injury, or illness.

Sickness benefit (*Sjuklön*) is the benefit that employed people receive from their employer for the first two week of sickness, and Sickness pay

(*Sjukpenning*) is received after two weeks (for a maximum 450 days) and by unemployed people. These benefits are paid at 80% of previous earnings. For those not established in the labour market and therefore without a previous wage there is a small 'guarantee income', which can be supplemented by social assistance.

## Disability benefits

Disability benefits are paid at 64% of previous earnings and are adminis-trated by the Social Insurance Agency (Försäkringskassan). Until 2005 there were different Social Insurance Associations in different counties under one national agency. Since 2005 there has been a single centralised national Social insurance Agency. There are two disability benefits in Sweden: Activity compensation (*Aktivitetsersättning*) and Sickness compensation (*Sjukersättning*). Together, these two schemes include approximately 440,000 people, based on 2010 figures (Försäkringskassan, 2011c), representing slightly less than 10% of the total workforce.

Activity compensation is a benefit for those 19–29 years of age, while Sickness compensation can only be granted to those aged 30–64. The other main difference between the schemes is that the activity compensation is much more 'active' in the sense that individuals are encouraged to take part in measures such as rehabilitation or education. These 'activation' measures are voluntary and non-conditional, that is, do not affect the level of the benefit (Försäkringskassan, 2011b).

Medical assessments are conducted every three years to judge an indi-vidual's ability to work. Medical assessments make reference to possible new medical treatments or new forms of rehabilitation that may have become available since a claimant's last assessment. To be eligible, the Social Insurance Agency must decide that there is no ability to work even after medical treatment or rehabilitation. The benefit can be granted at a full- or part-time rate, depending on the hours an individual is deemed able to work.

## Recent reforms

There is a close connection between disability benefits and the labour market. This connection has changed since the beginning of the 1990s (Försäkringskassan, 2007a). Until 1991, unemployed people aged 60–64 could claim disability benefits without giving any medical reason. Between 1991 and 1997, a minor incapacity coupled with an inability to find a job (referred to as 'labour market reasons') was sufficient to claim disability benefits for this age group. In 1997, the exemptions for people aged 60–64 were removed, and since that year people aged 60–64 have been permitted to claim on the grounds of incapacity alone.

In the first half of the 1990s, changes were implemented that restricted eligibility by increasing the level and permanence of incapacity required to receive disability benefits. In 2003, there were more time limits introduced for remaining eligible for disability benefits. Disability benefits were moved from the pension system to the sickness insurance system, which affected the amount of benefit received by an individual.

In Sweden today employers have relatively limited responsibility for workers with long spells of sickness (SOU, 2011:11; Hägglund and Thoursie, 2010). Swedish employers pay for the first two weeks of sickness, but after that there is only a general responsibility to assist rehabilitation mainly through finding new suitable tasks. These responsibilities on employers were introduced in 2005 with the intention of motivating employers to take responsibility for the working environment. However, the reform may also have served to make employers less willing to hire employees with a high risk of sickness (see Hägglund and Thoursie, 2010; Palmer, 2005).

The major reform, however, came in 2008. The reform impacted sick-leave benefits (which affect the in-flow to disability benefits because almost all claimants initiate within the sick-leave system – see Palmer, 2005) as well as disability benefits. As a consequence of the 2008 reform, after six months within the sick-leave system, the Social Insurance Agency will consider the possibility of the sick person being offered more appropriate work with another employer. If an individual is considered fit to work with another employer, then their contract of employment with their current employer can be terminated. Therefore, some people who prior to 2008 would have received disability benefits now become unemployed.

In addition, as a result of the 2008 reforms, the Social Insurance Agency introduced guidelines for the health service for how different diagnoses could affect the length of sick-leave entitlement. Within the incapacity benefit system the eligibility criteria were also sharpened.

Prior to the 2008 reform, Sickness compensation with time limits (*Tidsb egränsadsjukersätting*) was available to claimants where the Social Insurance Agency judged that there was a chance that the individual will be fit to work full- or part time again. The possibility to get time-limited Sickness compensation ended for new claimants in 2008, and in 2012 those already in the system would cease to be eligible (Försäkringskassan, 2011b). As a result of the 2008 reform, only those permanently incapacitated with regard to all employment are entitled to disability benefits.

## The impact of high costs for disability benefits on the social insurance system

Throughout the 1970s the level of newly granted disability benefits was quite stable, although there was a downward trend for men and an upward trend for women (Försäkringskassan, 2007b). In the mid-1980s there was an increase owing to people being given disability benefits for labour market reasons (that is, inability to find a job) on a large scale. This was followed by a downward trend throughout most of the 1990s because of limited eligibility for incapacity benefit for labour market reasons, as described above.

Another period of rapid increase was between 1998 and 2005 when there was an unprecedented rise in the number of people with newly granted disability benefits. Much of the rise can be accounted for by long sick absences over previous years that were converted to disability benefits when the social insurance office no longer judged that there was a possibility for the incapacitated to return to paid employment. However, numbers had begun to fall once again before the reform in 2008. The most profound change in the types of diagnosis among those who had been newly granted benefits was a rise in psychiatric diagnoses and also diagnoses related to restricted mobility. This change in diagnostic pattern was more pronounced for women.

Figure 10.1 shows OECD (2011) data on incapacity-related public spending as a proportion of GDP from 1990 to 2007. It demonstrates the high costs in Sweden but also that costs in Sweden display greater volatility than those in other countries. In 2007, Sweden had significantly higher costs for incapacity-related public spending than any other country as a proportion of GDP. Other countries have also seen steady increases in costs, although the Netherlands and to a much lesser degree Germany, reduced costs.

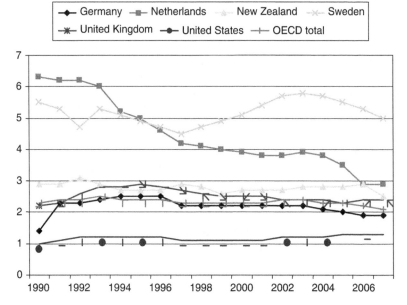

*Figure 10.1*   Incapacity-related public spending in seven OECD countries, 1990–2007 (% of GDP)
*Source*: OECD, 2011.

It is easy to understand that the high incapacity-related expenditure attracted the interest of economists, politicians, and the media. The chapter will return to the consequences of the political debate, but first disability benefits are discussed in the context of unemployment and disability insurance.

## Disability benefits and unemployment

There is a longstanding connection between social insurance and the labour market in the Nordic welfare states that dates back to the inception of these welfare systems. The Swedish welfare state is an archetype of a generous and universal welfare system but is also, as in other Nordic welfare states (see Esping-Andersen, 1990), based on citizens' position and earnings in the labour market. This was not a significant problem during the 'golden era' of the welfare state when there was very low unemployment, high labour market participation and ample resources for services to help unemployed people back to work (see Lindwall, 2004). Today, there are more people who have not yet established themselves in the labour market and are not eligible for unemployment insurance (Ulmestig, 2007).

Until the economic crisis of the 1990s, the unemployment rate in Sweden was around 3%. This rose to around 7% during the 1990s, where it has remained since, with severe consequences for the Swedish welfare state (Palme, 2000; Sjöberg, 2001). Unemployment is particularly high among young people (SCB, 2011).

Disabled people who have been in employment are offered better conditions within the unemployment insurance system compared to the incapacity benefit system. This may be one explanation of why people with disabilities have a high unemployment rate. The relationship with unemployment is therefore crucial to understand disability benefits in the Swedish welfare state.

## Policy for unemployment and incapacity

Issues around incapacitated workers were among a set of fundamental issues that the early designers of welfare states set out to tackle, as well as how to protect but incentivise the unemployed (Olsson, 1993; Nilsson, 2003). Social insurance systems and labour market policy expanded after the Second World War, and the systems for disability benefits became more generous and more inclusive. The Nordic welfare states have been described as 'decommodifying' – where the survival of workers is less dependent on their ability to sell their labour on the labour market, in comparison to other welfare states (Esping-Andersen, 1990). However, eligibility for benefits and the level of benefit received were, and remain, decided by position in the labour market and wages respectively.

Changes to labour market policy were made by both the right-wing government and the Social Democratic government that gained power in 1994. The changes can be described as moves towards welfare retrenchment and activation policy (Köhler et al., 2008; Giertz, 2004). Within unemployment insurance, benefit levels were cut and time limits were reduced and strengthened. Requirements on the unemployed to be 'active' in regaining employment were also strengthened. Activation policies blur the demarcation lines between social policy and labour market policy (Damgaard, 2003; Hvinden et al., 2001). According to Hvinden et al., 'The underlying message is that the social value of an individual is primarily determined by his/her potential contribution as a worker' (2001, p. 179). In 2008 the logic of activation was introduced in the social insurance system as a response to rising costs (Hetzler, 2009).

## The system for incapacity and unemployment benefits

In Sweden, when claiming disability benefits, there is always a connection to the labour market. The criteria of eligibility are not directly dependent on incapacity but instead on how the incapacity affects a person's ability to support themselves, full- or part-time, in the labour market. The ability of an individual is of course affected by how the labour market functions and by how the labour market institutions and organisations are constructed. So who qualifies for disability benefits in Sweden? Table 10.1 shows which groups were granted disability benefits in 2005.

For most Swedes, unemployment benefits are synonymous with unemployment insurance. Unemployment protection has two levels. One is for those who are members of an unemployment insurance fund and are eligible for benefits, and the other is a basic level of social assistance for those who are not members, or who are but do not meet the criteria for eligibility. The maximum benefit level is more than double that available from the basic level (SO, 2011a). However, the maximum level of benefits has not been adjusted according to inflation for many years, and only 12% of the working population in Sweden would get as much as 80% of their wage (SO, 2011b). This proportion was 75% in 1993 (Anderson and Löfgren, 2004, p. 28). Further, only 40% of the unemployed who are registered at the unemployment office are eligible for unemployment insurance funds (SO, 2011c).

Within the social assistance systems, to which unemployed people not eligible for unemployment insurance are referred, there are demands to take part in activation schemes in excess of what is dictated by national labour market policy. There are also different systems for supplementary unemployment insurance through agreements between the union and employers' associations for some sectors, and there is private or semi-private provision through the unions (SOU, 2011:11, p. 64). The supplementary systems

*Table 10.1*   Characteristics of incapacity benefit claimants (*N* = 5,025)

|  |  | Percentage |
|---|---|---|
| Sex | Female | 63 |
|  | Male | 37 |
|  | Total | 100 |
| Age | 20–29 | 4 |
|  | 30–44 | 19 |
|  | 45–54 | 25 |
|  | 55–64 | 52 |
|  | Total | 100 |
| Country of origin | Born within Sweden | 82 |
|  | Born outside Sweden | 18 |
|  | Total | 100 |
| Benefits | Full-time | 56 |
|  | Part-time | 44 |
|  | Total | 100 |
| Education | High school (Grundskola) | 37 |
|  | College (Gymnasium) | 40 |
|  | University (Högskola) | 23 |
|  | Total | 100 |

*Source*: Försäkringskassan (2010).

mainly cover those who are well established in the labour market. To be categorised as unemployed is less generous when it comes to benefits levels, and also there is more mandatory activation if an individual is categorised as unemployed rather than incapacitated. There is a greater stigma associated with unemployment than incapacity in Sweden (Svallfors, 1999, p. 38). To be recategorised as unemployed from being incapacitated can affect not only income but also status in the eyes of other people.

As demonstrated above, changes in employment and activation policy impact on benefit entitlement, particularly in the social insurance system. The next section of this chapter describes changes to the social insurance system in more detail, including therefore activation requirements.

## Changes to the social insurance systems

It is difficult to fully grasp the multiple connections between policy and outcomes in the welfare state (Pierson, 2003). However, there were clear and significant changes made in the social insurance system that are likely to have had a discernible impact, although the effects of these changes have not been fully evaluated. Data available from the Social Insurance Agency are therefore presented and discussed here.

The changes made by the government in 2008 to meet the high costs and address the criticism of a 'passive' welfare state were aimed at making the social insurance system more demanding for claimants but also more tailored to personal circumstances, and at providing stronger economic incentives for people to work (for example, Försäkringskassan, 2010). The Swedish scholar of social policy, Antoinette Hetzler, concludes in an analysis of the 2008 reform that higher thresholds for eligibility, demands for activity, introducing time limits in social insurance, and changing the definitions of incapacity and sickness all represent major changes to one of the basic components of the Swedish welfare state (Hetzler, 2009). This new policy regime was paralleled by similar changes to social policies and labour market policies for unemployment benefits in many other western countries – specifically increased demands for activity and tightened eligibility criteria under the banner of 'personal responsibility' (see van Berkel and Hornemann Møller, 2002; Lødemel and Trickey, 2000).

There is also, as suggested in the introductory section, a connection between labour market policy and the social insurance system on a systemic level where unemployment and incapacity benefits become 'communicating vessels'. For example, many people become registered as unemployed after meeting the time limit for disability benefits. People who do not have any work or are unable to return to their previous employment (for example, owing to health problems) become regarded as unemployed and transferred from the jurisdiction of the social insurance office to that of the unemployment office (Försäkringskassan, 2010). Without any change in capacity for work, people are transferred from disability benefits to a system governed by regulations intended for the unemployed.

There is a lack of systematic evaluation of the impacts of the 2008 reforms. However, the Social Insurance Agency has produced numbers of individuals that have been granted disability benefits during the period 1994–2010 (Försäkringskassan, 2011d). All new benefits are accounted for, and the frequency of approved benefits is analysed in relation to change over time, gender, age, and regional distribution. The on-flow to the incapacity benefit system peaked in the middle of the first decade of the 2000s and fell thereafter. In 2004, the rate of new claims for disability benefits was 15.1 per 1,000 inhabitants. By 2010 this had decreased to 2.8 new disability benefit claimants per 1,000, representing a substantial drop.

However, the decrease in the numbers coming into the incapacity system is unevenly distributed across Sickness Compensation (payable to those aged 30–64 years) and Activity Compensation (payable to those aged 16–29 years). In Sickness Compensation, which represents the largest part of the disability system, the decrease is very marked. But in Activity Compensation, the system for those between 19 and 29 years old, there has been a strong increase in numbers claiming (Östh and Olofsson, 2010/S 2010:4). For example, between 2003 and 2011 there was a 79% increase in the number granted Activity Compensation. According to the same report, historically, only 2% of youth that have been granted disability benefits established themselves later in life on the labour market, making the scale of the increase of considerable concern for these individuals' future prospects.

There is not incontrovertible evidence that this decrease is an effect of the reforms in 2008, but it is reasonable to assume that when the thresholds are higher, fewer people will be eligible. This is of course a financial saving within the incapacity benefit system, but to some extent the cost has been transferred to the unemployment insurance and social assistance systems.

Until 2010, women were more likely to claim disability benefits than men (Försäkringskassan, 2011d). In 1994, 11% more women than men made new claims for disability benefits. By 2004, this gap had increased to 62% more women than men. This large difference between women and men has since narrowed, and by 2010 had disappeared. In terms of age, those 60–64 years of age have a higher number of approved disability benefits, peaking in 2004 at 42.2 approved disability benefits per 1,000 inhabitants (Försäkringskassan, 2011d). Relatively few individuals aged 19–29 years receive disability benefits, although, as noted previously, there have been large increases in the numbers claiming among this age group in percentage terms.

The social insurance system, including disability benefits, have complex regulations and have seen many reforms, hence conclusive evidence on outcomes is limited. The system is also affected by local variation in labour market conditions, sickness and in how the system is implemented – as chapters in this book on the situation in the UK highlight. These issues are discussed in the following section.

## Local variation and implementation

There are local variations within the Social Insurance system that are evident in the statistics published by the Social Insurance Agency. There are for example regional variations in terms of grants awarded in the National Health Insurance (Försäkringskassan, 2009; Bjerstedt, 2009), with disproportionately high levels in northern counties (Försäkringskassan, 2011d). In 2010, the northern county of Jämtland had 25% more grants in comparison to the national average. The Social Insurance Agency concludes that local variation in outcomes is a result of variation in health and ability to work (Försäkringskassan, 2011d).

Geographical differences in terms of sickness and incapacity have been identified and, as a consequence, different Social Insurance Associations were centralised in 2005 (Bjerstedt, 2009). The aim of this organisational reform was to combat geographical variation. Examples of 'problems' include that the assessment of applications was apparently not uniform for the whole country. According to the Social Insurance Agency (Försäkringskassan, 2011d), the reduction in geographical differences in the number of granted benefits shows that such uniformity is now becoming a reality. The reduction has mainly been in urban areas where fewer people receive Sickness benefits and Disability benefits (Hägglund, 2010).

Haugen et al. (2008) studied geographical differences in attitudes towards Sick absence in Sweden. Their empirical data is from 2005, prior to the main reforms. Haugen et al. conclude that their results support the view that geographical factors have an influence on individual *attitudes*, although their results show no clear evident patterns in terms of *outcomes* – for example, they found no more acceptances for using the sickness benefits in rural and northern parts of Sweden.

The academic debate in Sweden on local variation within the social insurance system has in the 2000s been dominated by a research programme in which four different municipalities in Sweden were compared (Frykman et al., 2009). The results from this research programme came to play a significant role in the debate on fraud and on the view that people were willing to use the social insurance system in order to wilfully remain 'passive' (Johnson, 2010).

One urban and one rural municipality in Jämtland were compared with an urban and rural municipality in Småland (Frykman et al., 2009). Jämtland is a county in northern Sweden with high levels of sickness and incapacity and high unemployment, while Småland is in the south with low levels of sickness and incapacity and low unemployment. The results showed that differences were very pronounced, with almost twice as many days of sickness benefits and disability benefits together in Jämtland compared to Småland.

The conclusion of the research programme was that differences in sickness and incapacity patterns are related to regional variations in people's attitudes towards sick leave and incapacity (cf. Frykman and Hansen, 2009). The pattern of attitudes as demonstrated here indicates greater acceptance of sick leave in the north, while the south has more negative perceptions of sick leave. The research programme also concluded that sick 'culture' also affected local officials (Olofsdotter Stensöta, 2009), with local officers sharing the norms of the local community of which they were part. However, there were differences between officials in the northern and the southern counties. In interviews with officials, the northern officials were much more open to use the social insurance system to support people and their individual needs. They also provided services to individuals that were not part of their remit and to seek the support of other authorities to help their clients. In the southern county the officials more often, but not always, upheld boundaries more firmly between clients and themselves, and more often prioritised regulations before the individual needs of their clients (Olofsdotter Stensöta, 2009).

It can be argued that to some extent there was a misconception about the results and even more about what conclusions to draw from them. One interpretation is that social insurance and other welfare systems in northern

Sweden were used to maintain social cohesion (see Frykman et al., 2009). In areas with structural problems such as unemployment, low income, and low educational attainment, the welfare system became an important factor in supporting a basic income. The results were not about normative assumptions about how people used welfare systems but instead how structural causes made some communities dependent on welfare. However, the members of such communities, and the communities as a whole, were in the long run faced with the negative sides of welfare dependency, both economically and culturally.

One of the possible reasons for local variation within the social insurance system is, as discussed above, local interpretations of regulations. The content of Social Insurance, and other areas of social policy, are to some degree 'made' in the local context and in local officials' interpretation of regulations (see Lipsky, 2010; Hjertner Thoren, 2008). Melén (2008) and Hultgren (2010) show the importance of officials and how they interpret and use disability benefits and related systems. Melén (2008) analyses officials in the Social Insurance Agency and the Employment Office, and Hultgren (2010) analyses the decisions made by officials in the Social Insurance Agency. While care needs to be taken in generalising from these two case studies, the geographic patterns of how Social Insurance is implemented are suggestive of institutional and structural factors influencing the rise in numbers on disability benefits rather than changes in individuals' 'work ethic' and behaviour.

Who receives benefits is partially dependent on how regulations are implemented by individual officials. One common conclusion is that social status affects how people are treated by officials, with those with low educational and occupational status being more likely to have their benefit entitlement questioned. For instance, poorly educated immigrant women are often expected to take any work but well-educated native-born men can wait for the 'right' job while on sickness benefits (Melén, 2008, p. 249).

Structural problems being presented as individual and medical problems are described in a public report on youth and disability benefits (Östh and Olofsson, 2010/S 2010: 4). This report highlighted that poor psychological health among some younger people can explain some cases of incapacity, alongside low education, low socio-economic status, and unemployment. Especially problematic is young people who only have nine years of mandatory schooling, who are over-represented in the incapacity system. The report authors (Östh and Olofsson, 2010/S 2010: 4) argue that there is a risk that structural problems like exclusion from the labour market are presented as medical problems. There are other researchers who point out that the medicalisation of labour market exclusion becomes an individualisation of structural problems (Peralta, 2006; Holmqvist, 2009). For instance, the welfare state makes demands of sick and disabled people to retrain and search for work. Employers may use narratives of individual shortcomings and medical diagnoses to conceal their own demands for high productivity and reduced acceptance and accommodation of sickness and incapacity in the workplace.

Another example on the importance of implementation from Melén (2008) is that officials adapt their clients' capacity for work to labour market conditions. So, instead of trying to rehabilitate them to a labour market with low demand for labour, their incapacity is described in a manner that allows them to get access to subsidiary employment through the Employment Office. Hultgren (2010) exemplifies variations in the power that individual officials have to reject applications for benefits. The analysis of all rejections in two counties in southern Sweden shows that there were only a handful of officials and physicians involved who were labelled as 'moral entrepreneurs' by Hultgren, that is, those who took an 'interpretative' stance in implementing policy.

In this section local variation and implementation has been discussed and analysed. It is reasonable to conclude from the studies presented here that the system, in the sense of the rights bestowed upon and duties expected of people, is affected by where individuals live, educational and occupational status, and the beliefs and practices of the particular official representing the social insurance agency.

## The high costs for disability benefits – some answers

The high costs for disability benefits in Sweden the first decade of the twenty-first century have shaped the political debate and discourse, and have dictated the direction of reform of the Swedish welfare state, including beyond the disability benefits system. In this section, research is drawn upon to give some answers as to why Sweden faced these very high costs for Social Insurance. Björn Johnson (2010) tests the competing explanations of bad working conditions versus an increase of passivity and abuse of the systems – the latter being the main explanation among economists, the media, and politicians. He concludes that it is not reasonable, and there is very weak empirical evidence, to assume that either the working environment or Swedish norms about abusing the system have changed as rapidly as the costs have risen. Johnson's explanation is instead more nuanced, drawing on work by Larsson et al. (2005).

The rise in sick leave (see Figure 10.1) was not mainly a consequence of more people calling in sick but a consequence of people being sick for longer periods. So the key question for Larsson et al. (2005) is why is it difficult for people to get back to work? The explanation for the high costs for the social insurance is complex and consists of two important elements (Larsson et al., 2005).

One is the economic strain on the public sector in the municipalities arising from the economic recession in the 1990s but also economic strains in other parts of the public and private sectors. Retrenchment programmes in the municipalities did worsen the work environment and the demands on the staff were higher. The willingness and ability of employers to hire less productive workers was reduced in both the public and private sectors (Marklund et al., 2005). It also became more common for employers to give people notice to quit or to pay them off. It is hard to find work if jobs are scarce and an individual is not fully able, so the risk of unemployment or very long periods on sick leave with people ending up in incapacity benefit systems rises (Melén, 2008; Marklund et al., 2005). This is especially visible in periods of high unemployment when the labour market becomes more competitive.

The other reason given by Larsson et al. (2005) is changes in the laws and the organisation for rehabilitation. Until the early 1990s there had been special local rehabilitation and adaptation groups for getting people back into the labour market. In these groups the employers had meetings a few times a year with the Social Insurance Agency and Public Employment Service, and often with representatives from occupational health services to discuss rehabilitation among the employed. These groups were very common; for example in 1983 almost three-quarters of all employers with more than 50 employees were involved in such a group. These adaptation groups disappeared in the early 1990s and were replaced with other less effective ways of fostering cooperation and good practice. Laws and regulations were changed. The Social Insurance Agency pointed out more strongly the responsibility on employers for rehabilitation, the public employment service started to prioritise the unemployed over the disabled, and the state subsidy for the occupational health service was withdrawn.

In his doctoral thesis Urban Lidwall (2010) has similar findings to Larsson et al. (2005) but gives less significance to the changes in the laws and rules, and instead puts more emphasis on demographic change. Over time, the labour force has become older, and one of the reasons for falling numbers was that those born in the 1940s 'baby boom' left the workforce.

However, Johnson (2010), Lidwall (2010), and Larsson et al. (2005) could not find any empirical support for the explanation that people had a higher propensity to use the system than in the past. Rather, increasing workplace demands, unemployment levels, rising mental ill-health, changes to regulations, and demographic change appear to be the main drivers of the numbers on disability benefits in Sweden.

## Conclusions

Sweden is an example of a disability benefit system that was put under heavy pressure. High costs in the first half of the first decade of the 2000s 'forced' a policy change towards time limits and tougher criteria of eligibility. However there is little evidence, contrary to the dominant political discourse, that there was widespread abuse of the system or that 'passivity' was an important factor behind the rising costs. There is not enough solid evidence to explain the rise in the costs for disability benefits beyond any doubt. However, when Johnson (2010) evaluated the studies and the empirical data he came down in favour of two main explanations, based on Larsson et al. (2005). Both point to tougher working environments in the labour market and cuts and changes in the organisations of labour market rehabilitation programmes. Lidwall (2010) also highlights the significance of demographic change, with the workforce becoming older and therefore having more health problems.

Despite the lack of evidence, the government chose to handle the problem based on the assumption that people were using the system more than they 'needed' to. However, the rhetoric prior to the policy change was not only, or even chiefly, about fraud but more about people becoming passive as a result of being on sick leave. When the main problem was presented as passivity, the Swedish welfare state had a ready-made 'solution' in the form of activation policies. Even if these policies had to go through some remodelling, the bulk of them were deemed to be applicable. It is reasonable to assume that the reform in 2008 was successful in lowering the costs for disability benefits (although costs had begun to decrease before the reform). When the thresholds get higher and the demands on recipients more pronounced, fewer people will be eligible or choose to claim.

In the opening chapters of this book, evidence is presented that the unemployed are 'hidden' within the incapacity system in the UK. A similar process is detectable in Sweden prior to the reforms, although since the reforms people with incapacity are increasingly forced to quit their contract of employment (if they have one) and look for other more suitable work as unemployed. This now serves to 'hide' incapacity among the unemployed – a process that may occur in the UK with the raised medical threshold to be eligible for disability benefits and the introduction of increased activation measures on claimants of disability benefits. This is a similar process but with an opposite flow compared to the one described by Beatty, Fothergill, and Macmillan (2000). This can be understood in relation to the very high confidence Swedish governments have in active labour market policy.

But there is also some flow in the opposite direction owing to the medicalisation of unemployment and increased workplace demands (Peralta, 2006; Holmqvist, 2009). This medicalisation can be understood as an attempt from the state to hide unemployment within the disability benefits system. In this chapter it has been argued that there is a relation between incapacity and unemployment, here labelled as 'commuting vessels'.

It is clear that disability benefits are closely connected to the labour market and are in that respect a labour market issue. There are few people that have such limited capacity that they could not be employed if there was a will to adapt work environments and a greater will to employ those not fully abled. As a consequence of this, the Social Insurance Agency does not base the criteria of eligibility on how incapacitated people are but on their capacity. If there is work capacity but not with the current employer, people have to quit and look for other employers. The unemployed, in cases where the Social Insurance Agency assesses that they have some work capacity, look for work they can manage. This policy can easily be challenged on the basis that employers are unlikely to employ a disabled person when an able-bodied person is also available. This then raises the question of whether and to what extent the state should subsidise, otherwise support or mandate such employment. In this respect disability benefits represent an employ-ability issue, but one requiring policy action *both* by employers and benefit recipients.

One of the basic ideas behind active labour market policy is to give unem-ployed people knowledge and experience that makes them attractive in the labour market and effectively match them with suitable job vacancies. However, for people with a lack of education, poor health or disability and close to retirement age, active labour market policy carries a risk of only serving to humiliate. For other people, active labour market policy can be a way to avoid disability benefits and to become established, or re-established, in the labour market.

The changes within Swedish the welfare state are path-dependent but also to some degree a break with the past. The high confidence in 'activation' measures is closely connected to the core of the Nordic welfare model, as is the close connection between the labour market and the system of social insurance. However, the individualisation of responsibility in which struc-tural problems are presented as personal shortcomings, passiveness, and incapacity do break with the principles of the Nordic welfare type portrayed by Esping-Andersen (1990).

## References

Andersson, D. and Löfgren, A.-K. (2004) *Arbetsmarknadspolitiken Vid ett Vägskäl* (Stockholm: Landsorganisationen i Sverige).
Bjerstedt, D. (2009) *Tryggheten inför rätta. Om Rätten till Förtidspension enligt Förvaltningsdomstolarna under tre Decinnier* (Lund: Department of Sociology, Lund University).
Damgaard, B. (2003) *Social- og Arbejdmarkedssystemerne – En Flerstrenget Historie* (Köpenhamn: Socialforskningsinstituttet).
Esping-Andersen, G. (1990) *The Tree Worlds of Welfare Capitalism* (Cambridge: Polity Press).
Försäkringskassan (2007a) *Inflödet till sjuk- och aktivitetsersättning – har reglerna någon betydelse?* Rapport 2007:13 (Stockholm: Försäkringskassan).
Försäkringskassan (2007b) *Diagnosmönster i förändring. Nybeviljade förtidspen-sioner, sjukersättningar och aktivitetsersättningar.* Rapport 2007:3 (Stockholm: Försäkringskassan).

Försäkringskassan (2009) *Trygghetens variationer.* Socialförsäkringsrapport 2009:2 (Stockholm: Försäkringskassan).

Försäkringskassan (2010) *Hälsa, arbetsmarknadsanknytning och behov av stödjande insatser hos personer med sjuk- och aktivitetsersättning* (Stockholm: Försäkringskassan).

Försäkringskassan (2011a) Försäkringskassan website at: http://www.forsakrings kassan.se/sprak/eng 2011-03-18.

Försäkringskassan (2011b) Försäkringskassan website at: http://www.forsakrings kassan.se/privatpers/sjuk/sjuk_lange_sa2011-03-24.

Försäkringskassan (2011c) Försäkringskassan website at: http://statistik.forsakrings kassan.se/rfv/html/2_sjukakters_ar_2010.html.

Försäkringskassan (2011d) *Nya ohälsomått inom sjukförsäkringen*, Socialförsäkring srapport 2011:6 (Stockholm: Försäkringskassan).

Frykman, J., Hammarlin, A.-M., Hansen, K., Rothstein, B., Olofsdottter Stensöta, H., and Schirenbeck, I. (2009) *Trygghetens Variationer*, Socialförsäkringsrapport 2009: 2 (Stockholm: Försäkringskassan).

Frykman, J. and Hansen, K. (2009) *I Ohälsans Tid. Sjukskrivningar och Kulturmönster i det Samtida Sverige* (Stockholm: Carlsson Bokförlag).

Giertz, A. (2004) *Making the Poor Work: Social Assistance and Activation Programs in Sweden* (Lund: Socialhögskolan).

Hägglund, P. (2010) *Rehabliteringskedjans Effekter på Sjukskrivningstiderna, Ifau-Rapport 2010: 1* (Uppsala: IFAU).

Hägglund, P. and Skogman Thoursie, P. (2010) *Reformerna inom sjukförsäkringen under 2006–2010: Vilka effekter kan vi förvänta oss? Ifau-Rapport 2010:17* (Uppsala: IFAU).

Haugen, K., Holm, E., Lundevaller, E., and Westin, K. (2008) 'Localised Attitudes Matter: A Study of Sickness Absence in Sweden', *Population, Space and Place*, 14, 189–207.

Hetzler, A. (2009) 'Labor Market Activation Policies for the Long-Term Ill – A Sick Idea?', *European Journal of Social Security*, 11 (4), 369–403.

Hjertner Thorén, K.H. (2008) *Activation Policy in Action: A Street-Level Study of Social Assistance in the Swedish Welfare State* (Göteborg: Växjö University Press).

Holmqvist, M. (2009) 'Medicalization of Unemployment: Individualizing Social Issues as Personal Problems in the Swedish Welfare State', *Work, Employment and Society*, 23, 405–421.

Hultgren, P. (2010) *Det Dubbla Statushandikappet och Sjukförsäkringens Moraliska Praktiker – En Aktstudie om Sjukpenningsärenden som får Negativa Beslut på Försäkringskassan* (Växjö; Linnaeus University Press).

Hvinden, B., Heikkilä, M., and Kankare, I. (2001) 'Towards Activation? The Changing Relationship between Social Protection and Employment in Western Europe' in M. Kautto, J. Fritzell, B. Hvinden, J. Kvist, and H. Uusitalo (eds) *Nordic Welfare States in the European Context* (London: Routledge).

Johnsson, B. (2010) *Kampen om Sjukfrånvaron* (Lund: Arkiv förlag).

Junestav, M. (2010) *Sjukskrivning som Politiskt Problem i Välfärdsdebatten: det Politiska Språket och Institutionell Förändring*, Rapport 2010:16 (Uppsala: IFAU).

Köhler, P., Thorén, K., and Ulmestig, R. (2008) 'Activation Policies in Sweden: Something Old, Something New, Something Borrowed and Something Blue' in W. Eichhorst, O. Kaufmann, and R. Konle-Seidl (eds) *Bringing the Jobless into Work* (Berlin: Springer).

Larsson, T., Marklund, S., and Westerholm, P. (2005) *Den Galopperande Ajukfrånvaron. Sken, fenomen och väsen* (Stockholm: Arbetslivsinstitutet).

Lidwall, U. (2010) *Long-Term Sickness Absence* (Stockholm: Karolinska Institutet).

Lindwall, U. (2004) *The Politics of Purpose: Swedish Macroeconomic Policy After the Golden Age* (Göteborg: Department of Political Science).

Lipsky, M. (2010) *Street-Level Bureaucracy: Dilemmas of the Individual in Public Services* (New York: Russell Sage Foundation).

Lødemel, I. and Trickey, H. (2000) *An Offer You Can't Refuse* (Bristol: Policy Press).

Marklund, S., Bjurvald, M., Hogstedt, C., Palmer, E., and Theorell, T. (eds) (2005) *Den Höga Sjukfrånvaron – Problem och lösningar* (Stockholm; Arbetslivsinstitutet).

Melén, D. (2008) *Sjukskrivningssystemet: Sjuka som blir Arbetslösa och Arbetslösa som blir Sjukskrivna* (Lund University: Department of Sociology).

Nilsson, R. (2003) *Kontroll, makt och Omsorg* (Lund: Studentlitteratur).

OECD (2011) *Social Expenditure Database*, http://www.oecd.org/document/9/0,3746,en_2649_34637_38141385_1_1_1_1,00.html, date accessed 11 November 2011.

Olofsdotter Stensöta, H. (2009) 'Om Medikalisering' in J. Frykman, A.-M. Hammarlin, K. Hansen, B. Rothstein, H. Olofsdottter Stensöta, and I. Schirenbeck (eds) *Trygghetens Variationer, Socialförsäkringsrapport 2009:2* (Stockholm: Försäkringskassan).

Olsson, S.E. (1993) *Social Policy and Welfare State in Sweden* (Lund: Arkiv förlag).

Östh, J. and Olofsson, J. (2010) *Förtidspensionering av unga. En Fråga om Utsortering efter Utbildningsnivå och Sociaoekonomisk Bakgrund? Statens Offentliga Utredningar, S 2010:4* (Stockholm: Fritzes).

Palme, J. (2000) 'Socialförsäkring och Kontanta Familjestöd' in A. Bergmark (ed.) *Välfärd och Försörjning* (Stockholm: Fritzes förlag).

Palmer, E. (2005) 'Sjukskrivning och Förtidspension de Närmaste åren' in S. Marklund, M. Bjurvald, C. Hogstedt, E. Palmer, and T. Theorell (eds) *Den Höga Sjukfrånvaron – Problem och lösningar* (Stockholm; Arbetslivsinstitutet).

Peralta Prieto, J. (2006) *Den Sjuka Arbetslösheten – Svensk Arbetsmarknadspolitik och Dess Praxis 1978–2004* (Uppsala: Uppsala Universitet).

Pierson, P. (2003) *Dismantling the Welfare State? Reagan, Thatcher, and the Politics of Retrenchment* (Cambridge: Cambridge University Press).

SCB (2011) *The Labour Force Surveys (LFS) 50 Years* (Stockholm: Statistics Sweden).

Sjöberg, O. (2001) 'Välfärdens Finansiering under 1990-talet' in J. Fritzell and J. Palme (eds) *SOU 2001:57: Välfärdens Finansiering och Fördelning* (Stockholm: Statens offentliga utredningar).

SO (2011a) *Swedish Federation of Unemployment Insurance Funds (SO) website*, http://www.samorg.org/so/Index.aspx?id=137, date accessed 24 March 2011.

SO (2011b) *Swedish Federation of Unemployment Insurance Funds (SO) website*, http://www.samorg.org/so/Index.aspx?id=1151, date accessed 24 March 2011.

SO (2011c) *Swedish Federation of Unemployment Insurance Funds (SO) website*, http://www.samorg.org/so/filer.aspx?typ=dokument&id=-16343648943806, date accessed 24 March 2011.

SOU 2004:2 *Försäkringskassan: Slutbetänkande av Utredningen om inrättande av en sammanhållen statlig myndighet för socialförsäkringsområdet* (Stockholm: Fritzes offentliga publikationer).

SOU 2004:127 *Vem tjänar på att arbeta? Bilaga 14 till Långtidsutredningen 2003/2004* (Stockholm: Fritzes offentliga publikationer).

SOU 2011:11 *Långtidsutredningen 2011, Huvudbetänkande* (Stockholm: Fritzes offentliga publikationer).

Svallfors, S. (1999) 'The Middle Class and Welfare Retrenchment: Attitudes to Swedish Welfare Policies' in S. Svallfors and P. Taylor-Gooby (eds) *The End of the Welfare State? Responses to State Retrenchment* (New York: Routledge).

Ulmestig, R. (2007) *På Gränsen Till Fattigvård? En Studie Om Arbetsmarknadspolitik Och Socialbidrag* (Lund: Socialhögskolan, Lund University).

van Berkel, R. and Hornemann Møller, I. (2002) *Active Social Policies in the EU: Inclusion through Participation?* (Bristol: Policy Press).

# 11
## From Dutch Disease to Dutch Fitness? Two Decades of Disability Crisis in the Netherlands

*Rik van Berkel*

### Introduction

In 1990, the then Dutch prime minister, Ruud Lubbers, declared that 'the Netherlands is ill'. In that year the number of recipients of the Dutch Disability Benefit was close to 900,000, representing almost 15% of the working population. Twelve years later, the 2 May 2002 issue of *The Economist* published an article, in which the following statement concerning the Dutch disability system was made: 'it is the very need for consensus that has inhibited further reforms to the much-abused and excessively generous disability system, which pays out to a ludicrous one in seven Dutch people of working age'. These quotes illustrate that the Dutch 'disability crisis' is far from a recent phenomenon and that the reforms introduced during the 1980s and 1990s had not been able to turn the tide. Nevertheless, as will be elaborated below, the current picture is more positive – although the risk of a 'new' disability crisis lies in wait.

This chapter will analyse Dutch disability benefit dependency and, more specifically, the social security reforms introduced to reduce benefit dependency. First, we will present some core characteristics of the Dutch disability system and data on how disability benefit dependency has developed. Second, the most important reforms introduced to reduce benefit dependency and promote labour-market participation – the two main objectives of the reforms – will be discussed. Rather than providing a complete overview of the reforms, our discussion will focus on the reform *strategies* that successive Dutch governments have used to deal with the disability crisis. The third section will look at the reforms from a different perspective, by trying to analyse what the reforms tell us about the ways in which the disability crisis has been defined in the Netherlands. Specifically, we will show how the three explaining key factors discussed in the introductory chapter have played a role in Dutch reforms. The final section concludes this chapter.

## Dutch disability benefits: Some introductory comments

The Dutch disability benefit system consists of two separate schemes. The main scheme is a benefit for (former) employees who, after a certain period of receiving sickness benefits (currently two years), may claim disability benefits: the WAO (*Wet op de Arbeidsongeschiktheidverzekering*, Disability Insurance Act) and its successor since 2006, the WIA (*Wet werk en inkomennaararbeidsvermogen*, Act for Work and Income according to Work Capacity). A separate benefit exists for what are called the 'early disabled': people who are disabled when they reach the age of 17, or people who become disabled during their studies but before reaching 30 years of age (*Wet Arbeidsongeschiktheidsvoorzieningjonggehandicapten* or *Wajong*, Act Disability Provision for the Young Handicapped). To avoid confusion: people receiving the latter benefit are not necessarily young, but became disabled when they were young, which is why we talk about 'early disabled'. It is interesting to note that whereas in the period between the 1980s and 2006 (the year WIA was implemented) the emphasis in the debates concerning the disability crisis was on the WAO/WIA, and benefits for long-term sick employees, the emphasis since then has shifted to the early disabled, as the number of people receiving the benefit for the early disabled has grown considerably during the first decade of the twenty-first century. This seems to underline Van Oorschot and Boos' characterisation of Dutch disability reforms as a 'battle against numbers' (Van Oorschot and Boos, 2001).

Within both benefit systems, two further categorisations are of importance. Firstly, both systems distinguish between fully and party disabled benefit recipients. The degree of disability is based on people's earning capacity. For employees, the reference income is their former income: when a person's earning capacity is less than 20% of former wage, he or she is considered fully disabled. For the early disabled, the reference income is a percentage of minimum wage. This way of determining the severity of disability implies that someone who is considered fully disabled is not necessarily unable to work. The partly disabled who have work receive a benefit that supplements their wage; those who are unemployed receive unemployment benefits. A second categorisation distinguishes those who are considered permanently fully disabled from those whose full disability is regarded as temporary. The degree of disability of the temporarily fully disabled is, as is the case for the partly disabled, re-examined after a certain period of time. Within the WIA, the latter categorisation is reflected in two different benefits: one for the permanently fully disabled and one for the other groups of disabled, the temporarily fully disabled and the partly disabled. For the early disabled, this categorisation will be introduced in 2013 (see below).

Contrary to what is the case in several other countries, the Dutch disability system does not use the distinction between *risqué professionel* and *risque social*. Whether disability is work-related or not is not taken into consideration when a person claims disability benefit. According to Muysken and Rutten (2002), one of the consequences of this is that whereas Dutch disability payments are, in an international perspective, relatively low for those whose disability is work-related, they are relatively high for people whose disability is related to other causes than work.

In Table 11.1, we present an overview of numbers of recipients of disability benefits during the last two decades. Apart from the WAO/WIA and Wajong benefits, the table also presents data on the numbers of recipients of a specific disability benefit for the self-employed (WAZ) – in the remaining parts of this chapter, no further attention will be paid to this benefit.[1] In Table 11.2, we present data on disability benefit recipients as a proportion of the working population.

The figures in these tables show that the number of disability benefit recipients increased throughout the 1990s, reaching almost one million recipients in 2002. After that, a gradual decline took place. This was specifically the case for the WAO/WIA, where the decline has been rather spectacular. In contrast, the number of early disabled has increased explosively and doubled within 15 years.

When we compare Tables 11.1 and 11.2, the picture changes somewhat. Despite the increase of benefit dependency during the 1990s, the proportion of the working population depending on disability benefits gradually decreased, showing that the increase partly reflected the growth of the total working population. During the 2000s, we see an acceleration of the decline of the proportion of the working population depending on disability benefits.

*Table 11.1*  Disability benefit recipients in the Netherlands, 1990–2010 (x1,000)

|  | 1990 | 1994 | 1998 | 2002 | 2006 | 2010 |
|---|---|---|---|---|---|---|
| WAO/WIA | 731 | 736 | 729 | 803 | 639 | 596 |
| Wajong | 91 | 100 | 118 | 134 | 156 | 205 |
| WAZ | 59 | 58 | 58 | 57 | 47 | 30 |
| Total | 881 | 894 | 905 | 994 | 842 | 831 |

*Source*: UWV, 2007; CBS Statline (http://statline.cbs.nl).

*Table 11.2*  Disability benefit recipients in the Netherlands as a proportion of the working population, 1990–2010 (%) (own calculations)

|  | 1990 | 1994 | 1998 | 2002 | 2006 | 2010 |
|---|---|---|---|---|---|---|
| Proportion | 14.5 | 13.8 | 13 | 13.3 | 11.2 | 10.6 |

*Source*: UWV, 2007; CBS Statline (http://statline.cbs.nl).

As the quote from *The Economist* cited before illustrated, Dutch disability benefit dependency is considered high in an international perspective. However, one should be cautious in making international comparisons of benefit dependency without taking into account how national social security systems deal with social issues (Jehoel-Gijsbers, 2007). Thus, the emerging disability crisis of the 1980s was not (merely) a sudden crisis of the health of Dutch workers, but (also) related to the economic and labour-market crisis of this decade. In this 'pre-activation' period, providing redundant older workers with labour-market exit options and encouraging them to make way for the young unemployed were seen as legitimate and accepted policy strategies – in this context, disability benefits functioned as one of the available exit routes. What turned rising disability benefit dependency into a 'crisis' was not simply the increasing numbers of older workers receiving the benefit and the rising public expenses that were the result, but also the introduction of the 'activation paradigm' in the Netherlands in the late 1980s and early 1990s. This new social policy paradigm transformed what used to be considered a policy solution – reducing the labour participation rates of older workers – into a major policy problem.

## Main reforms of the Dutch disability system

The reforms in the Dutch disability system that were introduced during the 1990s and early 2000s, mainly affected the scheme for long-term sick employees (WAO/WIA). Only more recently, the reform emphasis shifted towards the scheme for the early disabled (Wajong). We will discuss both schemes separately in this section.

### Reforms of the WAO/WIA benefit

Reforms of the main Disability Benefit scheme in the Netherlands affected the scheme itself, the way in which its implementation is organised, and the Sickness Benefit system, which is the benefit sick employees receive during the first period of sickness, preceding Disability Benefit dependency. In general, the reforms were aimed at:

- reducing the numbers of new entries into the Disability Benefit scheme
- reducing the numbers of *fully* disabled persons receiving the benefit
- promoting (partial) labour-market participation.

An underlying objective of the reforms was, of course, to reduce the expenditures on disability benefits.

### Reducing the number of entries into the Disability Benefit scheme

One of the core conclusions of a parliamentary inquiry that took place in the early 1990s into the increase of the numbers of Disability Benefit recipients was that social partners had, as it was called, 'misused' the benefit system to mitigate the consequences of the economic crisis and increasing unemployment in the 1980s.[2] Until then, Disability Benefits were implemented and administered by sectoral organisations managed by representatives of the trade unions and employers' organisations (Berghman et al., 2002), which gave them significant impact in decision-making processes concerning the ways in which eligibility tests were taking place. In order to put an end to this, social partners' role in implementing social security was abolished. Eventually, this resulted in the full dismantlement of the sectoral implementation organisations and the establishment of one national organisation for the administration and implementation of social insurance (Disability Benefit and Unemployment Benefit), the UWV. UWV functions under the responsibility of the Minister of Social Affairs and Employment; social partners have no involvement in the management of this agency.

Making the criteria to access Disability Benefits stricter has been another reform. The aim was to reduce the number of successful new benefit claims, as well as limit the discretion of the medical professionals who are responsible for disability assessments by making assessments more 'objective': 'This means that doctors not only have to determine whether clients' complaints are *caused* by a medical condition, but also whether the functional limitations that result are severe enough to render them incapable of working' (Van Meershoek et al., 2007, p. 498, italics added). Van Meershoek et al. argue that the model of rational, objective medical decision-making that policy makers apparently assume, is inadequate: 'In most cases doctors consider the relationship between health complaints and functional limitations as complicated and unclear' (Van Meershoek et al., 2007, p. 502). Nevertheless, it is exactly this model that the reforms attempted to impose. According to the authors, the model not only denies the inherently normative character of the assessment process by treating it as merely technical, it also renders the norms used by professionals in the assessment process invisible. They argue 'that contemporary society is too complex to control be defining a priori rules and procedures, that procedures based on mechanical objectivity are inadequate instruments for generating trust through transparency, and that they have to be replaced by procedures that make physicians accountable' (Van Meershoek et al., 2007, p. 510).

Several reforms aimed at reducing Disability Benefit claims by strengthening efforts focused on prevention. During the late 1990s, the Dutch Sickness Benefits Act was abolished for most groups of employees (cf. Yerkes and Van der Veen, 2011): a collective, public 'safety net' provision only exists nowadays for people working as a temp, people with temporary work and the sick unemployed. Since then, employers are obliged to pay sick employees 70%[3] of their wages during the first year – later this period was extended to two years – of sickness. This privatisation of sickness benefits was expected to provide an incentive for employers to prevent sickness and to promote the quick reintegration into work of sick employees. Eventually, this should reduce the numbers of new Disability Benefit claims.

Similar effects were expected from another reform, the so-called Gatekeeper protocol, which made the access to Disability Benefits of employees after two years of sickness dependent on the efforts of employers and employees during the period of sickness to reintegrate the sick employee in his own company or in another company (called first track and second track reintegration respectively). This means that when applying for Disability Benefits, the employer and employee have to submit evidence of the reintegration efforts to the benefit agency (UWV). When the benefit agency considers these efforts insufficient, the employer will have to continue to pay the employee sickness benefits beyond the two-year period. Initially, the UWV decided to introduce a light evaluation of reintegration efforts. Nevertheless, it was expected that a more intensive evaluation process would strengthen efforts to prevent disability entry, and would thus result in a reduction in Disability Benefit claims. To test this expectation an experiment was conducted to compare the results of light and intensive evaluation (Bolhaar et al., 2005). The experiment did indeed have the expected result: the intensity of the process turned out to be an important factor in determining the outcome of the evaluation of reintegration efforts.

A final reform that aimed to reduce new benefit entries concerns changes in the minimum degree of disability that is required for successfully claiming disability benefit. Whereas in the former disability benefit scheme (WAO), people were entitled to disability benefits when their degree of disability was 15% or higher, the new benefit (WIA) increased the threshold to 35%. According to the evaluation study for the WIA, about 45% of WIA claims are rejected because the degree of disability of the claimants is assessed as being below 35% (Cuelenaere and Veerman, 2011).

Figures show that the numbers of new entries into the disability benefit scheme reduced significantly, especially after 2001, when more than 100,000 people entered the benefit scheme. Since 2005, the number of new entries has fluctuated around 20,000, one-fifth of what it was only four years before. To put these figures in a more long-term perspective, whereas the average number of yearly entries into Disability Benefits was 86,000 in the 1990s, in the 2000s it was around 54,000 (UWV, 2007; Cuelenaere and Veerman, 2011). According to De Jong (2008), 1.4% of the workforce entered the disability benefit system in 2001; in 2006, this was only 0.4%. Although this reduction cannot fully be attributed to policy reforms, De Jong estimates that about half of the reduction is the result of the Gatekeeper protocol discussed above and the strengthened efforts to reintegrate sick workers it intended to realise. Similar figures on the effects of the other 'strand' of reforms, making access criteria for Disability Benefits stricter, are not available, but as the figures concerning the impact of a higher threshold mentioned above illustrated, it can be expected that these effects are considerable.

This marked decrease in new disability benefit recipients also implied that WIA dependency remained below expectation. However, the WIA evaluation study (Cuelenaere and Veerman, 2011) also points to a worrying trend concerning the position of non-regular workers who, during the first period of sickness, depend on the sickness safety net provision mentioned preciously. Whereas this group constitutes about 15% of the Dutch labour force, it constitutes 46% of the WIA entries. According to the evaluation study, lack of a bond with an employer – employers do not have to continue to pay wages to non-regular workers during periods of sickness, which implies that these workers are not subject to the Gatekeeper protocol – makes re-entering the labour market difficult: reintegration will have to take place with a new employer. This illustrates that reintegration attempts with sick employees' current employers are more likely to succeed than reintegration attempts taking place when a bond with employers no longer exists. This is a rather alarming conclusion for those already depending on Disability Benefits and considered not fully disabled (reforms at increasing the proportion of partially disabled people are discussed below and affected new claimants as well as those already receiving Disability Benefits), for the increasing numbers of non-regular workers, and for the rapidly increasing numbers of early disabled who also do not have a bond with an employer. Prevention strategies may be useful for workers with a relatively stable labour-market position, but apparently not for those who for whatever reason do not manage to realise this position. We will return to this issue below.

### Reducing the number of fully disabled persons

The second group of reforms tried to reduce the proportion of disability benefit recipients who are considered to be fully disabled. In the late 1980s, a reform had already been introduced that abolished the opportunity to provide partially disabled people with a full disability benefit when there was a lack of opportunities in the labour market. As a consequence of this reform, labour-market conditions were no longer taken into consideration when determining benefit entitlements. From then on, unemployed partially disabled people were obliged to combine their partial disability benefit with unemployment benefit and, when their unemployment benefit entitlements were exhausted,[4] with social assistance.

The reforms aimed at making access criteria for Disability Benefits stricter (see above) not only focused on reducing new entries into Disability Benefits, but also affected the position of people already receiving the benefit. The two reforms of the access criteria (in 1994 and 2004) were accompanied by a re-examination of all people already dependent on Disability Benefits below a certain age threshold, now using the adjusted instead of the original access criteria to assess their degree of disability. These re-examinations were massive operations, involving hundreds of thousands of disability benefit recipients. Many recipients saw their degree of disability being reduced under the new criteria, or even lost their entitlements altogether. For example, Van Oorschot and Boos (2001) mention that after the 1994 reform, half of all re-examined fully disabled persons saw their total benefit withdrawn; during the 2004 reform, almost 40% of those re-examined saw their degree of disability being reduced (Kok and Hop, 2008). Given the problematic nature of work reintegration for those who no longer have a bond with employers (see above), for many of the people whose degree of disability was reduced, the re-examination process changed a situation of full disability into one of partial disability and partial unemployment.

As we saw before, the new 2006 Disability Benefit (WIA) introduced two sub-schemes: one for the fully *and* permanently disabled, and one for the other groups. Yerkes and Van der Veen (2011) interpret the new benefit as a clear example of the welfare/workfare divide characterising the current Dutch welfare state: only a select needy group receives full state support (the fully and permanently disabled), whereas all others are subjected to a workfare regime. Disability Benefit recipients who are not considered fully and permanently disabled are confronted with regular re-examinations of their degree of disability.

As can be expected, the proportion of partially disabled benefit recipients among all disability benefit recipients increased gradually through the years: during the period 1991–2006 the proportion of partially disabled increased from 21% to 33% (Table 11.3), which is the combined result of re-examinations of *current* recipients as well as stricter criteria used to assess the severity of disability of *new* claimants. According to De Jong (2008), in 1990 20% of new benefit recipients was partially disabled; in 2004, this proportion had doubled.

These figures cannot be compared with the proportion of people receiving either of the two benefits in the new WIA system, as WIA not only looks at severity but also at permanence of disability. Of all WIA recipients in 2010, a quarter were considered fully and permanently disabled (http://statline.cbs.nl).

## Promoting (partial) labour-market participation

Promoting the labour-market participation of disabled people was a third objective of the policy reforms. Once again, a range of reforms has been

*Table 11.3* Proportions of recipients receiving a partial and full disability benefit (WAO), 1991–2006

|       | Partially disabled (%) | Fully disabled (%) |
|-------|------------------------|--------------------|
| 1991  | 21                     | 79                 |
| 1996  | 28                     | 72                 |
| 2001  | 32                     | 68                 |
| 2006  | 33                     | 67                 |

*Source*: UWV, 2007.

taking place. First, the generosity of benefits was reduced, which is supposed to stimulate recipients to find a job as it makes benefit dependency less attractive (although it also had consequences for the benefits of the fully disabled). This affected the wage replacement rate of the benefit as well as the duration of the period during which people were entitled to a wage-related benefit. In the 1990s, this duration was made dependent on age. After the period of entitlement to a wage-related benefit expired, people would receive a lower-level disability benefit.

De Jong (2008) has illustrated the size of the income effects of the reforms of the 1980s and early 1990s by looking at the after-tax replacement rate of fully disabled workers. This dropped from 90% in the period before 1980 to 75% in 1994. Of course, many disabled people were confronted with the combined effects of lower benefits on the one hand, and reductions of their degree of disability (as a consequence of stricter access criteria; see above) on the other, which intensified the impact of the reforms on their income.

The new benefit, the WIA, introduced even stronger work incentives for those who are not fully and permanently disabled. The system is rather complex (for more detailed information, see De Jong, 2008), but the general idea is that benefits are more generous for disabled people who manage to realise a larger proportion of their assessed residual earnings capacity. As De Jong (2008, p. 12) concludes: 'work pays, and working more, pays more'.

Since the second half of the 1980s, several measures have been taken that should stimulate employers to hire disabled workers and that should support the disabled in finding a job. Employers, for example, can receive a budget for workplace adjustments. They can also get a wage subsidy when hiring a disabled person, which lasts for a maximum period of one year and amounts to a maximum of 50% of minimum wage. In addition, employers do not have to continue paying wages in periods that a disabled person is on sickness leave. Van Oorschot and Boos (2001) noted the option that was introduced to impose a quota on branches of industry that realise insufficient progress in reintegrating disabled workers, but a quota has never been implemented. Dutch policy makers and politicians are reluctant and sceptical when it comes to introducing obligations for employers. They may have good reasons for this attitude; but in a context of increased pressures on the disabled to reintegrate, the issue of alternative policies, especially for those already on Disability Benefits, becomes more urgent. For disabled people, the instrument of a so-called personal reintegration budget was created (Bosselaar and Prins, 2007), which allows disabled people to develop a reintegration plan and gives them resources to fund the expenses needed to realise the plan.

But despite these measures, the work reintegration of the disabled is not evaluated very positively in the literature. For example, Jehoel-Gijsbers (2007) found that only one in four of all people who entered the disability benefit scheme between April 2002 and December 2003 had been involved in a reintegration programme by April 2006. Furthermore, she is rather critical about the effectiveness of these reintegration programmes, which seem to extend the duration of benefit dependency rather than shorten it. Another study of the effectiveness of activation reached a more positive conclusion (Kok and Hop, 2008), which is explained as a consequence of different effect indicators (return to work plus full benefit independence in Jehoel-Gijsbers' study; return to work in the study by Kok and Hop).

In her study, Jehoel-Gijsbers investigated full return to work of disability benefit recipients, that is, return to work that resulted in disability benefit independence. Her study reached a similar conclusion to that mentioned above: most of the people fully returning to work (85%) had a bond with an employer, either because they were working partially already, or because they were receiving a supplement to their disability benefit from an employer. This indicates again that for work reintegration to be successful, efforts should start early, as reintegration becomes far more difficult when a bond with employers no longer exists.

In a more recent study Jehoel-Gijsbers (2010) concludes that progress has been made concerning the aim of reducing benefit dependency (with the noticeable exception of the benefit for the early disabled) and that dependency on the 'new' benefit (WIA) is even lower than initially expected. The WIA evaluation study shows that expenses on disability as a percentage of GDP have decreased: whereas this percentage amounted to more than 4.5% in 1990, it was below 2.5% in 2005 (Cuelenaere and Veerman, 2011). In other words, from a financial point of view, the reforms have been successful on their own terms. However, both studies also make it clear that the objective of raising the labour-market participation of disabled people has not been realised. Jehoel-Gijsbers' study found that the labour-market participation rate (weekly 12 hours or more) of people on disability benefits even declined in the period 2002–2008: from 24% in 2002 to 20% in 2008. Once again, the position of non-regular workers is particularly vulnerable, as the WIA evaluation study shows (Cuelenaere and Veerman, 2011): of the regular workers among the partially disabled WIA recipients in 2009, 63% was participating in paid work, whereas only 27% of non-regular workers receiving the WIA benefit for partially disabled employees had a job.

### The early disabled: The Wajong

As we saw in Table 11.1, the decrease of WAO/WIA recipients sharply contrasts with the increase of recipients of the benefit for the early disabled, Wajong. Jehoel-Gijsbers (2010) discusses several studies that point at similar causes for this sharp increase:

- The strong increase in the numbers of pupils in special education, which is secondary education for children with a physical or intellectual handicap, a chronic disease, severe behavioural disorder, and so on. About half of the pupils leaving special education become dependent on a Wajong benefit.

- As a consequence of a decentralisation of financial responsibilities for social assistance expenses to Dutch municipalities (2004), local welfare agencies started to refer increasing numbers of young unemployed people claiming social assistance to the Wajong benefit (which is not paid out of municipal budgets).
- An increase of the number of young people depending on institutionalised care (that is, young people living in institutions for youth care) has contributed to an increase in Wajong dependency as well. In 2006, about one quarter of all Wajong recipients lived in organisations providing institutionalised care.
- Young early disabled people living at home claim Wajong benefits more frequently as well, probably as a consequence of the fact that people have become better informed about the existence of this benefit.
- 'New' diseases such as autism and attention deficit hyperactivity disorder (ADHD) could explain part of the increase of Wajong dependency as well. Nevertheless, according to Jehoel-Gijsbers (2010) the strongest increase is found for young people with an intellectual disability.

The labour-market participation rate of Wajong recipients is not much different from the labour-market participation of disabled persons receiving a WAO/WIA benefit: about 25% of people entitled to Wajong have a job. Interestingly, in regions with high numbers of Wajong recipients, labour-market participation rates are higher as well.[5] Most Wajong recipients work in so-called sheltered employment, although their participation in regular work increased during the 2001–2006 period: in 2001, 28% of Wajong recipients worked in regular work while in 2006 this was 39%.[6] Analysing labour-market participation in more detail, Jehoel-Gijsbers (2010) reaches the conclusion that apart from support in finding a job, Wajong recipients need support in *keeping* their job. In particular Wajong recipients working in regular jobs run a high risk of losing their job.

Currently, the Dutch government is preparing far-reaching reforms of Wajong, which are expected to become effective in 2013. For all new cases, Wajong will only remain accessible for those who are fully and permanently disabled (compare the WIA system discussed previously). All others will be integrated together with Social Assistance recipients into a new benefit system, the *Wet WerkennaarVermogen* (WWnV, Work according to Capacity Act). It is expected that the income consequences will be considerable, when comparing the WWnV benefit with the former Wajong benefit. Apart from reducing social security costs, one of the main aims of this reform is to increase the labour-market participation of the early disabled. As we saw before, currently about 25% of the Wajong recipients are working; the current Dutch government argues, following a report of the Socio-Economic Council (a tripartite institute advising government), that this can be raised to about 60%. At the same time, labour-market participation should be realised in the regular labour market, not in sheltered employment (where currently most working Wajong recipients find their job): as a matter of fact, government intends to reduce the number of sheltered work places considerably. Employers will be stimulated to promote the labour-market participation of future WWnV recipients (the early disabled plus social assistance recipients) through a so-called wage dispensation system. This system allows employers to pay wages below the minimum wage when a worker's productivity is below average. Employees will receive a WWnV supplement to their wage, so that their total income will not be below the social minimum. Nevertheless, the 60% participation rate for early disabled people seems very ambitious, especially under current economic conditions: promoting their sustainable regular labour-market participation will most likely require more innovative policies than the wage dispensation system only.

## Dutch disability benefit reforms: An analysis

After having sketched the main reform trends in Dutch disability benefits during the last decades, this section will analyse how the Dutch disability crisis has been interpreted by successive Dutch governments. More specifically, we will analyse to what degree the central thesis of this book – that the disability crisis should be understood as a result of labour-market processes, gaps in individuals' employability and health problems – is reflected in Dutch reforms.

It is evident that the explosive growth of disability benefit dependency in the 1980s has explicitly been related in the Dutch policy debate to high unemployment and economic restructuring processes during that decade. However, the strategy to mitigate the social consequences of these labour-market processes by providing redundant workers with a relatively generous labour-market exit route was, as we saw, at some point in the reform process considered as misuse of the disability benefit scheme, which provided an important trigger for the policy reforms discussed above. Not coincidentally, this interpretation of the causes of the disability crisis coincided with the rise of the activation discourse in Dutch social policies: instead of providing redundant workers with favourable labour-market exit routes (disability benefits functioned as a kind of early retirement scheme), reintegration and labour-market participation became priorities.

One of the core arguments used by successive governments to legitimate this policy shift was that demographic developments will result in labour shortages, which will increase the labour-market opportunities of people with disabilities. Until now, however, these demographic developments seem to have had little impact on the labour-market participation rates of people (partly) depending on disability benefits. Besides it should be noted that although geographical variation does exist in benefit dependency and the labour-market participation of disabled people, this has never been a major issue in the Dutch policy debate. In this respect, the Dutch case is clearly different from the UK case discussed in previous chapters.

The sustainability of the Dutch disability benefit schemes against the background of increasing labour-market flexibility seems to be an important issue. The WIA evaluation study as well as several other studies have shown that reintegration of sick employees who have a bond with employers is considerably more successful and likely compared to the reintegration of sick employees who need to reintegrate with a new employer. According to these studies, this helps to explain the success of the privatisation of sickness pay and the Gatekeeper protocol: the bond between employer and employee is maintained, and both have an interest in making efforts to reintegrate the sick employee. It is exactly this bond with employers that flexible workers (as well as sick unemployed people) lack. This hampers reintegration during the period of sickness (thus making entry into disability more likely): preventive reintegration (that is, reintegration before disability benefit dependency starts) is more difficult to realise for these groups of workers. Furthermore, the WIA evaluation study showed that non-regular workers are not only more likely to become dependent on the disability benefit, but the partially disabled among them are also less likely to work, compared to regular workers.

As far as the explosive increase of the numbers of Wajong recipients is concerned, the political debate pays little attention to the issue of how this phenomenon is linked to labour-market processes. The main focus is on the assumed 'labour-market participation potential' of this group: the dominant political opinion is that many more Wajong recipients could work than is currently the case. In the literature, several authors have related the increasing number of Wajong recipients to broader processes taking place in society. For example, Besseling et al. (2009) suggest that the increasing complexity of society and the increasing requirements employees have to meet may be part of the explanation, although they point out that clear evidence for this is hard to provide. The authors mention several measures directed at employers that could promote the labour-market participation of Wajong recipients, such as introducing quota regulations or to expect from employers that the composition of their workforce reflects the composition of the regional population of working age. However, as we mentioned before Dutch policy makers and politicians are highly unlikely to introduce this type of obligation for employers.

These considerations concerning the increase in Wajong recipients point out that the employability of disability benefit recipients is an important issue in increasing their labour-market participation. Something similar may be at stake for recipients of the WAO/WIA benefit, especially those who have been out of work for a longer period. For example, a considerable proportion of disability benefit recipients is older than 45 (in 2006, this proportion amounted to 80%), and it is well known that employers are not eager to hire older workers, especially when they have been out of work for several years. In addition, employers may believe that hiring disabled workers involves risks, such as lower productivity or a higher probability of sickness-related absence. But even though Dutch governments have introduced several policy reforms that should stimulate employers to hire disabled workers (see above), in most reforms employability seems to be primarily seen as a motivation rather than an opportunity issue. Most reforms have reduced the generosity of disability benefits considerably, and strengthened the work obligations of recipients – reflecting the policy assumption that a lack of work incentives in the disability scheme stops people from reintegrating into the labour market, and therefore reduces their employability.

The health factor is present in the policy discourse on the disability crisis and in policy reforms as well. First of all, as we saw it was argued at the start of the debate about the crisis that many people entered disability benefits for other than health reasons. It is very likely that there was a core of truth in this argument, given the fact that disability benefits were used as an 'economic shock absorber' during the 1980s. Another way in which the health factor played a role in the policy reforms considered the assessments of disability during medical examinations preceding the decisions about disability benefit entitlements. According to policy makers, professionals included too many 'non-medical' considerations in their decisions, which stimulated policy makers to formulate stricter conditions for benefit entitlements, among others, the requirement that work impairments should be causally related to objective medical conditions. As we saw previously, the re-examinations of people already dependent on disability benefits had significant consequences for the degree of disability of many of them. Definitions and operationalisations of disability apparently matter a great deal where the accessibility of disability benefits is concerned.

A final issue related to the health factor concerns the perception of the relationship between work and sickness/disability. Whereas in the past, sickness and work were considered to be incompatible – work became an issue only after recovering from sickness – and the emphasis was on the impediments of disability for work, the policy reforms discussed in this chapter imply a clear 'recursive shift'. Policy makers nowadays emphasise the work capacities of disabled people, rather than their work impediments, and argue that work and sickness/disability are not incompatible. In itself, this 'new' way of looking at the relationship between work and disability is not simply a 'neo-liberal' strategy to move people out of social security into whatever jobs are available: interest organisations of disabled and handicapped people have often argued in favour of more job opportunities and jobs adjusted to their capacities, and often felt permanently excluded from the labour market. The core issues here are, of course, the meticulousness with which the work capacities of disabled people are assessed, as well as the degree to which work and work circumstances can be and actually are adjusted to people's capacities. As we have seen in this chapter, increasing numbers of people have been declared 'fit for work', at least partially; but the prospects of a sustainable return to work are rather gloomy, especially for those who no longer have a bond with an employer.

## Conclusion

The Dutch disability crisis has been on the political agenda now for over two decades. Numerous reforms have been introduced, which had little impact on the volume of disability benefits during the 1990s, but became considerably more effective during the 2000s – at least, when we disregard the issue of the increasing numbers of early disabled persons. What seems to have been one of the most successful reforms is the increasing focus on preventing disability by implicating employers strongly in the reintegration of sick employees in the sickness period preceding disability benefit dependency. At the same time, the position of those who have no bonds with employers, remains vulnerable: the early disabled (who do not have a work history), flexible workers, and those already dependent on disability benefits. For these groups, benefits have become considerably less generous, whereas their labour-market opportunities remain weak.

The three factors that were discussed in the introductory chapter of this volume as the key factors for understanding the disability crisis have certainly played a role in the Dutch political reforms, but in a rather different way than the authors of the introductory chapter interpret them. In the Dutch reforms, these factors were seen by policy makers and politicians as strengthening the disability crisis in the following ways:

1. For too long, the Dutch disability benefit scheme has been used to solve other societal and labour-market problems than its purported target goals.
2. For too long, the Dutch disability benefit scheme contained too few incentives for benefit recipients to return to work, thus reducing instead of promoting their employability.
3. For too long, the emphasis has been on the impediments rather than the capacities of sick and disabled people to work.

At the moment, the debate concerning the WAO/WIA has calmed down, after having dominated the political social policy agenda for many years. Even though the number of people dependent on these benefits is still considerable, the inflow in the new benefit system has decreased beyond expectation. Because of that, and because of the gradual retirement of those dependent on disability benefits (especially recipients of the old WAO), the volume of disability benefit recipients is likely to decrease further in the years to come. Nevertheless, the position of flexible workers raises new challenges for the Dutch disability system, especially in the context of an increasingly flexible labour market. As we saw, there are two aspects to flexible workers' vulnerability: efforts aimed at preventing disability are much less institutionalised as in the case for regular workers, and once flexible workers become dependent on Disability Benefits, their reintegration opportunities are weaker.

Most reforms in the near future will focus on the early disabled. As things look now, people confronted with early disability will experience a serious deterioration of their benefit entitlements and conditions starting in 2013, especially when their disability is assessed as partial or non-permanent. In addition, the current government wants early disabled people to participate in the regular labour market – whereas most early disabled who have a job now do so in sheltered employment. In our opinion, raising the regular labour-market participation of the early disabled is going to be a major challenge. The Dutch success formula of prevention and early reintegration is difficult to realise for the early disabled, who have no bonds with employers; and the availability of the type of jobs most of them participate in now, sheltered jobs, will be reduced considerably.

New and innovative solutions will be needed to deal with this potential 'new' disability crisis of the labour-market participation of flexible workers and the early disabled, especially in a country that has become rather lavish in imposing obligations on people receiving benefits, but remains reluctant, if not hostile, towards obliging employers to hire vulnerable labour-market groups. One of the initiatives taken in this context is what is called the 'employers' approach' in activation and reintegration services. Several agencies and organisations involved in providing activation and reintegration are starting to develop services specifically aimed at supporting employers in finding solutions for work organisation and labour-market problems in such a way that these solutions create new opportunities for vulnerable groups in the labour market. In itself, this shift of the focus in activation and reintegration from employees to employers is an interesting trend. Whether it will be effective in the sense that it can open up new opportunities for the sustainable labour-market participation of vulnerable groups on a sufficiently large scale will have to become clear in the next few years.

## Notes

1. As of 1 August 2004, no new WAZ claims were allowed, so that collective arrangements for the disabled self-employed no longer exist.
2. The use of the term 'misuse' is rather remarkable given the wide public and political support for the 'older workers make way for younger workers' strategy in the 1980s.
3. Collective agreements between employers and trade unions often regulate that employees receive a higher percentage of their wages during sickness periods.
4. In the 1980s, wage-related Disability Benefit entitlements still lasted until retirement.

5. Contrary to what one might expect, Wajong dependency is lower in the highly urbanised western part of the Netherlands, and even lower in the four largest Dutch cities (Jehoel-Gijsbers, 2010).
6. Own calculations based on data presented in Jehoel-Gijsbers (2010).

# References

Bergman, J., Nagelkerke, A., Boos, K., Doeschot, R., and Vonk, G. (eds) (2002) *Social Security in Transition* (The Hague: Kluwer).
Besseling, J., Andriessen, S., and Wevers, C. (2009) *Contourennotitie Wajong-risicomodel* (Hoofddorp: TNO).
Bolhaar, J., de Jong, Ph., van der Klaauw, B., and Lindeboom, M. (2005) 'Strengere Poortwachtersfunctie UWV Leidt tot Lagere WAO-instroom', *Economisch Statistische Berichten*, 90 (4459), 200–203.
Bosselaar, H. and Prins, R. (2007) 'Personal Return to Work Budgets for Persons with Disabilities: Demand-Based Delivery of Re-integration Services in the Netherlands', *European Journal of Social Security*, 9 (2), 111–127.
Cuelenaere, B. and Veerman, T. (2011) *Onderzoek Evaluatie WIA* (Leyden: Astri).
De Jong, P. (2008) *Recent Changes in Dutch Disability Policy* (The Hague: APE).
Jehoel-Gijsbers, G. (ed.) (2007) *Beter aan het Werk. Trendrapportage Ziekteverzuim, Arbeidsongeschiktheid en Werkhervattin* (The Hague: SCP/CBS/TNO).
Jehoel-Gijsbers, G. (ed.) (2010) *Beperkt aan het Werk. Rapportage Ziekteverzuim, Arbeidsongeschiktheid en Arbeidsparticipatie* (The Hague: SCP/CBS/TNO).
Kok, L. and Hop, P. (2008) *Langdurig in de WAO* (The Hague: RWI).
Muysken, J. and Rutten, T. (2002) *Disability in the Netherlands: Another Dutch Disease? METEOR Research Memorandum, No. 2002–051* (Maastricht: Maastricht University).
UWV (2007) *Kroniek van de Sociale Verzekeringen 2007. Wetgeving en Volume-ontwikkeling in Historisch Perspectief* (Amsterdam: UWV).
Van Meershoek, A., Krumeich, A., and Vos, R. (2007) 'Judging without Criteria? Sickness Certification in Dutch Disability Schemes', *Sociology of Health and Illness*, 29 (4): 497–514.
Van Oorschot, W. and Boos, K. (2001) 'The Battle against Numbers: Disability Policies in the Netherlands' in W. van Oorschot and B. Hvinden (eds), *Disability Policies in European Countries* (The Hague: Kluwer).
Yerkes, M. and van der Veen, R. (2011) 'Crisis and Welfare State Change in the Netherlands', *Social Policy and Administration*, 45 (4): 430–444.

# 12
# New Zealand's Reform of Sickness Benefit and Invalid's Benefit

*Neil Lunt and Daniel Horsfall*

## Introduction

In common with many other OECD states, policy makers in New Zealand have struggled to reduce the numbers of people in receipt of long-term disability benefits. Disability benefits reform is a wide and challenging agenda and remains at the forefront of social security reform within New Zealand. Successive governments have sought to address the rise in numbers with only limited success. This chapter overviews the New Zealand situation and seeks to:

- outline the development of measures aimed at reforming New Zealand's main disability benefits, namely Sickness Benefit (SB) and Invalid's Benefit (IB), including the underpinning rationales
- situate these changes within the broader context of both active labour market policy and disability initiatives
- assess the continuing challenges that exist within the New Zealand context.

## Background

Following the colonisation of Aotearoa/New Zealand by British settlers in the nineteenth century there emerged a derivative legal system and a set of Westminster-type political institutions. New Zealand earned a reputation for being a social welfare laboratory, and pioneering welfare state developments included the introduction of Old Age Pensions (1898), Widows Pensions (1911), Miners Pensions (1915), and a system of wage arbitration from 1894. During the economic Depression, the First Labour Government from 1935 consolidated these earlier developments, legislating the 1938 Social Security Act and free public health care and education. In line with other Keynesian welfare states, post-war intervention was underpinned by an assumption of income and employment security. Social services were not viewed as a residual safety net, but seen instead as an encouragement to economic growth and development, and a core component of citizenship rights (Castles and Shirley, 1996; Lunt et al., 2002).

Sickness Benefit and Invalid's Benefit were introduced during the first Labour Government. The Pension Amendment Act 1936 saw provision extended beyond war veterans, miners, and the visually impaired to include 'invalids', and rates were increased and measures expanded to those with sickness in the Social Security Act 1938 (McClure, 1998). 'Invalid' benefici-aries were defined as permanently incapable of work and viewed as part of the deserving poor, and necessitating support and also insulation from the rigours of the competitive jobs market. SB was payable in respect of tempo-rary 'incapacity' for work through sickness or accident, that is, off work or working at a reduced level.

The 1970s were turbulent economic times, with rising unemployment and inflation and slowing growth. Both rising oil prices and the entry of the UK into the European Economic Community (EEC) impacted on New Zealand's traditional export markets. The election of the Fourth Labour Government in 1984 saw an end to the previous economic and welfare settlement, and led to wide-ranging economic and public sector manage-ment reform. Underpinning this neo-liberal agenda, whose proponents now controlled the NZ Labour Party, were theoretical commitments around the market, public choice theory, and principal–agency theory. Policy implica-tions were widespread deregulation of the banking and financial system, transport, energy, and privatisation. The top rate of income tax was slashed, and indirect taxation was increased. Overseas, New Zealand was presented as the model for rapid and effective 'structural adjustment' advocated within the 'Washington consensus'.

After the 1990s attention began to shift to the social policy arena with the newly elected National Government and subsequent National-led Coalitions (1990–1999) continuing along the path cut by Labour. Attempts were made to free up the labour market through decentralised wage bargaining, with its model being the individualised worker negotiating with their employer. The 1991 'Mother of all Budgets' cut welfare benefits levels with a view to increas-ing incentives to enter paid work, improving intergenerational equality, and bolstering moral responsibility (Kelsey, 1997, p. 280). Elsewhere, attempts were made to introduce market-like conditions into health services, accident compensation, education and state housing.

## Sickness Benefit and Invalid's Benefit

New Zealand faces a continuing problem of labour market inequalities for people experiencing ill-health and disability. The disadvantaged position of disabled people is well documented. Disabled adults are far less likely to be in the labour force than non-disabled adults (36% of disabled adults were not in the labour force compared to 16% of non-disabled adults).

Disabled people are less likely to be employed than non-disabled peers (59% compared to 76%) (Office for Disability Issues, 2011). Disabled people are more likely to have no formal educational qualifications (35% of disabled adults, 20% in non-disabled adults). Just under half (38%) of disabled adults reported gross personal incomes less than NZ$15,000 for the year ended 31 March 2001, compared with 27% of non-disabled adults. Women with a disability are particularly disadvantaged in terms of income, as are other groups including Māori, Pacific Peoples, and older workers (Ministry of Health, 2001; Statistics New Zealand, 2008).

In the three decades post-war SB and IB receipt remained relatively constant at under 1% of the working age population (Fletcher, 2009). Beginning in the mid-1970s, numbers began to rise steadily. Since then growth has occurred at what has been seen as an alarming rate (see Fletcher, 2009, p. 4; Shaw et al., 2011, pp. 568–9), which currently stands at over 5% (Ministry of Social Development, 2012a, 2012b). OECD comparison rates should be interpreted with care given the fact they include IB but exclude SB with durations less than two years. They also do not count Accident Compensation Corporation scheme weekly compensation recipients (adding these would bring New Zealand far closer to average OECD rate) (Fletcher, 2009, pp. 10–11).

The proportion of the working age population receiving IB has increased steadily between 2002 and 2008, though it reduced slightly since that point (Ministry of Social Development, 2012a). Nevertheless, the increase from 2.5% of the working age receiving IB in 2001to 3.2% in 2008 has hardly been bucked, with 3.1% receiving it in 2011. Similarly, numbers on SB rose sharply in the early 1990s and continued to increase between 2000 and 2012. Figures for SB and IB, to the year ending December 2012, stood at 83,571 people aged 18–64 in receipt of IB and 61,245 people (aged 18–64) in receipt of SB (Ministry of Social Development, 2012a, 2012b). It is worth noting that self-reported health is especially low among IB and SB recipients (Pledger et al., 2009), and those in receipt of SB/IB face a risk of mortality that is three times higher than that faced by those not in receipt of either IB or SB (Shaw et al., 2011).

Recent analysis of the rise in numbers on IB and SB suggests that around half of the rise in IB is explained by population growth, the ageing of the population, and the rise in the age of eligibility for New Zealand Superannuation (Wilson et al., 2005; Shaw et al., 2011). There has been a rise in almost all incapacities for IB (Wilson et al., 2005). While not explicitly examining causation, the authors suggest that there are several factors correlated with benefit growth, including the changing structure of employment and types of work available, employer recruitment and retention practices, and changing wage/replacement income ratios. The interaction of SB and IB with other programmes and shifts in organisational practice may also be significant. For example, the introduction in 1998 of social assistance with community work and training obligations, reforms to Accident Compensation eligibility, changes in case management, and changed operational focus may all contribute to cross-benefit transfers. Changes in the prevalence of inca-pacity caused by de-institutionalisation, the changing nature of work, and recognition of previously little understood impairments are further possible reasons (Wilson et al., 2005; Shaw et al., 2011). Fletcher (2009, p. 4) in his review concludes that: 'The biggest driver of long-run growth [however] appear to be changes in the labour market and in the interaction between those changes and the operation of the benefit systems.'

In light of the above, contributory factors towards the growth in disability rolls are the triad of considerations outlined in Chapter 1:

- labour market processes of job destruction, polarisation, and work inten-sification that have limited opportunities for work in post-industrial labour markets, particularly for those with poor health
- gaps in individuals' employability and skills that mean that they are left at the 'back of the queue' for those jobs that are available
- health problems that both explain why people claim disability benefits in the first place and limit their prospects of returning to work.

What appears clear is that just as there is unlikely to be one single expla-nation of the rise (Wilson et al., 2005; Shaw et al., 2011) neither is there one simple solution – changing attitudes, providing services, or fostering incentives are by themselves unlikely to be 'golden bullets'.

For SB and IB, greater inflows between 1993 and 2002 rather than increased durations have fuelled the increase (Wilson et al., 2005). Research also suggests that 81% of the IB growth for those aged between 15 and 59 is associated with current or recent contact with the benefit system, indi-cating transfers from elsewhere in the benefits system (particularly SB, but also Unemployment Benefit (UB), Domestic Purposes Benefit and Widow's Benefit) rather than new flows from the workplace (Wilson et al., 2005, p. 26). The Ministry of Social Development points out that only 2% of those receiving SB in 2012 (0.05% of the general population) had been in receipt for a continuous period of 10years or more. When other benefits were taken into account, however, that figure rose to 9% of those claiming SB had been in continuous receipt of a benefit for 10 years or more (Ministry of Social Development, 2012b). This figure is much higher for IB recipients, 34% of whom have received continuous IB for 10 years or more (Ministry of Social Development, 2011a). Estimates from a cohort of beneficiaries granted IB in 1993 suggest that over a 10-year period around 40% of those granted IB remained on the benefit nine years later, and around 17% of the total cohort of IB recipients had left for employment (Wilson et al., 2005, pp. 54–5). For the 1993 cohort, the median IB duration was six years; for the SB cohort it was 19 weeks (Wilson et al., 2005, p. 63).

From the 1990s, increased numbers moving onto disability benefits and the relatively long stays on IB and growth in inflows of SB have been perceived as a major thorn in the side of successive governments (McClure, 1998; Shaw et al., 2011). There are clearly financial costs in terms of the taxpayer burden of spiralling benefit payments, as well as the forgone fiscal take of beneficiary inactivity. But there are also the broader social costs, including the wasted potential of individuals languishing on benefits, and associated health costs that are known to arise from long-term sickness and distance from the labour market. It has long been apparent that many disabled people in receipt of disability benefits wish to work (Office for Disability Issues, 2002; Welfare Working Group, 2011).

The difficulties of SB and IB emanate from how such benefits are labelled, defined, and conceptualised. To qualify for IB, a person must have a condition that is defined as 'permanent' and 'severe', that is, be unable to work for 15 hours a week. SB requires a condition or disability that limits capacity to seek or undertake full-time employment (30 hours) (Shaw et al., 2011). In line with many systems of disability support, criticisms include a failure to recognise partial capacity, ignoring the spectrum of capacity; and that it does not account for the fluctuating nature of impairment and changes over time (Thornton, 1998). Despite employability being contingent on support, the irony is that those that find themselves on SB and IB may need more support but have received less.

Until recently there has typically been a lack of policy attention to SB and IB recipients who have not been expected to produce return-to-work plans and who have not been able to access the broad range of labour market programmes (Fletcher, 2009). This focus on unemployment has been common across the OECD. The less frequent attention and lack of planning and job-search obligations associated with SB and IB is an incentive for those who are discouraged from seeking work, and who can obtain a medical certificate, to apply for or transfer to one of those benefits. In the case of IB, the payment differential provides a further incentive. Second, the incentives on case managers are to allow clients entry onto SB or IB in order to focus on the UB caseload.

New Zealand's SB and IB policy has developed through three phases. We discuss each of these in turn and conclude with a discussion of the ongoing issues that impact on the implementation of SB/IB policy. The intention is to situate the discussion of disability benefits within the combination of three key factors outlined by the editors in Chapter 1.

## Phase 1: Minimal social policy

Given concerns about capture, the National policy introduced a new approach to medical certification for SB and IB with the introduction of the Designated Doctor Scheme in 1995. Designated doctors had responsibility for assessing benefit eligibility, certifying applications for SB at 13 and 52 weeks, and certifying grants for IB, and recommending a possible review (12, 18, 24 months). From 1998, there was an alignment of SB rates with UB rates for new grants and the introduction of a new variant of social assistance, the 'Community Wage' (with expectations of training, engagement, and job search) in place of UB and SB. In October 1998, the designated doctor review scheme was revised, and doctors signing the certificate were able to certify SB for four weeks and then at 13-week intervals. For IB, designated doctors certify the granting of a benefit, with review being recommended by these doctors for two years, five years, or never. During the first part of 1999, there was also the trial of work capacity assessment for those with sickness, disability, or injury. A Phase one trial was undertaken but Phase two was never completed. The work capacity process for IB and SB sought to identify the level of work, if any, a beneficiary was capable of, and to determine what assistance would help them move into paid work (abridged from Wilson et al., 2005). Thus, the first attempts at emphasising work capacity were established.

These approaches sought to narrow the gateway to benefits and to ensure those with work capacity did not avoid the obligations that were at this time being placed on other groups of beneficiaries, including those in receipt of UB and Domestic Purpose Benefit. The approach was individualised and an underpinning assumption saw 'problems' as located in individual claimants, particularly in their attitudes towards work and unwillingness to meet their obligations. At root, it can be argued that National's policy towards SB and IB was 'minimal social policy', underpinned by a thrust towards cutting and reducing wherever possible, and overlaid with discursive articulations of beneficiary obligation. Such an approach emphasised welfare provision as a 'safety net' and saw intervention as primarily ameliorative. Cutting benefits was seen to provide incentives, and workfare/worktest were developed under such thinking. Thus under minimal forms of intervention there was relatively little attention paid to skills, support, health problems, and labour market deficiencies identified by Lindsay and Houston in Chapter 1 as core pillars of contemporary policy intervention.

## Phase 2: Social development

Between 1999 and 2008 Labour-led administrations sought to develop a social development approach to social policy and welfare reform. This paradigm shift can be placed within the broader 'Third Way' approach: linking economic and social policy; development of a preventative welfare state; the centrality of paid work; opportunities replacing income redistribution; the language of inclusion/exclusion displacing equality; a pragmatism of 'what works'; and attention to citizens' rights *and* responsibilities (cf. Driver and Martell, 2001; Powell, 2002; Lister, 2004).

Policy entailed a commitment to 'employability' focused on intensive case management and personal development plans (Lunt, 2006). These were combined with a range of supply-side initiatives such as attempts to 'make work pay', As part of the commitment towards human capital development, social security is seen as requiring updating and modernisation in terms of administration, delivery, and *purpose*. Labour administrations prioritised welfare reform (including tackling numbers on SB and IB), emphasising active labour market policy and enhancing 'employability' of all disadvantaged groups. Increased numbers in receipt of SB and IB were in stark contrast to the Labour's social development aspirations.

The shift that took place around SB and IB must also be placed in the broader context of changes that have occurred in how 'disability', 'disabled people', 'ability' and 'capacity' are conceptualised. There have been significant developments across the field of disability policy and strategy. The New Zealand Disability Strategy *Making a World of Difference* (Ministry of Health, 2001) was underpinned by a commitment to the social model of disability and was the result of lengthy consultation with the disability sector. The document's 15 key dimensions included education, health, employment, rights, and leadership. There is a broad commitment to a non-disabling society, and addressing the participation of particular target populations within the broader disability community.

From the 1990s, a dominant theme of welfare reform focused on shifting from passive welfare delivery and minimal social policy. Welfare policy is seen to require a better linkage with economic policy, as well as being in need of some 'modernisation' to bring it in line with changed social, economic, demographic, and attitudinal realities of the twenty-first century. A constituent of the realignment between economic and social policy has been the 'work-first' approach to reducing poverty, and attempts to widen labour market opportunities as a route to fostering social inclusion. An investment approach was explicitly signalled in relation to SB and IB, concerned with 'how we should invest in people receiving a Sickness or Invalid's Benefit at an individual client level and identify the type of services and programmes we should fund for people in this client group'(Ministry of Social Development, 2004).

In contrast to earlier individualised understandings, the new terrain was the social model and recognition of structural inhibitors and complex decision-making contexts. The issue is reframed, thus it is not that people are claiming such benefits inappropriately, but that the structure of benefits are themselves inappropriate for many of the people claiming them (cf. Social Market Foundation, 2005). Within New Zealand, the Sickness and Invalid's Benefit Strategy (later the *New Service for People Receiving Sickness and Invalid's Benefits*) further emphasised the importance of recognising the *potential* for work, and of removing barriers and building bridges for those that wish to avail themselves of such opportunities. Since 1999, this view was supported by a number of changes to the benefits system and in the delivery of service supports: increased regional flexibility in delivering employment services and addressing skill shortages. At the micro level there were ongoing attempts to introduce tailored case management. Key changes introduced by Labour included:

### Benefit eligibility

There were attempts to 'rewire' the benefit system to allow individuals to take risks and try out labour market opportunities. From 2004, IB recipients could trial a return to work of over 15 hours per week for six months without losing benefit entitlement if they need to access the benefit later on for the same disability or condition.

### Benefit gateways

Labour allowed local general practitioners and case managers to seek a second opinion where doubt exists about new and continued eligibility for SB, thus pre-empting patient 'capture' that is said to result from close or long-standing personal relationships between claimants and their doctors.

### Case management and work capacity

There have been ongoing debates around the appropriate balance within case management of client support and ensuring client compliance, and whether specialist case management for particular benefit types and those with complex needs is more effective than generic provision. Enhanced case management ascertains potential for work and to individualise provision for recipients. The 2003 Jobs Jolt initiative trialled sites to deliver employment-related services to SB and IB clients. This included specialist case management for SB and IB recipients with lower target caseload ratios. Specialist case managers work with medical practitioners and job brokers to devise return-to-work strategies. For SB and IB recipients, the emphasis is upon recognising the potential individuals may have for work, and providing more effective and personalised services for those that wish to make use of them. It may also include services aimed at retention for those at risk of losing jobs on grounds of ill-health and disability (Maharey, 2005). Moves to encompass work preparation, return to work, and retention (within the new Support to Work programme) were extensions of previous Work and Income roles.

### Vocational assessment and service wraparound

Preparing for Work is a vocational assessment tool to help case managers identify the skills and aspirations of those who want work. To encourage SB and IB beneficiaries to enter the paid workforce, pilot projects have been used (employABLE projects, 2002–2004). Four were centrally funded but offered by community-based groups (targeting either Māori or people with mental health problems).

There have been a series of developments aimed at wrapping specialist support services around clients who are identified as being close to the labour market and potentially benefiting from enhanced and intensive support – whether health, motivational, or vocational. These 'Innovative Employment Assistance' initiatives include the piloting of PATHS (physical health), ProCare (mental health services), Work First (mental health), Workwise (mental health), Te Rau Pani (mental health), and Kaleidoscope (spinal injury) (Ministry of Social Development, 2005).

Open labour market solutions to disability employment policy were emphasised and vocational services without transitions intent were no longer funded through the Government agency Work and Income. Sheltered workshops lost their exemption from minimum wage and holiday legislation (Department of Labour, 2001).

### Mutual obligations

The 2007 Social Security Amendment Act introduced planning and activity requirements for those in receipts of SB, IB and consolidated the obligations of Domestic Purposes Benefit recipients. While this development is not work-testing per se and does not demand pre benefit activity, there are requirements to comply with the demands of the Personal Development and Employment Plans when in receipt of benefit. These requirements may include engaging with Work and Income, undertaking planning and developing formal plans, potentially undertaking a work-related activity, and showing commitment to the plan. From 2006 there were attempts to place beneficiaries in one of three categories: Work support, for people who could work immediately; Work Development Support, for people who might be able to work if they had extra support to do so; and Community Support, for those who were not considered able to work in the near future. Personal Development and Employment plans aimed to identify measure and supports to enable a person to move into employment. In 2007 such case management was extended to include SB and IB who could now participate in the process and receive regular reviews. While there was a capacity for SB and IB to be sanctioned, in practice those on SB/IB would take part voluntarily.

In summary, a great deal of emphasis was placed on developing case management and specialist support to assist those transitions into employment. While there were greater opportunities for more proactive engagement with SB and IB clients (within the balance of *rights and responsibilities*), there was a reluctance to pursue such an approach. More broadly, macroeconomic policy and employability retained a supply-side focus.

## Phase 3: National's policy priorities post-2008

The National Party won the 2008 election and formed a Coalition agreement amid what were seen as 'extraordinarily difficult times for the country and the world'(Key, 2008). Recent policy developments have been shaped by an 'unrelenting focus on work'. The Future Focus Bill, which has been incorporated in the Social Security (New Work Tests, Incentives, and Obligations) Amendment Act of 2010, represents a legislative effort to reduce long-term welfare dependency through stricter eligibility criteria for IB and by seeking to facilitate a shift to work for those who are registered as disabled but are willing and able to work.

Of particular relevance are the changes to the administration of and eligibility criteria for SB. The Act codifies the aim of improved management of SB via a second four-week medical assessment period and a review after 12 months on SB. While there are no fundamental changes for those in receipt of IB, eligibility initial assessment of claims will become more stringent with the focus very much placed on what a person can do rather than what they are unable to do. A departure from previous practice sees those deemed capable of part-time work within a two-year period after assessment being placed on SB rather than IB, on which recipients will face more frequent reviews of their condition and a strong expectation that they will get back into work when they can.

Alongside the Act the Welfare Working Group (WWG), which was established by Cabinet and mandated to directly investigate strategies to reduce long-term welfare dependency (WWG, 2010), has proposed further changes although their implementation is far from assured. The most notable suggested change is perhaps the consolidation of disparate 'main' benefits with a single jobseeker's allowance, supplemented by a secondary payment for those in receipt of IB (WWG, 2011). Both the Future Focus elements of the Social Security Act (2010) and the debates that were held during its reading stage, and the WWG report (2011) stress the economic, moral, and social cases for returning as many people to work as possible, although this has not been without criticism (O'Brien et al., 2010). In July 2013 SB is replaced by Jobseekers Support, a work-focussed benefit with work expectations according to capability. IB becomes Supported Living Payment with no work expectations.

Detailed scrutiny has been paid to Ministry of Social Development's benefit assessment and case management practices by the Office of the Auditor General (OAG) (2009). In particular, a range of concerns were raised around failure to 'proactively' engage and case-manage beneficiaries, with frontline staff not identifying sickness and invalid's beneficiaries who are most likely to participate in work-planning activities (with both work capacity assessments and vocational assessments as possible options). As a result of the OAG report, a target group has of 3,000 sickness beneficiaries has been selected who hold medical certificates confirming they are currently available for part-time work. Staff will also receive training on the 'proactive engagement' approach, including the types of conversations that need to occur, the expected outcomes, and the expectation of regular engagement with each beneficiary. The Ministry is also continuing to strengthen the use of regional health advisors and regional disability advisors, and to bolster the guidance on staff referral to these specialists. The OAG has encouraged the Ministry 'not to lose sight of this group of beneficiaries and to continue to improve its processes, despite the challenges of the current economic environment'. While case management lies at the heart of development, these more proactive interventions mark a departure from previous voluntary approaches. Changes to the benefit architecture – particularly to restrict routes onto IB – and increased emphasis on work capacity are further notable developments.

## Enduring themes and challenges

### The 'social model' and employment

A major challenge is to maintain the social model at the centre of SB and IB reforms, and to avoid making individuals the sole locus of intervention despite the importance of 'individualised' provision. The social model of disability leads to a policy of alleviation rather than compensation, and calls for policymakers and society to 'redesign, reframe, reconstruct and reconstitute inclusionary policies'(Lunt and Thornton, 1994). Difficulties of engaging small firms may doubly disadvantage particular groups that are more likely to be over-represented in such employment opportunities: women, older workers, and those from minority ethnic groups.

The social model is focused on environments and rights, and emphasises education, transport, health and community care services, and housing. Given labour market status is strongly related to educational experience, a quality education is the crucial first step to ensuring employment opportunities. Inflexible transport remains a major barrier to the social and labour market participation of disabled people, with such groups less likely to be car owners and more likely to use public transport when travelling to work. The 2006 Disability Survey found that 81,300 (20%) disabled adults and children would travel on buses if they were made easier for disabled people to use (Office for Disability Issues, 2009). The future responses of the New Zealand disability community to attempts to tackle SB and IB issues are likely to be conditional on the wider transformations occurring in terms of implementation of the social model and progress of the Disability Strategy.

### Partnerships and/or obligation

In seeking to tackle SB and IB responsibility must be apportioned between a range of stakeholders – beneficiaries, government departments and agencies, employers, and the health sector. Employers can be seen as users of incapacity services because the initiatives may reduce labour shortage, turnover, and absenteeism (Corden and Sainsbury, 2001). Employers are diverse, and small employers may present a particular challenge in forging working partnerships around issues including sickness, ill-health, and disability. Small employers and their recruitment practices present particular issues for New Zealand, given that, in 2010, there were 250,000 enterprises, and of these, 90% employed five or fewer persons, and 99% employed 50 or fewer(Statistics New Zealand, 2010). Some steps have been introduced in New Zealand ('Service to Employers') whereby employers are supported and given information to help in their hiring and retention of staff with ill-health or a disability.

### 'Healthy welfare'

Policy is moving beyond the belief that the individual beneficiary is the only component subject to 'activation'. As well as a role for employers, active engagement is also being sought from a range of medical professionals, particularly in primary health care, including better assessment and communication of information (OAG, 2009).

The majority of working age disabled people have incurred their impairments at work (OECD, 2003), and the workplace and health systems are becoming crucial sites for the delivery of employment-focused services. Recognising the importance of prevention, early intervention, and the role of health services has prompted new trials focused on the role of primary and secondary medical practitioners ensuring quick return to work.

Professionals differ about the extent to which they see work rehabilitation as part of primary care. Overseas research suggests general practitioners were concerned about the conflict of certification activity with a therapeutic role (Hiscock et al., 2005).

Ongoing engagement with the medical profession is likely to be required to clarify general practitioners' roles of clinician, advocate, and adjudicator in relation to health and wellbeing (OAG, 2009). General practitioners often feel pressured and are also inclined to take the wider views of claimants/ patients into account, perhaps not wanting to commit them to searches for scarce work or where services are poor (Social Market Foundation, 2005). A fuller notion of employability clearly encompasses the supply, demand, and matching of labour (Lunt, 2006).

It seems likely that prevention and managing long-term sickness-related absence will be increasingly important areas, with medical practitioners encouraged to do more to help workers stay in and retain work. Previously, general practitioners have not seen such dimensions as part of their role and have lacked the tools, training, and financial incentives to offer such support. District Health Boards are not funded or responsible for helping individuals to access a range of health services to ensure an employment outcome (Ministry of Social Development, 2005, p. 83).

### The scope of mutual obligation

'Mutual obligation' and 'conditionality', and the appropriate blend of 'rights and responsibilities' is central to discussions of welfare reform, including reform of the disability benefits (OECD, 2003; Stanley et al., 2004). While Labour resisted pressures to move from voluntary to compulsory initiatives for SB and IB recipients, continued reform of the benefit and support system has brought such issues back into the spotlight since 2008. The relationship of citizens to their social security systems and entitlement is thus reconfigured to become a relationship 'at a distance' via obligations to exhibit increased attachment to the labour market.

## Investing in social policy

To tackle the differences in labour market outcomes and jobs, it is necessary to consider school, education, skills, and broader social attitudes. Many disabled people view their own lack of confidence as a major barrier to accessing employment (cf. Barnes et al., 1998). Singley (2003) notes that most beneficiaries want to work but a range of personal, family, community and work-related (skills, experience, education) considerations interact with demand for labour to produce less than optimum outcomes. Multiple barriers and entrenched discrimination may require considerable ongoing investment. Of those on IB, around 7% are aged over 40, 36% aged over 55, and 8% are aged 18–24. Some 23% of IB recipients are Māori. In relation to impairments, 31% of IB claimants had psychological or psychiatric impairments, and 12.8% had an intellectual disability. For SB recipients, 15% were aged between 18 and 24, and of total recipients 42.5% had psychological or psychiatric impairments, and 15.3% musculoskeletal conditions. One in four SB recipients was Māori and 7% were of Pacific Island ethnicities (Ministry of Social Development, 2012a, 2012b). There is a raft of international evidence that suggests people who were in employment prior to receiving a disability benefit are more likely to return to employment, so what a person was doing before receipt has a bearing on likely success (Johnson, 2001). Many of those arriving on disability benefits have poor work histories, and there is clearly plenty of scope for investment to ensure they are not left behind as the economy grows.

Overall, the configuration of benefits and services has been rigid, perverse, and constraining, when what is required is a dynamic and transformative system. A flexible system of benefits would recognise partial capacity, and encourage risk-taking within the labour market by offering a sufficient 'trampoline' (rather than merely a 'safety net') should it be required. Under historical arrangements, individual incapacity is reinforced at every turn of the benefit system, crowned in no small part by the very naming of a benefit as the 'Invalid's Benefit', which demeans recipients and reinforces a view that those with disability and long-term illness have solely benefit futures. However, for effective transitions (or 'trampolines') to be effective opportunities must exist, be regionally dispersed, and provide the right workplace context for people to make sustainable transitions. Investment in case managers, the linchpins of developments, is crucial, as is resisting the increase of workloads, and providing supervision and adequate support for those engaged in intensive case management activities.

On the theme of investment, it is important not to write off the work prospects of those who do not face a specific obligation to work, while recognising that outcomes other than employment may also be appropriate. Overseas research also suggests funding mechanisms need to be sensitive to ensure that more difficult cases are supported, and recognise that 'slow burners' can be helped to move towards work (Knight et al., 2005; Lewis et al., 2005; cf. OAG, 2009). Integrating disabled people in the workforce has been a strand of welfare reform and also a broader social priority, with the New Zealand Disability Strategy (2001) making a commitment to the social model of disability.

Increased attention is being paid to the role of part-time work and recognition of potential capacity and transitions towards full-time work. In June 2005, one in seven IB recipients and one in eight SB recipients had current earnings declarations, meaning that they had earned some income in the last 12 months. As Jensen et al. (2005) note, the impact of disability is more modest when employment is measured as part-time rather than full-time hours (2005). They suggest that part-time participation rates beg interesting policy questions around how support services and employers may be able to facilitate transitions to full-time work (2005).

The OAG (2009) was critical on the possibilities of determining policy effectiveness, with major implications for research and evaluation strategy. There are key gaps in the statistical information available on the characteristics of Sickness and Invalid's beneficiaries. For example, there is very little information available on the educational qualifications and labour market experience and skills of SB and IB recipients – because it is not central to administrative needs (cf. Fletcher, 2009). If reforms of disability benefits are not driven by a good understanding of the problems and well grounded in evidence, there is a danger that groups already at risk of poverty and social exclusion are further disadvantaged (cf. Stanley and Maxwell, 2004).

## Conclusion

To pick up on the central themes of this book, what is the prognosis of the policy and initiatives detailed in this chapter? First, with the end of macro-level ambition, there is now an emphasis on micro interventions targeted at *particular* groups experiencing *particular* difficulties in *particular* markets when engaging with *available* economic opportunities. This individualisation identifies attitudes, motivation, information, and better access to information, skills, education, mobility, incentives, disincentives, habits, and traits (Lunt, 2006). Local labour market processes are entrusted to produce opportunities, and individuals are expected to slot themselves into those opportunities, albeit with governmental encouragement and support.

Second, in terms of gaps in employability, policy has clearly begun to tackle a major contradiction – those who find themselves on SB and IB may need more support but have received less. Third, with respect to health problems explaining why people initially claim disability benefits and have limited their prospects of returning to work, there is growing attention to how a more joined-up system of benefit delivery and health support can ensure transitions towards successful labour market outcomes.

## References

Barnes, H., Thronton, P., and Maynard Campbell, S. (1998) *Disabled People and Employment: A Review of Research and Development Work* (Bristol: Policy Press).

Castles, F.G. and Shirley, I. (1996) 'Labour and Social Policy – Gravediggers or Refurbishers of the Welfare State' in F.G. Castles, R. Gerritsen, and J. Vowles (eds) *The Great Experiment: Labour Parties and Public Transformation* (Auckland: Auckland University Press).

Corden, A. and Sainsbury, R. (2001) *Incapacity Benefits and Work Incentives* (London: DWP).

Department of Labour (2001) *Pathways to Inclusion: Improving Vocational Services for People with Disabilities* (Wellington: Department of Labour).

Driver, S. and Martell, L. (2001) 'Left, Right and Third Way' in A. Giddens (ed.) *The Global Third Way Debate* (Cambridge: Polity).

Fletcher, M. (2009) *Addressing the Growth in Sickness and Invalid's Benefit Receipt* (Auckland: New Zealand Treasury).

Hiscock, J., Hodgson, P., Peters, S., Westlake, D., and Gabbay, M. (2005) *Engaging Physicians, Benefitting Patients: A Qualitative Study* (London: DWP).

Jensen, J., Sathiyandra, S., Rochford, M., Jones, D., Krishnan, V., and McLeod, K. (2005) *Disability and Work Participation in New Zealand: Outcomes Relating to Paid Employment and Benefit Receipt* (Wellington: Centre for Social Research and Evaluation, Ministry of Social Development).

Johnson, A. (2001) *Job Retention and Advancement in Employment: Review of Research Evidence* (London: DWP).

Kelsey, J. (1997) *The New Zealand Experiment: A World Model for Structural Adjustment* (Auckland: Auckland University Press).

Key, J. (2008) *Speech from the Throne* (Wellington: New Zealand Parliament).

Knight, T., Dickens, S., Mitchell, M., and Woodfield, K. (2005) *Incapacity Benefit Reforms: The Personal Advisor Role and Practice: Stage Two* (London: DWP).

Lewis, J., Corden, A., Dillon, L., Hill, K., Kellard, K., Sainsbury, R., and Thornton, P. (2005) *New Deal for Disabled People; An In-Depth Study of Job Broker Service Delivery* (London: DWP).

Lister, R. (2004) *Poverty* (Bristol: Polity).

Lunt, N. (2006) 'Employability and New Zealand Welfare Restructuring', *Policy and Politics*, 34 (3): 473–494.

Lunt, N., Spoonley, P., and Mataira, P. (2002) 'Past and Present: Reflections on Citizenship within New Zealand', *Social Policy and Administration*, 36 (4): 346–362.

Lunt, N. and Thornton, P. (1994) 'Disability and Employment: Towards an Understanding of Discourse and Policy', *Disability and Society*, 9 (2): 223–238.

Maharey, S. (2005) *Extending Opportunities for Social Developments and Employment* (Wellington: Office for the Minister For Social Development and Employment).

McClure, M. (1998) *A Civilised Community: A History of Social Security in New Zealand, 1898–1998* (Auckland: AUP).

Ministry of Health (2001) *New Zealand Disability Strategy: Making a World of Difference* (Wellington: Ministry of Health).

Ministry of Social Development (2004) *What We Are Doing: Independence Works* (Auckland: Ministry of Social Development).

Ministry of Social Development (2005) *Jobs Jolt 2005 – Update* (Wellington: Ministry of Social Development).

Ministry of Social Development (2012a) *National Fact Sheet – Invalid's Benefits, December 2011* (Wellington: Ministry of Social Development).

Ministry of Social Development (2012b) *National Fact Sheet – Sickness Benefits, December 2011* (Wellington: Ministry of Social Development).

O'Brien, M., Bradford, S., Dalziel, P., Stephens, M., Walters, M., and Wicks, W. (2010) *Welfare Justice for All – Reflections and Recommendations: A Contribution to the Welfare Reform Debate* (Wellington: Welfare Justice: The Alternative Welfare Working Group and Caritas Aotearoa).

OECD (2003) *Disability Programmes in Need of Reform: Policy Brief* (Paris: OECD).

Office for Disability Issues (2002) *Fully Inclusive New Zealand: Briefing to the Minister for Disability Issues* (Wellington: Office for Disability Issues).

Office for Disability Issues (2009) *Disability and Travel and Transport in New Zealand in 2006: Results from the New Zealand Disability Survey* (Wellington: Statistics New Zealand).

Office for Disability Issues (2011) *Indicators from the 1996, 2001 and 2006 New Zealand Disability Surveys for Monitoring Progress on Outcomes for Disabled People* (Wellington: Ministry of Social Development).

Office of the Auditor General (2009) *Ministry of Social Development: Changes to the Case Management of Sickness and Invalids' Beneficiaries* (Wellington: Office of the Auditor General).

Pledger, M., Cumming, J., McDonald, J., and Poland, M. (2009) 'The Health Status of New Zealand Workers: An Analysis of the New Zealand Health Survey 2002/03', *Kotuitui: New Zealand Journal of Social Sciences Online*, 4 (1): 55–70.

Powell, M. (2002) *Evaluating New Labour's Welfare Reforms* (Bristol: Polity).

Shaw, C., Blakely, T., and Tobias, M. (2011) 'Mortality among the Working Age Population Receiving Incapacity Benefits in New Zealand, 1981–2004', *Social Science and Medicine*, 73 (4), 568–575.

Singley, S. (2003) *Bariers to Employment among Long-Term Beneficiaries: A Review of Recent International Evidence* (Wellington: Centre for Social Research and Evaluation, Ministry for Social Development).

Social Market Foundation (2005) *The Incapacity Trap: Report of the Social Market Foundation Commission on Incapacity Benefit* (London: SMF).

Social Security (New Work Tests, Incentives, and Obligations) Amendment Act (2010) (Wellington: Parliamentary Counsel Office).

Stanley, K. and Maxwell, D. (2004) *Fit for Purpose: The Reform of Incapacity Benefit* (London: IPPR).

Stanley, K., Asta Lohde, L., and White, S. (2004) *Sanctions and Sweetners: Rights and Responsibilities in the Benefit System* (London: IPPR).

Statistics New Zealand (2008) *Disability and the Labour Market in New Zealand in 2006* (Wellington: Statistics New Zealand).

Statistics New Zealand (2010) *New Zealand Business Demography Statistics: At February 2010* (Wellington: Statistics New Zealand).

Thornton, P. (1998) *Key Issues: International Research Project on Job Retention and Return to Work Strategies for Disabled Workers* (Geneva: International Labour Office).

Welfare Working Group (2010) *Reducing Long-Term Welfare Dependency: The Options* (Wellington: Welfare Working Group).

Welfare Working Group (2011) *Reducing Long-Term Welfare Dependency: Recommendations* (Wellington: Welfare Working Group).

Wilson, M., McLeod, K., and Sathiyandra, S. (2005) *Growth in Numbers of Sickness and Invalids Benefit Recipients 1993–2002* (Auckland: Centre for Social Research and Evaluation: Te Pokapū Rangahau Arotaki Hapori).

# 13
# Fit for Purpose? Lessons for Policies to Address the Disability Benefits 'Crisis'

*Donald Houston and Colin Lindsay*

> Social and employment policy is characterised by its avoidance of questions about the wider system, in favour of a focus on the 'margins', and its downplaying of the involuntary dimension of unemployment while opting for a very subjective and personalised approach to the problem.
>
> (Walters, 2000: 9)

## Introduction

The chapters in this book have examined the disability benefits 'crisis' in the UK from a number of perspectives: the labour market, employability, and health. Evidence presented indicates that all three perspectives are important in understanding the rise in the numbers claiming disability benefits. Furthermore, and crucial to an understanding of the nature of the crisis, these three issues interact with each other and have acted *together* to move a significant proportion of the UK's working age population on to disability benefits, in many cases never to work again. Large-scale deindustrialisation has been an underlying driving force in the UK context. Mass job destruction and long-term implications for employability and health have combined to produce geographical concentrations of interrelated problems of low demand for labour, low labour market participation, low skills, poor health, and low incomes. Addressing the disability benefits crisis therefore unavoidably confronts longstanding problems in Britain of low investment in industry, weak vocational training infrastructure, poor working conditions and practices, entrenched inequalities in health, and an inflexible benefits system.

The chapters in this book on the experiences outside the UK suggest that policy too can have a substantial influence on numbers on disability benefits. Various employment and social policies combine to influence whether those unable to work owing to sickness or disability end up on disability benefits, unemployment benefits, early retirement, or outside the benefits system altogether.

The disability benefits crisis is not unique to the UK. However, some advanced economies – notably Germany – have avoided it completely, and in others it has been less acute, for example New Zealand. It is perhaps significant that these countries have not deindustrialised in the way the UK has. On the other hand, nor have the Netherlands or Sweden, yet both these countries have higher rates of disability benefit claims than the UK.

The three causes of the disability benefits crisis in the UK – weak demand for labour, low employability, and poor health – are all outcomes of a wider failure of policy to deliver strategic investment in a number of sectors. This is as true of industrial policy and regional policy as much if not more so than of strategies for employment, training, and public health.

Industrial policy has wantonly allowed large swathes of manufacturing and engineering to wither on the vine for over three decades. Regional policy oversaw the large-scale destruction of jobs concentrated in the UK's former industrial heartlands, which decimated the employment base in many towns over a prolonged period spanning from the late 1970s to the mid-1990s. Some of these towns had only just begun a fragile recovery in the latter part of the UK's 'long boom' a short time before the 2008 recession hit, choking off any further growth.

The UK has historically had low levels of investment in infrastructure, technology, and vocational training. As a consequence, opportunities to create new industrial bases and to retrain manual workers are limited, particularly in former industrial parts of the country. Deregulation of the labour market and the encouragement of work intensification as routes to raising labour productivity, rather than capital investment and upskilling, have led employers to prefer hiring workers who are young, fit, and flexible – but ultimately disposable. New EU Member States from eastern Europe provided a flow of migrants fitting this description in the 2000s. This facilitated the latest round of low-cost, low-investment retrenchment in British industry, following previous rounds in the 1950s and 1960s characterised by mass immigration of cheap labour from former British colonies. Ultimately, however, competing on cost alone is a route to low productivity, low incomes and, in the long run, poor health.

Public health policy has focused on promoting lifestyle change at the level of the individual, with little attempt to promote health through the regulation of employment practices or of processed food and drink products prevalent in the British diet. Yet workplace stress, poor diet, and excess alcohol consumption are endemic, indeed epidemic, in parts of the UK.

In one sense, that 2.6 million people are on disability benefits in the UK is simply a reflection of the failure in these other policy areas. However, the welfare system *itself* has failed to demand the measures required in other policy areas to prevent the flow of people into the system. Welfare reform has not recognised the need to consider job availability in some parts of the UK. Nor has it ever seriously supported the attainment of marketable new qualifications for claimants (that may take some time, even years, to attain) as a feasible route off disability benefits. Nor has it placed any significant demands on employers to accommodate those with poor health or disability. Nor have occupational health or public health professionals been tasked with designing preventative measures that might help stem the diversion of sick and disabled people on to social security benefits.

Instead, the response to the crisis has been a double knee-jerk reaction of restricting eligibility and introducing mandatory activation. These responses tackle the immediate symptoms of the problem that manifest themselves on the individual but do nothing to address the underlying causes, which are systemic and structural in origin. These approaches are also rather inflexible and do not allow tailored support measures appropriate for particular individuals to be developed on a case-by-case basis.

## A labour market problem

This book provides convincing evidence of the importance of economic opportunities in influencing numbers claiming disability benefits in the UK. The chapter by Beatty and Fothergill illustrates the very powerful concentration of disability claims in districts ravaged by deindustrialisation and job loss – even after allowing for underlying differences in population health. Macnicol's chapter demonstrates a clear long-run temporal link between job opportunities and numbers of 'disabled' workers out of the labour market – with strong rises in disability benefit claims coinciding with periods of significant job loss and economic restructuring in the 1880s, 1930s and again during the 1970s and 1980s. When Britain's former industrial areas eventually began a fragile economic recovery in the early 2000s, numbers claiming disability benefits finally started to fall, but only after the more employable group of unemployed ahead of them in the 'jobs queue' had moved off the queue and into work.

For a long time in the UK, manufacturing was seen as unimportant to the 'new' economy, which it was assumed could be based on the service sector. This has produced substantial skills and spatial mismatches between labour demand and supply, which have both arguably acted as brakes on economic growth in the UK since the beginning of the 1980s. Only since the start of the current financial crisis and recession has the importance of manufacturing to economic recovery begun to be taken more seriously again.

As well as job destruction, work intensification has also played a role in limiting access to employment for sick and disabled people. As Beatty and Fothergill note in their chapter, mundane and repetitive work at the bottom end of the labour market is demanding and requires a degree of physical robustness. New work pressures in the service sector also place demands on employees, but requiring mental rather than physical robustness. Ulmestig's chapter highlights how in Sweden measures to support sick and disabled people in employment have been eroded over time, with fewer occupational health officers and the removal of local adaptation groups to work with employers to make workplace adaptations to accommodate workers with disabilities.

## An employability problem

Claimants of disability benefits are characterised as tending to have few qualifications, having formerly worked in manual occupations, being older, and – of course – having poor health (as outlined in the chapter by Green and Shuttleworth). Consequently, Beatty and Fothergill's chapter argues that they are placed at the back of the 'jobs queue' when it comes to their chances of being hired by an employer. This does not imply that their low employability per se has caused the rise in disability claims – indeed, this would be absurd since qualifications and many other measures of employability have improved over time. Rather, low employability relative to other workers can explain why certain individuals as opposed to others come to be squeezed out of the labour market when jobs disappear or are in short supply. People with poor health and/or disability can perform many types of employment, but they are vulnerable to downturns in the economy, often being the first to be made redundant and the last to be hired. Consequently, insufficient demand for labour and work intensification coupled with poor health in a population can combine to move substantial numbers on to disability benefits.

Although older men, often with occupation-specific skills, working in heavy engineering and coal mining were those predominantly affected by job loss initially, the current wave of inflated disability claims has come to include more women, younger people, and those with lower skills. Through time a persistent shortage of jobs in former industrial areas has come to exclude those most marginalised in the labour market – the sick and disabled, older workers, and those with few qualifications.

Underdeveloped vocational education and training in the UK has arguably made it more difficult for redundant industrial workers to retrain. Many such workers have narrow occupation-specific skills and a lack of opportunities and confidence to retrain.

## A health problem

Warren, Garthwaite, and Bambra's chapter presents evidence on the extent of the health gap between those on disability benefits and the rest of the working age population. However, as with low employability among claimants of disability benefits, this is not indicative of a driving force behind the long-term rise in the number of claims. Indeed, as Macnicol's chapter states, 'it is unconvincing to argue that health would suddenly worsen for a population sub-set within one generation'. Rather, as identified in Beatty and Fothergill's chapter, the disability penalty in the labour market has increased over time. This is likely to be the result of an increasingly tight and competitive labour market, and increasing demands from employers for flexibility and productivity.

The role of health in the riddle of the UK's disability benefits crisis is complex. On one hand, poor health is a direct cause of an *individual's* claim for disability benefits, but there is not much evidence to support the view that health trends represent a direct causal mechanism behind the long-run rise in numbers claiming disability benefits, with life expectancy rising and the health of the working age population if not improving then certainly not deteriorating. That said, it could be that worklessness and work intensification have had deleterious impacts on health for some individuals, particularly at the bottom end of the labour market, but these have been masked by a general trend driven by other factors towards improvements in health across the population as a whole.

Notwithstanding any negative consequences for health of labour market restructuring and work intensification, the disadvantages faced by sick and disabled people in securing employment have evidently risen over time, with a marked reduction in their employment rate and rise in their propensity to be on disability benefits since the 1970s. An added twist is that as job opportunities diminish, sick and disabled people become more likely to describe their illness or impairment as 'limiting', as described in the chapter by Webster et al.

Thus, there are important interactions between labour market conditions, the employment prospects of sick and disabled people, levels of ill-health, and people's perception of how disabling their illness or impairment is.

## What can policy achieve?

Given how powerful the trio of labour market, employability, and health are in producing large numbers on disability benefits facing considerable barriers to re-employment, it is tempting to be defeatist and assume that there is little the welfare system can do to combat these structural issues. However, the experience of other countries – and arguments and evidence presented by UK-based authors in this book – points to some important roles for policy.

In order to be successful, policy must be based on an accurate diagnosis of the nature of the problem, and based on a clear view of what outcomes are desirable. After a careful consideration of the evidence and arguments presented in this book, it is difficult to conclude anything other than that the UK policy response misdiagnoses the cause of the problem and is focused primarily on reducing numbers of benefit claimants rather than increasing employment or incomes among sick and disabled people. The problem is viewed by policy primarily as a problem of low motivation and insufficient incentives to work among those receiving disability benefits, with little consideration of the effects of labour market conditions, employability, and health. The response to perceived low work incentives is a punitive cutting of benefit levels and entitlement rather than increasing earnings at the bottom end of the labour market. Tax Credits and the Minimum Wage in the UK went a small way towards addressing this, but tackle the symptoms rather than the causes of low pay. Increased investment and improved labour productivity would do more to boost earnings and therefore increase work 'incentives'.

The policy response in the UK (and some other countries) has been cast in too narrow terms. For instance, Green and Shuttleworth's chapter identifies that the policy focus on building the 'motivation' to work of those on disability benefits is only a small part of the jigsaw. Low motivation is as much, if not more so, a symptom as a cause of low employment prospects. Political debates around malingering, low motivation, passiveness, and dependency are at best simplistic, and at worst inaccurate, diagnoses of the nature of the disability benefits crisis. This has been very much the debate in a number of countries, but particularly the UK and Sweden. However, the survey evidence presented in Green and Shuttleworth's chapter indicates that the majority of claimants of disability benefits value work, and that there is a strong correlation between *expectations* of likelihood of ever working again with an objective assessment of *actual* likelihood of working again. In other words, claimants' own perceptions and consequent motivation are quite accurate – the product of rationality rather than 'dependency' or malingering.

The strong 'case management' approach in New Zealand to tailor support services to the needs of the individual outlined in Lunt and Horsfall's chapter and the Dutch success of engaging employers in the reintegration of sick employees identified in van Berkel's chapter both provide examples of what holistic and personalised support can achieve. Crucially, there is a need to tackle employability *and* health (as identified by most chapters in this book), and a need to work with individuals *and* employers (identified specifically in chapters by Ulmestig and van Berkel).

Particularly in the UK context of strong geographic variation in job opportunities and levels of receipt of disability benefits, there is a need for welfare policies to be implemented flexibly and with discretion to take account of individual and geographic circumstances. If suitable jobs are not available, activation measures will be counter-productive in terms of benefit claimants' motivation. Personalised back-to-work plans (if indeed a return to work is appropriate for a given individual) need to be designed that have a clear desired outcome as the final goal. What is realistic to define as the final goal will depend greatly on the local employment and training opportunities available. On a more fundamental level, there is a need for policies to promote the economic regeneration of the UK national economy, but with particular attention to former industrial areas. Otherwise, as identified in the chapter by Beatty, Fothergill, and Houston, the current reforms of disability benefits in the UK will simply move large numbers out of the benefits systems altogether and into poverty rather than into employment.

The benefits system sets up false dichotomies between sick and healthy, and between employed and workless. In reality, people have a range of capabilities for work, not least determined by the work conditions offered by employers. Similarly, many people are underemployed in terms of hours worked or the utilisation of their skills, yet are classified as 'in work' by the benefits system and in social surveys. Many of the involuntarily underemployed may describe themselves as 'self-employed' or 'carers' if they, even for only a certain number of hours per week, fit these categories. Yet many have low, precarious, and variable incomes and may work very few hours.

## Conclusion

The UK has never really got to grips with dealing with sick and disabled people of working age. The sick and disabled do not fit the model of efficient, flexible, and substitutable workers on which the UK's neo-liberal economy and laissez-faire labour market are based. Employers therefore find it difficult to reconcile taking on sick or disabled people with their desire to be efficient and flexible. The welfare state has come to see the sick and disabled essentially as unmotivated to work and therefore undeserving of adequate income protection. Although entitlement is in part determined by National Insurance contributions, payment level and funding are not based on an insurance system, which may have contributed to a reduction in solidarity for disability benefits.

Rather than focusing on the low and declining employment prospects of the sick and disabled, many governments, although particularly the UK government, have instead concentrated on manipulating definitions of incapacity and eligibility criteria for benefits in order to control the numbers receiving disability benefits. The increased level of ill health or disability required in order to qualify for the new Employment and Support Allowance (ESA) in the UK will mean that recipients of ESA will have higher levels of incapacity than those on the old Incapacity Benefit. Consequently, this will become a more marginalised and challenging group to support and average duration on benefit is likely to increase.

What has gone wrong? We believe two intertwined discourses have led over the last three decades to produce a welfare system and labour market that have both systematically failed to address the needs of people of working age suffering from sickness or disability. First, the UK's hegemonic adherence to the normative principles of the neo-liberal economy and laissez-faire labour market leave little sympathy or flexibility towards those with particular needs in the workplace. It is deeply ironic that in the name of economic flexibility employers have become so socially inflexible. This neo-liberal hegemony now extends even to many parts of the political left in the UK.

Second, a pejorative discourse of 'dependency' has developed in response to people receiving long-term disability benefits in a model much more akin to stigmatised 'social assistance' than a collective Bismarckian insurance system. A contributions-based universal income protection scheme for the sick and disabled, however, is not necessarily 'soft' on claimants and must inevitably have tough controls to avoid 'moral hazard'. Indeed, Brussig and Knuth in their chapter on the disability benefits system in Germany argue that the distinction between a generous Bismarckian insurance-based system and a tough 'Work First' welfare system is largely false. Indeed, Germany has very tight controls on eligibility to disability benefits and 'Work First' style measures to ensure any possible employment prospects are explored – as does the at one time (financially) relatively generous universal Nordic model in operation in Sweden.

We, along with many other researchers and commentators, have a concern at the failure in the UK to correctly diagnose the causes of the disability benefits crisis. As a consequence, restrictions on access to benefits and activation policies have gone hand in hand as part of an 'incentives' framework. However, it is entirely possible, indeed desirable, to decouple income protection from activation. A Bismarckian universal insurance-based system with *both* strong income protection *and* strong activation and support towards re-employment is in many ways appealing compared to the current system. Such a scheme would be contributions-based, so would reduce stigma of benefit receipt. Individuals' incomes would be better protected against sickness and disability. Strong activation and rehabilitation would support return to work. We support the view that there is a moral responsibility on individuals of working age to find work if their family and health circumstances permit it. However, there is also a moral responsibility on employers to support sick and disabled people in the workplace, a moral responsibility on the state to provide a welfare system that will protect its members when they are unable to work owing to ill-health or disability, and a further moral responsibility on the state to provide appropriate and high-quality services to enable people to retrain, manage their conditions, and find suitable employment. Only the state can act on the systemic and strategic factors that are required to support a healthy population, cohesive society, and well-functioning economy and labour market.

Although much is now known about the disability benefits 'crisis' of the last 30 years in the UK and beyond, the future is less certain. Important questions for future research relate to changing occupational hazards in the service economy and where, once benefit reforms bite, involuntary unemployment and underemployment will be 'hidden' next, for instance among the precariously self-employed and/or those who may describe themselves as carers or early retired.

We make two pleas of future research. One is that the fundamental importance of the demand for labour is never overlooked – both in terms of the quantity and quality of jobs available. Not only does the demand for labour have a direct impact on the number of people claiming disability benefits, the consequent long-term worklessness has second-round impacts on employability: 'the maintenance of overall unemployment rates at two per cent or less for years at a time may be the single most important factor in minimising the number of hard-to-employ' (Reubens, 1970: 384).

Our other plea for future research is that analysis considers the distribution of employment and income across the population as a *whole*, not just disadvantaged groups such as the 'sick' or 'disabled'. The outcomes affecting particular individuals are the product of whole *systems*, encompassing the economy, the labour market, employers' practices, the health service, and the benefits system.

## References

Reubens, Beatrice (1970) *The Hard-to-Employ: European Programs.* New York: Columbia University Press.

Walters, William (2000) *Unemployment and Government: Genealogies of the Social.* Cambridge: Cambridge University Press.

# Index

Printed and bound in Great Britain by
CPI Antony Rowe, Chippenham and Eastbourne